PREDICTING T
ARTIFI

A THESIS
SUBMITTED FOR
THE AWARD OF THE DEGREE OF
DOCTOR OF PHILOSOPHY
IN
STATISTICS

SUBMITTED BY
Sneh Saini
Research Scholar

UNDER THE SUPERVISION OF:

Supervisor	Co-Supervisor
Dr. (Mrs.) Ratna Raj Laxmi	Dr. N.P. Singh
Professor	Professor
Department of Statistics	Department of Information
Maharishi Dayanand University	and Management
Rohtak, Haryana	Management Development
	Institute, Gurgaon, Haryana

DEPARTMENT OF STATISTICS
MAHARISHI DAYANAND UNIVERSITY
ROHTAK-124001, (HARYANA)

Acknowledgment

Research Thesis, a part of academic curriculum of the doctor of philosophy is a challenging task for any Ph.D. student. With blessings of the Almighty God, it gives me immense pleasure to pen down my imprints of heartfelt gratitude for those who played a remarkable role in the journey of designing this precious manuscript.

I am extremely fortunate to have Prof. (Mrs.) Ratna Raj Laxmi as my my supervisor and mentor. She has always been a great inspiration to me. I am grateful to her, for the professional guidance, candid advice, optimistic outlook, constant support and real encouragement. Her involvement in the project triggered and nourished my intellectual maturity. I feel blessed to have her as my guide.

It has been a privilege to prepare this thesis under the able guidance of my co-supervisor Prof. (Dr.) N.P. Singh. His in-depth knowledge in the subject, systematic guidance, patience and critical evaluation during preparation, gave this thesis its present form. I express my gratitude and heartfelt thanks to him for his valuable guidance, suggestions, encouragement and constant support. I feel privileged and honoured to be associated with him.

I am grateful to Prof. (Dr.) Priti Gupta, Head, Department of Statistics, the faculty and the entire staff of Department of Statistics, for their consistent support and interminable encouragement during my difficult hours.

I extend my heartfelt thanks to Mr. Sachin Varshney and Mr. Naresh Bansal who had always been with me at every difficult hour.

Any kind of work is impossible without the support of one's pillars, i.e., family. I bow down before my parents who actually, ignited the spark of this research work. A very special note of thanks and heartfelt gratitude to my father, Advocate(Sh.) P.S. Saini and my mother, Mrs. Shakuntla Saini ,who motivated and encouraged me throughout this journey.

I am immensely grateful to my husband Mr. J.B. Saini who always stood by me in time of crisis. I would not have been able to complete my work without his valuable criticism, ideas and most important, the moral support. I am really blessed to have my daughters Khyati Saini and Niyati Saini from whom I always received full support, cooperation and motivation to complete this research.

This list of acknowledgement would be incomplete without paying gratitude to my sisters Mrs. Santosh Saini, Dr. Suman Saini, Dr. Rajni Saini and all my family members, who always supported, encouraged and believed in me in all endeavours.

Finally, once again I thank Supreme God, Lord Shiva for always being with me and showering all his blessings on me and my family throughout the journey of my research.

Date:

Place: (Sneh Saini)

List of Research Papers Published

1. Saini Sneh, Singh N P and Laxmi Ratna Raj (2016): "Application of ARIMA Models in Forecasting Stock Prices". International Journal of Mathematics and Computer Application Research (IJMCAR), ISSN(P)2249-6955; ISSN(E): 2249-8060, Vol. 6, Issue 6, Dec 2016, 1-10.(Published)
2. Saini Sneh, Laxmi Ratna Raj, and Singh N P (2016): "Prediction of Stock Prices using Artificial Neural Networks". International Journal of All Research Education and Scientific Methods (IJARESM), ISSN: 2455-6211, Vol. 4, Issue 10, October-2016, Page 20-25 (Published)

CONTENTS

Chapter I: INTRODUCTION   Page No.

    1.1 Introduction   1
    1.2 Objectives of the Study   1
    1.3 A Brief About Technical Development in Prediction of Stock Prices 2
    1.4 Preliminaries   4
    1.5 Summary of the Present Scope of Study   6

Chapter II: REVIEW OF LITREATURE

    2.1 Introduction   9
    2.2 ARIMA Models   9
        2.2.1 Summary of review of literature - ARIMA Models   10
        2.2.2 Literature Reviews of ARIMA Models   13
    2.3 Artificial Neural Networks (ANN)   18
        2.3.1 Summary of review of literature – ANN Models   19
        2.3.2 Literature Reviews of Artificial Neural Network   22
    2.4 GENETIC ALGORITHM   29
        2.4.1 Summary of review of literature - Genetic Algorithm 29
        2.4.2 Literature Reviews of Genetic Algorithm Models   32

Chapter III: DESCRIPTIVE ANALYSIS OF TIME SERIES DATA

    3.1 Introduction   38
    3.2 Time Series   38
    3.3 Sector Wise Data   41
    3.4 Descriptive Statistics Prices of Stocks   42
        3.4.1 Analysis of measure of central tendency and dispersion 42
        3.4.2 Observations   45
        3.4.3 Measure of Skewness and Kurtosis   45
        3.4.4 Test Statistics of Skewness and Kurtosis   47
    3.5 Outlier Test   54
    3.6 Stationarity Check   59
    3.7 Utility of Descriptive Statistics   62

Chapter IV: ANALYSIS OF TIME SERIES DATA WITH ARIMA MODEL

    4.1 Introduction   63
    4.2 Brief overview of some related literature   64
    4.3 ARIMA Model   66
        4.3.1 Autoregressive (AR) and its basic concepts   66
        4.3.2 Moving Average (MA) Modelsand its basic concepts 68
        4.3.3 ARMA modelsand its basic concepts   69

4.3.4 Autoregressive Integrated Moving Average (ARIMA) models	69
4.4 General process of forecasting using ARIMA models as perBox-Jenkins Methodology	69
4.4.1 Types of models or ModelIdentification	71
4.4.2 Model Parameter Estimation	72
4.4.3 Diagnostics Checking	72
4.4.4 Forecasting stock prices of selected Indian companies- An Empirical Evidence	74
4.5 Development process and results of ARIMA models	79
4.6 Experimental Process and Resultsof Sun Pharmaceutical (Normal Distribution)	79
4.6.1 Graphical Analysis	79
4.6.2 Illustrate and interpretation of the experimental results of Sun Pharmaceutical	95
4.7 Experimental Process and Results of Lupin Limited (Non- Normal Distribution)	103
4.7.1 Graphical Analysis	103
4.7.2 Illustration and interpretation of the experimental results of Lupin limited	118

Chapter V: ANALYSIS OF TIME SERIES DATA USING ARTIFICIAL NEURAL NETWORKS

5.1 Introduction	127
5.2 Artificial Neural Network	128
5.3 Architecture of Artificial Neural Networks	128
5.4 Training of Artificial Neural Network	131
5.5 Characteristics of Artificial Neural Networks	132
5.6 Antiquity of Artificial Neural Networks	132
5.6.1 Multilayer Perceptrons and Back Propagation Algorithm	132
5.6.2 Radial Basis Function	134
5.6.3 Hopfield Network	136
5.6.4 Self organizing Maps: Kohonen Algorithm	136
5.7 Methodology for Stock Price Data Forecasting	136
5.8 Analysis of Results and its Interpretation	142
5.8.1 Analysis of results obtained of Lupin Limited (Normal Distribution)	142
5.8.2 Analysis of results obtained of Sun Pharmaceutical (Non-normal Distribution)	143
5.9 Conclusion	148

Chapter VI: TIME SERIES ANALYSIS USING GENETIC ALGORITHMS

6.1 Introduction	149
6.2 Brief Overview of Some Related Literature	149
6.3 Terminology used inGenetic Algorithm	152
6.4 Elements of Genetic Algorithm	153
6.5 Functioning of Genetic Algorithm	154

6.6	Application of Genetic Algorithm	155
6.7	Experimental Process	156
	6.7.1 Graphical Representation of Sun Pharmaceutical	157
	6.7.2 Experimental Results of Sun Pharmaceutical	158
	6.7.3 Graphical Representation of Lupin Limted	161
	6.7.4 Experimental Result of Lupin Limited	162

Chapter VII: RESULTS AND DISCUSSIONS

7.1	Introduction	165
7.2	Evaluation of results forecasted using ARIMA models	166
	7.2.1 Results of time series data of Sun Pharmaceuticals (for normal distribution) at first difference based on the statistics of goodness of fit / accuracy using ARIMA models	166
	7.2.2 Results of time series data of Sun Pharmaceuticals (for normal distribution) at second difference based on the statistics of goodness of fit / accuracy using ARIMA model	168
	7.2.3 Comparison between first and second difference resultsanalysed of ARIMA	170
	7.2.4 Results of time series data of Lupin Limited (for non-normal distribution) at first difference based on the statistics of goodness of fit / accuracy using ARIMA model	172
	7.2.5 Results of time series data of Lupin Limited (for non-normal distribution) at second difference based on the statistics of goodness of fit / accuracy using ARIMA model	174
	7.2.6 Comparison between first and second difference of analysed ARIMA model	176
7.3	Evaluation of Results Forecasted Using Artificial Neural Networks	178
	7.3.1 Results of time series data of Sun Pharmaceuticals (for normal distribution) based on the statistics of goodness of fit / accuracy using ANN models	179
	7.3.2 Results of time series data of Lupin Limited (for non-normal distribution) based on the statistics of goodness of fit / accuracy using ANN models	184
7.4	Evaluation of Results Forecasted Using Genetic Algorithms	188
	7.4.1 Evaluation of the results of Sun Pharmaceuticals (normal distribution) based on statistics of goodness of fit/accuracy	189

7.4.2 Evaluation of the results of Lupin Limited (non-normal distribution) based on statistics of goodness of fit/accuracy	191
7.5 Comparison of results obtained from ARIMA, ANN, GA	193
7.6 Conclusion and Suggestions	200
Chapter VII: BIBLIOGRAPHY	**203-220**

CONTENTS OF TABLES

Table Number	Description of Table	Page No.
3.1	Sectors-wise classified BSE stocks	42
3.2	Measures of central tendency and measures of dispersion	44
3.3	Measures of Skewness, Kurtosis	47
3.4	Test statistics of Skewness	49
3.5	Descriptive analysis- Kurtosis and Test statistic of kurtosis	51
3.6	Chi square distribution values	52
3.7	Analysis of Jarque-Bera Test Statistics	53
3.8	Results of the companies having outliers in the data	59
3.9	Results of Augmented Dickey-Fuller (ADF) Test at different levels	60
4.1	Theoretical Box-Jenkins model	71
4.2	Measures of error for forecasting accuracy	75
4.3	Augmented Dickey-Fuller Statistics	80
4.4	ARIMA models at First Difference for opening price of Sun Pharmaceutical stock at BSE	80
4.5	ARIMA models at Second Difference for opening price of Sun Pharmaceutical stock at BSE	81
4.6	Descriptive Statistics of opening price of Sun Pharmaceutical stock at BSE	82
4.7	ARIMA Models at First Difference for opening price of Sun Pharmaceuticalstock at BSE	95
4.8	ARIMA Models at Second Difference for opening price of Sun Pharmaceutical stock at BSE	95
4.9	Dickey-Fuller Statistics	104
4.10	ARIMA Model at First Difference for opening price of Lupin	104
4.11	ARIMA Model at Second Difference for opening price of Lupin	104
4.12	Descriptive Statistics of opening price of Lupin stock at BSE	105
4.13	ARIMA Model at Second Difference for opening price of Lupin limited stock at BSE	118
4.14	ARIMA Model at Second Difference for opening price of LUPIN stock at BSE	119
5.1	Parameters used to train the input data set	138
5.2	Analysis of results of Lupin Limited	142
5.3	Analysis of results of Sun Pharmaceutical	143
6.1	Descriptive Statistics for goodness of Fit	158
6.2	Statistical Results of different Genetic Algorithms for Sun Pharmaceutical Stock index	158

6.3	Descriptive Statistics for goodness of Fit	160
6.4	Statistical Results of different Genetic Algorithms for Lupin Stock index	162
6.5	Statistical Result of different genetic algorithms foLupin Limited	162
7.1	Analysis of stocks (normal distribution) using ARIMA models	172
7.2	Analysis of stocks (non-normal) using ARIMA models	178
7.3	Analysis of stocks (normal distribution) using ANN models	183
7.4	Analysis of stocks (non-normal) using ANN models	188
7.5	Analysis of stocks (normal distribution) using GA models	191
7.6	Analysis of stocks (non-normal) using GA models	193
7.7	Results analysis of Predicted Prices of stock under different models for time series of normal distribution stocks	193
7.8	Results analysis of Predicted prices of stock under different models for time series of Non-normal distribution stocks	195
7.9	Snapshot of algorithms, goodness of fit models and normality of stock prices	200
7.10	Snapshot of analysis in relation to algorithms and voting of best fit based on different criteria	200

CHAPTER I
INTRODUCTION

1.1 INTRODUCTION

In a world of gizmos where everyone is running after technology and where data processing has been going through tremendous growth and changes, forecasting of stock prices is getting an ever-increasing importance. Be it the investors who are guided by the prediction of movement in stock prices or the companies who depend upon its accuracy, everyone secure their existence by giving a close look to what will happen in their future.

The stock market is comprised of a number of market participants (investors) with various risks and return characteristics with their own expectations about the stock of a particular company. They understand and react to the news of a company in different ways at different points of time. In such circumstances, it is very difficult to predict stock prices accurately. An investor can be guided to take buy and sell decision with the help of stock prediction system developed for predicting the trends or movement of dynamic stock prices accurately and consistently. Moreover, predicted trend in the stock prices will also help the regulators such as Securities Exchange Board of India (SEBI) of the stock market in taking many corrective measures. Keeping these facts in mind, this research is an attempt to forecast the future trends/values of given stock prices.

This chapter is divided into various sections where each section gives us a deeper look into the subparts of the thesis. The main theme of each section is as follows: Section1.1 gives the importance of the study; Section1.2 specifies the objectives of research; Section 1.3 briefs about developments in prediction of stock prices through traditional models, artificial neural networks and genetic algorithm. Section 1.4 communicates about the pre requisites terms and techniques used in this research. Lastly, section 1.5 concludes the chapter by outlining the present scope of our study.

1.2 OBJECTIVES OF THE STUDY

The prime objectives of the present study are as follows:
a) Forecasting of Stock data with statistical tools such as ARIMA models.
b) Forecasting of stock market data with data mining models such an ANN and GA.

c) To make a comparative analysis of statistical tools and data mining for their suitability for forecasting stock market data.

1.3 A BRIEF ABOUT TECHNICAL DEVELOPMENT IN PREDICTION OF STOCK PRICES

Research in this field possesses many theoretical and experimental challenges that give us an incentive to delve more and more into it. The most important aspect of these is the Efficient Market Hypothesis (EMH); referring Eugene Fama's (1970) "Efficient capital markets". This premise says that in any competent market, stock market prices are available to all citizens, whether he or she is an investor or not. Thus, probability of earning excessive profit does not exist. None of the systems is expected to outperform the market predictability, accurately and consistently. Hence, modelling any market data specifically stock prices under the assumption of EMH is only possible on the speculative, stochastic component and not on the movement of the changes in the value or other fundamental factors (Heping, 2004). Another theory related to EMH is the Random Walk theory. It states that random behaviour of the prices, i.e., previous prices along with future prices do not follow any trend or pattern.

A great deal of research has been conducted in the past about the validity of the EMH and random walk theories. However, with the introduction of computational and intelligent finance and behavioural finance, economists have tried to establish an alternative hypothesis which is called as the inefficient market hypothesis. The market is not always in a random walk, and inefficiencies always exist (Heping, 2003). The origins of disparity were studied by Mandelbrot (1960), analysing the cotton prices in New York stock exchange for developing assumptions of EMH. In his study, the results obtained proved that the data did not fit the normal distribution and resulted in producing symmetry from the viewpoint of scaling. Mandelbrot also analysed the fractals of the financial markets. Subsequently, with evolution in this field of research Pan Heping postulated the Swing Market Hypothesis (SMH) in 2003. The study analysed the efficient and inefficient nature of market and the subsequent trends also fluctuate amongst these two modes recurrently. The theory categorized the market movement into four components: physical cycles, dynamical swing, abrupt momentums and random walks.

Stock market is considered to be a chaos system. Chaos is a non-linear deterministic system which because of its irregular fluctuation is random. They are also dynamic systems, periodic, complicated and are difficult to deal with normal analytical methods. Neural networks make fewer assumptions regarding dependencies and are proved to be very effective for learning such non- linear chaotic systems (Lawrence, 1997)

Many researchers and practitioners have proposed prediction models using various fundamental, technical and analytical techniques to give relatively an exact prediction. Fundamental analysis involves the in-depth analysis of the changes of the stock prices in terms of exogenous macroeconomic variables. It assumes the share price of a stock dependent on its inherent value and the expected return of the investors. But this expected return is subjected to change as new information pertaining to the stock is available in the market which in turn changes the share price. Furthermore, the analysis of the economic factors is also fairly subjective as the interpretation totally lays on the intellect of the analyst. On the other hand, technical analyses focus on using price, volume, and open interest statistical charts to predict future stock prices. The principle behind technical analysis is that all of the internal and external factors that affect a market at any given point of time are already factored into that market's price. (Mendelssohn, 2000).

Further, for prediction of stock prices, some traditional time series forecasting tools are also used. In time series forecasting, the historical data is analysed to see the dependency between data. A model is developed based on the historical data and build patterns. Based on the theory, these models are then used to anticipate the future prices of the stock.

Predominantly, two approaches of time series modelling and forecasting are used, namely, linear approach and non-linear approach. Mostly, moving average, exponential smoothing, time series regression etc. are the methods used for forecasting. Autoregressive Integrated Moving Average (ARIMA) model is one of the most common and popular linear method which is also known as the [Box and Jenkins (1976)]. These model scan be represented in different types of time series, , i.e., Autoregressive (AR), moving average (MA) and combined AR and MA (ARMA) series.

Many researchers and analysts have proposed the existence of the nonlinearity in the financial market (Abhyankar et al, 1997). However, there exist very few evidences that substantiate the linear nature of stock market returns. It has been found that the residual variance is very high between the predicted return and the actual return of the stocks. Few parametric models such as Autoregressive Conditional Heteroscedasticity and General Autoregressive Conditional Heteroscedasticity are used for financial forecasting.

During the last decade, many researchers have developed various models and techniques for predicting stock market indices using artificial neural networks (ANN), anticipating that the market trends can be captured correctly. ANN has been used as a widespread technique because of its ability to discover nonlinear relationship in the input data set without a prior assumption of the knowledge of relation between the input and the output (Hagen et al, 1996). Further, neural networks are analogous to non-parametric and non-linear regression model. It is proved that neural networks serve as better model in stock price prediction.

"A neural network is a massively parallel distributed processor that has a natural propensity for storing experiential knowledge and making it available for use. It resembles the brain in two respects: Knowledge is acquired by the network through a learning process and interneuron connection strengths known as synaptic weights are used to store the knowledge" (Haykin, 1994). Neural networks have the ability to interpret complex and inaccurate data. These models extract patterns and trends that are not noticeable by human or computer techniques. Neural networks are analogous to nonparametric and nonlinear regression model. Neural networks have the capability to understand the complex and chaotic nature of stock market whereas the conventional statistical models have limitations in complex relationship between the input and the output of the system. This weakness is taken care of by ANN models.

Neural Networks have a built in capability to adapt the network parameters to any change in the system under study. A neural network can be retrained and modelled to a new environment with a particular input data set to predict at the same level of environment. Further, neural networks can change its parameters, i.e., synaptic weights when the system is non-stationary and dynamic in nature.

1.4 PRELIMINARIES

In this section, the basic concepts and definitions to be used in this work are presented.

Time Series: "A time series is a collection of observations of well-defined data items obtained through repeated measurements over time" (Australian Bureau of Statistics- Statistical language of time series data).

Autoregressive (AR): Autoregressive model the series is regressed on to past values of itself. An Autoregressive (AR) Model of order p, or an AR (p) model, satisfies the equation:

$$y_i = \emptyset_0 + \emptyset_1 y_{i-1} + \emptyset_2 y_{i-2} + .. + \emptyset_p y_{i-p} + \epsilon_i$$

Moving Average (MA): Moving average models are the time series models which can be expressed as a function of previous forecasting errors (or noise) 'ϵ_i'. A moving average (MA) model of order q, or an MA (q) model can be expressed with the following equation:

$$y_i = \mu + \epsilon_i + \theta_1 \epsilon_{i-1} + \cdots + \theta_q \epsilon_{i-q}$$

Autoregressive Integrated Moving Average (ARIMA) models: In ARIMA Models future value of the variables is a linear combination of past values and past errors. Mathematically it can be represented as:

$Y_t = \Phi_0 + \Phi_1 Y_{t-1} + \Phi_2 Y_{t-2} + \ldots + \Phi_p Y_{t-p} + \epsilon_t - \theta_1 \epsilon_{t-1} - \theta_2 \epsilon_{t-2} - \ldots - \theta_q \epsilon_{t-q}$

where
Actual values of the data are taken as Y_t, coefficients are considered as Φ_i and θ_j. The Random error is denoted by ϵ_t and auto regressive and moving averages are represented by integer's p and q. (Ayodele et al., 2014).

Degree of Freedom: Degree of Freedom is known as the number of independent ways by which a dynamic system can move without violating any constraint imposed on it.

Final Prediction Error (FPE): It is a criterion to compare the quality of a model by simulating the situation where the model is tested on a different data set.

Akaike information criterion (AIC): It is a measure of the relative quality of statistical models for a given set of data. For a given collection of models for the data, AIC estimates the quality of each model, relative to each of the other models. Hence, AIC provides a means for model selection.

AICc is AIC with a correction for finite sample sizes. The formula for AICc depends upon the statistical model. Assuming that the model is univariate, linear, and has normally-distributed residuals (conditional upon regressors)

Schwarz Bayesian information criterion (SBC) is a criterion for model selection among a finite set of models; the model with the lowest BIC is preferred to be the best model.

Artificial Neural Networks (ANN): A neural network is a system composed of many simple processing elements operating in parallel whose function is determined by network structure, connection strengths, and the processing performed at computing elements or nodes. DARPA Neural Network Study (1988)

Multilayer Perceptrons and Back Propagation Algorithm: Multilayer Perceptrons (MLP) are usually layered Feed Forward networks. Static back propagation algorithm is always used in conjunction with MLP as the training of MLP is done with the help of back propagation algorithm. These networks are widely used in various applications requiring static pattern classification. Easy to use and approximation of input/output map is their distinct feature whereas the only disadvantages is that they are trained slowly and need a large training data set (Almeida, 1987).

Radial Basis Function is a type of non-linear hybrid networks which contains only one hidden layer of perceptron. The hidden layer in multilayer perceptron uses a standard

Sigmoidal functions whereas a radial basis function network uses Gaussian transfer functions.

RBF Neuron Activation Function calculates the degree of similarity between the input vector and its prototype which is taken from the training sets. Input vectors which are more similar to the prototype give a result closer to 1.

Hopfield Network artificial neurons are the basic building block of Hopfield. The total number of inputs is represented by N where i is the input and a weight w_i is associated with it. The output remains the same until the values of neuron is updated.

Kohonen Algorithm: It is an idea of Self Organizing Maps was given by Kohonen T (1990). This is a typical feed forward network with a single computational layer of neurons arranged in rows and columns.

Epochs: Epochsare full cycle of neural network training on the entire training set. This parameter defines the maximum learning epochs cycles to reach specifies minimum weights delta.

Genetic Algorithm (GA): It is an algorithm which gives us the most optimal solution which is produced from fittest of a potential solution obtained from various potential solutions.

Population: It is a collection of potential solutions in genetic algorithms

Selection: It is an operator that decides which chromosome will reproduce.

Generation: Each cycle through the genetic algorithm is called a generation.

Crossover: It is an operator that perform recombination, creates two new offspring by combining the parent's genes in new ways.

Chromosome: One of the candidate solutions to the problem is known as a chromosome.

Mutation: An operator which introduces new information to be genetic pool to protect against premature convergence is known as mutation.

Optimization: It is a feature in genetic algorithm which gives the best accurate solution after several iterations in the population. This feature is considered as the base-line of the genetic algorithm.

1.5   SUMMARY OF THE PRESENT SCOPE OF STUDY

All the chapters in this research are designed to give us better ways of predicting trends in stock market prices using artificial neural network. They are segregated on the basis of the various models used to explain different perspectives around which our study revolves. The succinct description of each chapter is mentioned underneath:

Chapter I: Introduction

This chapter draws around a brief introduction and the review of research work related to the forecasting of stock prices. It carries-forward the objectives defined for the study to identify the best forecasting methods of stock prices with the help of ARIMA models, artificial neural networks and genetic algorithms. It also presents the brief review about technical development in prediction of stock prices at different stages by different researchers. It narrates overview of the preliminary words used in this research. This chapter is summarised by giving a brief introduction of the chapter-wise research work to be carried forward to predict trends in the stock market using artificial neural network.

Chapter II: Review of Literature

This chapter presents the review of the research work carried out by various authors for using different models of forecasting, , i.e., ARIMA models, artificial neural network models and genetic algorithms. A concise description of ARIMA model, ANN and Genetic Algorithm has been given to provide us a clearer view. The chapter also consists of the analysis table which presents analysis of research work done on all three models by a range of authors. A brief review of all the models used in the past has also been illustrated.

Chapter III: Descriptive Analysis of Time Series data

This chapter gives a brief introduction of the descriptive analysis followed by a range of definitions of the time series as given by earlier researchers. It also includes review of literature in relation to the application of time series analysis using ARIMA models, ANN and Genetic algorithms with specific reference to stock market data analysis. It showcases sector wise stocks of 25 BSE Sensex companies of the Indian stock market. The chapter also includes various statistics together with interpretation, mainly about measure of central tendency, dispersion, skewness and kurtosis, followed by tests of normality and test for outliers. One of the requirements of usage of times series data analysis with ARIMA models is that, time series must be stationary. The test of stationarity called ADF test is conducted to make the data stationary. The results of the ADF test are also given with comments of utility of descriptive statistics in context of ARIMA models.

Chapter IV: Analysis of Time Series data with ARIMA Model

This chapter dispenses the extensive process of building ARIMA models for short-term price prediction. The results obtained from real-life data establish the potential strength of ARIMA models to provide stockholders a short-term prediction that could support investment decision making process.

It gives a brief impression of review of literature. It also describes the ARIMA model along with the identification of non-seasonal Box-Jenkins model. It further illustrates the methodology used and the process of experiments, its results obtained, and interpretation for non-normal time series stock, i.e., Sun Pharmaceuticals. Besides, it illustrates the same for the normal time series stock, i.e., Lupin Limited. Finally, the chapter predicts the stock prices of Sun Pharmaceuticals and Lupin Limited.

Chapter V: Analysis of Time Series Data using Artificial Neural Networks

This chapter begins with some definitions of artificial neural networks. It explains the application of neural networks and apprise about their characteristics. Subsequently, it presents the classification of artificial neural networks followed by neural network architecture. An overview of the neural network training is given which describes its methodology and data processing. The results obtained are discussed on the basis of descriptive analysis and then interpreted. Finally, the chapter concludes with the prediction of stock prices with the best ANN model.

Chapter VI: Time Series Analysis Using Genetic Algorithms

The chapter begins with the brief introduction of genetic algorithm followed by review of literature in relation to the application of time series analysis using genetic algorithms with specific reference to the stock market data analysis. It also specifies basic framework of a genetic algorithm succeeded by methodology and data processing. Further, descriptive analysis of experimental results obtained are shown and discussed. The chapter sum-up with the prediction of stock price based on the best selected method of genetic algorithm.

Chapter VII: Results and Discussions

This chapter comprises of the behaviour of stock market and the fundamental and technical analysis of stocks. It demonstrates the predicted prices of stocks forecasted on the basis of best models of ARIMA, ANN and Genetic Algorithm. In addition, it shows the descriptive analysis of predicted prices of stocks and their interpretation. Finally, the chapter concludes with inference of the study and some suggestions for future research work.

CHAPTER II
REVIEW OF LITERATURE

2.1 INTRODUCTION

This chapter reflects about the research work carried out by various authors for using different models of forecasting, i.e., ARIMA models, artificial neural network models and genetic algorithm models. This chapter has been divided into three subsections. Section 2.2 presents the review of research work carried out by the researchers, mainly in the context of applications of ARIMA models in forecasting the time series of financial and economic data. Section 2.3 is devoted to review of literature on the applications of ANN models, applied to forecast economic or financial data time series. Review of literature on genetic algorithm application is presented in section 2.4. The objective of review of literature is to find out the gap in literature order to channelize the research work.

2.2 ARIMA MODELS

As mentioned in chapter 1, Box and Jenkins (1970) introduced the ARIMA models. These are also referred to as Box-Jenkins methodology composed of a set of activities dedicated to identify, estimate and diagnose ARIMA models for forecasting time series data. These models are one of the most prominent methods in financial forecasting as well. In ARIMA models have been applied for generating short-term forecasts. These models have constantly outperformed complex structural models for short-term prediction. In ARIMA models, the future values of variables are a linear combination of past values and past errors. The step in building ARIMA predictive models consists of model identification, parameter estimation, diagnostic checking and forecasting. Analysis of research work carried out on ARIMA models by various authors is presented as under in brief in the next sub section of this chapter. Tabular presentation of research papers is given in table 2.2.1

2.2.1 SUMMARY OF REVIEW OF LITERATURE - ARIMA MODELS

Authors	Year	Model Used	Application
Ozaki	1977	ARIMA model -Box Jenkins method	Determination of ARIMA model
Tang, Chiu and Xu	2003	ARIMA model- ARMA-GARCH model	Stock price prediction
Rangsan and Titida	2006	ARIMA model -non-seasonal Box-Jenkins models	Oil palm prices
Valenzuela, Rojas, Rojas, Pomares, Herrera, Guillen, Marquez and Pasadas	2008	Hybrid ARIMA–ANN model- hybridization of intelligent techniques	Time series prediction
Erfani and Samimi	2009	ARFIMA and ARIMA model- general process	Forecasting of stock prices
Priya and Suresh	2010	Yield forecast model (ANOVA)	Sugarcane yield
Green	2011	ARIMA model -Box Jenkins method	Stock price forecasting
Jarrett and Kyper	2011	ARIMA model-Intervention analysis	Chinese stock price prediction
Ababio	2012	ARIMA and ARIMAX model- Geometric Mean Regression, Exponential Smoothing and Box Jenkins method	Stock price forecasting
Bagherifard, Nilashi, Ibrahim, Janahmadi, and Ebrahimi	2012	ANN, RN, ARIMA models- Multi-Layered Perceptron,	Forecasting of exchange rates
Khashei, Montazeri and Bijari	2012	Fuzzy Logic and Artificial Neural Network	Improvement of auto regressive Integrated moving average
Abdullah	2012	ARIMA Model - AR, MR, and ARMA	Forecasting of gold bullion coin selling price
Emamverdi, Araghi and Fahimifar	2013	ARIMA model-Fuzzy ARIMA model	Stock market price prediction
Forslund and Akesson	2013	Multiple Linear Regression-AIC	Share price prediction

		test, LINEST-function	
Adebiyi, Adewumi and Ayo	2014	ARIMA model, Augmented Dickey Fuller	Stock price prediction
Mondal, Shit and Goswami	2014	ARIMA and ARMA model - ACF and PACF	Stock price forecasting
Devi, Sundar and Alli	2014	ARMA & AR models -Time Series Analysis- Beta calculation	Stock price prediction
Xiaoguang, Yuzhen, Ting and Zhiyuan	2014	ARIMA model -SAS system,	Share price prediction
Abdullahi and Bakari	2014	ARMA and ARIMA model- Augmented Dickey-Fuller test, Box- Jenkins, modelling	Nigerian stock market
Isenah and Olubusoye	2014	ARIMA and ANN model-The random walk and efficient market hypotheses,	Nigerian stock market
Kwasi and Kobina	2014	ARIMA model -Autocorrelation (ACF) and Partial autocorrelation (PACF) functions	Forecasting of cassava prices
Dhaval, Mitul and Devendra	2014	ARIMA model -Box Jenkins method	Predict the time series value for rain attenuation
Kim, Davis and Moses	2015	ARIMA model - Box-Jenkins, Random Walk	Stock price prediction
Sahoo and charlapally	2015	ARIMA model-Auto Regressive model, Back Propagation algorithms	Stock price prediction
Ostadi and Azimi	2015	ANN and ARIMA model – Auto-regression Integration Moving Average	Forecasting of steel prices
Hossain, Kamruzzaman and Ali	2015	ARIMA-EGARCH model, ARCH (GARCH) and ANN model	Forecasting of steel prices
Konarasinghe, Abeynayake and Gunaratne	2015	ARIMA model -Auto Correlation Functions, Partial	Prediction of Sri Lankan share market returns

		Autocorrelation Functions	
Jadhav, Kakade, Utpat and Deshpande	2015	ARIMA model -(1,0,i)	Indian share market forecasting
Khasheia, and Bijari	2015	ARIMA and FARIMA model- Time Series Forecasting models, Hybrid model	Exchange rate forecasting
Verma, Goyal and Goyal	2015	ARIMA model -Analysis using the Box-Jenkins method	Prediction of sugarcane yield
Babu and Reddy	2015	Box-Jenkins methodology, hybrid ARIMA-ANN model,	Forecast accuracy of internet traffic data
Manoj and Edward	2016	ARIMA model - AR, MR, and ARMA, ADF test	Forecasting of india stock market (bse)
Ngan	2016	ARIMA model -ACF and PACF	Forecasting foreign exchange rate
Sengupta, Biswas and Gupta	2016	ARIMA model ANN model, ARIMA-Kalman model	Wind energy potential of silchar
Gautam	2016	ARIMA model-ACF and PACF	Gold price forecasting

2.2.2 LITERATURE REVIEWS OF ARIMA MODELS

Large number of researchers had been using ARIMA models for the prediction of time series data of stock prices. It is also being used in the fields of agriculture, weather forecasting, pharmaceuticals, etc. Research papers which are recent on the topic and relevant to carry out research work are reviewed in the subsequent section.

Ozaki (1977) ascertained that AIC is a powerful tool in identification of different ARIMA models. He used MAICE (minimum AIC estimation) procedure which selects a model by using Akaike's Information Criterion (AIC) for determining the best ARIMA Models. He obtained that MAICE procedure produces almost results similar to five ARIMA models [(1, d, 0), (2, d, 0[(0, d, 1), (0, d, 2) and (1, d, 1)] of B-J. Tang et al (2003) proposed the mixture model called as generalized expectation maximization (GEM) algorithm for the mixture of ARMA-GARCH model for the prediction of stock prices. Its relative empirical performance against the conventional ARMA-GARCH and mixture of AR-GARCH model was investigated for the financial exchange rates. They also concluded that their mixture model (ARMA-GARCH) produced better results than the combination of AR-GARCH models.

Rangsan and Titida (2006) developed various ARIMA models for forecasting oil palm prices of Thailand for a period of 5 years from 2000 to 2004. The criteria for choosing best ARIMA model was minimum of mean absolute percentage error (MAPE). They found ARIMA (2,1,0) for the farm price model, ARIMA (1,0,1) for whole sale price, and ARIMA (3,0,0) for pure oil price as the best model in their respective categories. Valenzuela et al (2008) suggested the use of hybrid ARIMA–ANN models for better accuracy than ARMA models which had been prominent by use in linear models of forecasting of time series. They used hybridization of intelligent techniques such as Evolutionary Algorithms, Artificial Neural Networks and Fuzzy systems.

Erfani andSamimi (2009) applied Box-Jenkins methodology to establish autoregressive fractionally integrated moving average (ARFIMA) and autoregressive integrated moving average (ARIMA) models using 970 daily in-sample data from 26th March 2003 to 8th July 2007 of Tehran Stock Exchange. Partial auto-correlation function (PACF) and Auto-correlation functions (ACF) were tested followed by estimation of the parameters of autoregressive and moving regression. Comparison of predicted values with actual observed values was done. ARFIMA model outperformed ARIMA model to predict more accurately. Priya and Suresh (2010) developed a model for prediction of pre-harvest sugarcane yield for Coimbatore (India) from 1981 to 2004 using the yield data. They used fortnightly weather variables such as daily mean temperature (maximum-minimum), relative humidity (morning-evening) and total rainfall (fortnightly). Different weights were used for weather variables as regressor for constructing the prediction model. The weather variable weights were co-related with yields. The results proved the ability of the methods to describe 87% of deviation in the sugarcane yield successfully 2 months before the actual harvest.

Green (2011) applied ARIMA models on prediction of stock prices of 8 different companies. The sampling interval was weekly, i.e.,the 1st trading day of the month and the 15th trading day of the month. The study examined ARIMA model on the time series data of stock prices. ACF and PACF tests were conducted to conclude the best ARIMA model for each stock and interval also tried to find out if there were any similarities between industries. Jarrett and Kyper (2011) analysed the Chinese equity market to understand the predictable properties of fast growing volatile market. The data under consideration was collected from Pacific-Basin Capital Markets (PACAP) affiliated with the China Center for Economic Research (CCER) for a period of 20 years from January 1990 to December 2009. Box and Tiao (1975) modelled the historical stock market price index using ARIMA model. Their results indicated its effects on china as well as its manufacturing industry at the time of world financial crisis.

Ababio (2012) evaluated the accuracy for prediction of two models namely ARIMA and ARIMAX and emphasised that linear correlation had slight or no effect on the in-sample forecast ability. The data was comprised of 72 observations of Oil and Gas Industry of London Stock Exchange from 2005-2010. It was adjusted for monthly closing price of four stocks. The study showed that AIC had significant influence on the error metrics. ARIMAX models produced better results in comparison to ARIMA Models. Bagherifard et al (2012) presented forecasting of stock prices of Iran-Tehran stock market with historical price data of 2008 and 2009 using two models namely ANN and ARIMA and predicted stock prices for the year 2010. It was observed that results obtained using ANN methods were more accurate. It used artificial intelligence with higher accuracy in forecasting the stock prices. Khashei et al (2012) also suggested that combination of various models can improve the accuracy of prediction. They carried out their research using 2 models namely ARIMA and FARIMA Model for forecasting exchange rates. Abdullah (2012) employed ARIMA model for forecasting gold bullion coins selling prices using classical data. ARIMA (2, 1, 2) was considered as the best fit model for selling prices of the gold bullion coins. This was found as very low cost and effective model.

Emamverdi et al (2013) studied the behaviour of stock market index for abrupt changes and volatility in relation to predicting stock prices. They introduced Fuzzy regression, a new mathematical method to forecast stock prices. Their results proved that suggested method is more efficient for prediction and can be very useful for decision and policy makers. Forslund and Akesson (2013) designed a multiple linear regression model for the prediction of closing price of shares of 44 companies of Stockholm OMX stock exchange. Adebiyi et al (2014) carried out research for prediction of stock prices using ARIMA Model on historical stock data collected from Nigeria Stock Exchange and New York Stock Exchange. They found that proposed method of forecasting on short term basis was satisfactory in comparison to existing technique for stock price prediction. The results compete reasonably well with emerging forecasting techniques in short term prediction with the result obtained from ARIMA model.

Mondal et al (2014) analysed 56time series of Indian Stocks from different sectors to determine the accuracy of forecasting methods using ARIMA model. They also mentioned that, results obtained in the study were accurate up to 85% of ARIMA model. Devi et al (2014) carried out their research on prediction of stock market indices. They considered the data of three indices, namely CNX Realty, BANK NIFTY and MIDCAP 50 for the period of 2009 to2011. They applied data mining techniques for analysis of data to show the ups and downs of particular index. The relationship between the index and company's stock price was identified by using correlation method and associated risk was identified using Beta.

Xiaoguang et al (2014) analysed the shares of China Merchants Bank shares at opening prices (04/01/2013 – 18/10/2013) and to predict the next five days (21/10/2013 – 25/0/2013) stock opening price data using ARIMA models-SAS system and concluded it to be very efficient and suitable model for short-term stock predictions. Abdullahi and Bakari (2014) examined the trend or pattern of Nigerian stock market for a period of 1985-2008. They examined the tendency of the Nigerian capital market by applying various ARIMA models. They concluded that ARIMA (2, 1, 2) model performed better on the basis of least MAPE and MAE.

Isenah and Olubusoye (2014) carried out research on the prediction of Nigerian stock market logarithmic returns time series. The test for presence of memory was conducted by using the Hurst coefficient before the series was trained for the application of models. They used ARIMA and ANN Model such as random walk and an efficient market hypothesis and deduced that artificial neural network models outshined the ARIMA models in anticipating future growth of the return process. Kwasi and Kobina (2014) described modelling of ARIMA Models and forecasting of wholesale cassava monthly prices in central region of Ghana on the basis of historical prices from January 2013 to December 2013. They reported that results of ARIMA (0,1,0) model were the best. The study concluded with a good accuracy in terms of explained variability and predicting capability. Dhaval et al (2014) analysed about the predicted models used for forecasting the time series values for rain attenuation on the basis of classical real rain fall data from National Weather Service Climate Prediction Centre of U.S and Maryland. They applied ARIMA model for prediction of rain attenuation. The experimental values of the ARIMA models were obtained from different data sizes. The best fit model was selected on the basis of analysis in error matrix which gave fairly accurate prediction.

Kim et al (2015) investigated the behaviour of stock prices and rates of return to predict stock market movements. The null hypothesis of no difference between two population proportions was tested to find whether the weekly stock prices for 500 firms of Fortune and 600 firms for S&P small cap differ with respect to the ARIMA patterns. The data of over forty years was used for the analysis. The results of 327 (69.13%) of 473 Fortune 500 firms and 365 (61.45%) of 594 S&P small cap 600 firms showed ARIMA (0,1,0) to be the best model for prediction.Sahoo and charlapally (2015) used auto regressive model to predict the stock prices. To estimate the co-efficient of the regression, Moore and Penrose technique was implemented. Technique of advanced intelligent i. e. expert system and pure mathematical models along with neural networks were proposed for financial trading system to predict stock prices.

Hossain et al (2015) carried out the research on statistical data of Mobarakeh steel company of Tehran stock exchange for the period of 2006-2013. They recognized that ARIMA with EGARCH model implied low mean square error (MSE), low mean absolute error (MAE), low bias proportion, and low variance proportion for share volume trades data for comparison to other models. The result showed that prediction error by neural network was less than that of usual ARIMA models. They concluded that ANN can predict better than ARIMA models. Konarasinghe et al (2015) focused on the forecasting of Sri Lankan share market returns using ARIMA models. The series were tested with partial auto-correlation functions and auto correlation functions for stationarity of time series. The total market returns, sector returns and individual company returns were forecasted. They have used mean square error, mean absolute deviation, Anderson-Darling test and residual plots were used for model validation.

Jadhav et al (2015) analysed the historical data of six years for Indian stock market using six different models on monthly closing stock indices of sensex and concluded that ARIMA model helped in predicting fairly accurate values of the future stock indice. Out of the initial six different models. They chose ARIMA (1,0,1) as the best model based on the fact that it satisfies all the conditions for the "goodness of fit unlike the rest". Khasheia et al (2015) analysed the performance of four interval ARIMA-base time series methods for predicting exchange rates. The considered methods were ARIMA, Fuzzy ARIMA (FARIMA), Fuzzy ANN (FANN) and Hybrid Fuzzy Auto-Regressive Integrated Moving Average (FARIMAH). The results based on Fuzzy ANN (FANN) method were found satisfactory than other methods for forecasting in this study.

Verma et al (2015) applied ARIMA and state space modelling models on historical time series yield data from 1960-61 to 2006-07 of sugarcane crop for three districts of Haryana. The study predicted future values on the basis of crop yield forecasting for the period from 2002-03 to 2007-08 and checked the validity of analysed models. The results were found to be close to the actual yields for ARIMA and state space models. Babu and Reddy (2015) explored various prediction models for data of internet traffic (TSD), which was very unstable in nature. Hybrid ARIMA- ANN model was deduced as the best model in terms of minimum MSE and MAE and found more fit for forecasting the unstable data of internet traffic.

Manoj and Edward (2016) developed and applied ARIMA models on the Indian sectorial stock prices in their sector specific study of 6 sectors namely automobiles, banking, healthcare, information technology, oil & gas and power for daily actual data of 9 years from February 2007 to April 2015 with 1996 observations to forecast stock prices. They performed sector-specific study for forecasting and suggested that (1, 1, 0) to be the most suitable ARIMA model. Ngan (2016) analysed foreign exchange rate actual data for three years from 2013 to 2015 of commercial joint stock banks in Vietnam to forecast foreign exchange rate between Vietnam Dong and United State Dollar (VND/USD) in successive 12 months of 2016 using ARIMA Models. Their results proved that ARIMA models to be most suitable for estimating foreign exchange rate in short-term period.

Sengupta et al (2016) forecasted wind energy potential of Silchar (Assam, India) by using ARIMA and other models for a period from 2008 to 2011. The wind data at 10 m height plus 25 m height had been obtained, compared and analysed in this study. The peak average wind speed of Silchar was found to be 1.48 m/s at 10 m height and 1.69 m/s at 25 m height close to end of dry season. The highest average power densities were found during the month of March, which were 2.1 W/m2 and 3.2 W/m2 at 10 m and 25 m heights respectively. It was observed that for forecasting of speed data, autoregressive integrated moving average (ARIMA) models were the only useful models. Banhi and Gautam (2016) examined the gold prices of Indian market for the period of 11 years from November 2003 to January 2014 to assess the risk by investors in purchase of gold. ARIMA models applied on six different model parameters to forecast the future gold prices and proved that ARIMA (1, 1, 1)to be the best model which satisfied all the criteria of a fit statistics and gave fairly accurate results.

2.3 ARTIFICIAL NEURAL NETWORKS (ANN)

An artificial neural network (ANN) is a computational model based on the structure and functions of biological neural networks. It has mechanism of many inputs with only one output. ANN models are based on this mechanism: ANN has a large number of elements that are interconnected with each other in different layers. ANN has neurons like biological neurons, which are artificial and receive inputs from other artificial neurons. Thereafter, the inputs are biased and further added and the outcome of results is then transformed by a transfer function, i.e., sigmoid or hyperbolic function etc. into the output. Analysis of research works carried out in the past on ANN models for forecasting by various authors are presented in the following table 2.3.1. Brief of these studies is presented in the subsequent sections.

2.3.1 SUMMARY OF REVIEW OF LITERATURE – ANN MODELS

Authors	Year	Model Used	Application
White	1988	Artificial Neural Network- modelling and learning techniques	Economic prediction using IBM daily stock returns
Narendra and Parthasarathy	1990	Artificial Neural Network- Multilayer Network, Recurrent Networks	Identification and control of nonlinear dynamical system
Werbos	1990	Backpropagation dynamical systems-neural networks, feedforward systems of equations	System pattern recognition and fault diagnosis.
Park, Sharkawi, Marks, Atlas and Damborg	1991	Artificial Neural Network- layered perceptron	Electric load and temperature forecasting
Kryzanowski, Galler and Wright	1993	ANN-Backpropagation, Boltzmann machine.	Prediction of market to pick stock
Hill, Marquez, Connor and Remus	1994	Artificial Neural Network- feedforward neural network	Share market price prediction
Connor, Martin and Atlas	1994	Artificial Neural Network- AFERFM, HFERFM	Forecasting foreign exchange rate
Abhyankar, Copeland and Wong	1997	One way multilayer network	Market trend of stock market prices
Adya and Collopy	1998	Artificial Neural Network	Information processing system (Neurons)
Tsaih, Hsu and Lai	1998	Artificial Neural Network	Introduction to ANN
Atiya, Shoura, Shaheen and Sherif	1999	KDD, Back Propagation Algorithm	Prediction of stock market
MarcekandMarcek	2000	Artificial Neural Network- feed forward and recurrent neural networks	Predicting the exchange rate EUR/RON and USD/RON

Lakshminrayanan	2005	Box-Cox Transformation-forecasting of macroeconomics time series	Stock prediction-dataset of 530 monthly time series.
Abraham	2005	Artificial Neural Network-Automata and Fuzzy Logic	Comprehensive study of ANN
Morariu, Iancu and Vlad	2009	Artificial Neural Network-multilayer perceptron	Time series forecasting
Hadavandi, Shavandi and Ghanbari	2010	Artificial Neural Network-Genetic Fuzzy System (GFS)	Stock price forecasting
Aamodt	2010	Artificial Neural Network-Swing Point, Trend line, Moving Average	Forecast financial time series
Naeini, Taremian and Hashemi	2010	Feed Forward MLP Neural Network, linear regression method	Stock market value prediction
Tarsauliya, Kant, Kala, Tiwari and Shukla	2010	ANN Model-BPA, LRN, RBF, GRNN	Forecasting of financial time series
Khan, Alin and Hussain	2011	Artificial Neural Network-feedforward neural network	Share market price prediction
Philip, Taofiki and Bidemi	2011	Artificial Neural Network-AFERFM, HFERFM	Foreign exchange rate forecasting
Lehmiri	2011	Artificial Neural Network (ANN) and Backpropagation Algorithm	Prediction of financial stock market
Sharma, Rai and Dev	2012	Artificial Neural Network-Automata and Fuzzy Logic	Comprehensive study of ANN
Oancea and Ciucu	2012	ANN-feed forward and recurrent neural networks	Predicting foreign exchange rate

Author	Year	Method	Topic
Simon and Raoot	2012	ANN-back propagation neural networks, radial basis networks	Stock market prediction
kumar and Elango	2012	ANN -Multi-layer perceptron	Stock market prediction
Strzelczyk and Strzelczyk	2013	One way multilayer network	Market trend of stock market prices
Yadav, Yadav and Jain	2013	Feed Forward and Feedback Networks	Basic study of artificial neural network
Proietti and Lutkepohl	2013	Box-Cox Transformation-forecasting of macroeconomics time series	Stock prediction-dataset of 530 monthly time series.
Patil and Yalamalle	2014	LIX15 of NSE, MLP, MATLAB	Prediction of stock prices
Chauhan, Bidave, Gangathade and Kale	2014	KDD, Back Propagation Algorithm	Prediction of stock market
Maind and Wanker	2014	Artificial Neural Network	Information processing system
Kumar and Sharma	2014	Artificial Neural Network	Introduction to ANN
Munasinghe and Vlajic	2015	Multilayer feed-forward Networks	Stock prediction
Grigoryan	2015	ANN based model NARX	Talit stock of NASDAQ OMX
Karlsson and Nordberg	2015	DAX and Nikkei indices	Prediction performance of foreign market
Saini, Parkhe and Khadtare	2016	Feed Forward and Recurrent Neural Network	Forecasting foreign exchange rates

2.3.2 LITERATURE REVIEWS OF ARTIFICIAL NEURAL NETWORK

Brief description of research work carried out by various authors in the past in context of forecasting using ANN models is as under:

White (1988) outlines some upshots of an evolving project emphasizing on IBM's common stock daily return, using ANN modelling and other learning technique to find out and unravel non-linear regularities in asset price movements. He suggested some new problems through statistical solutions which help to decide on the exclusion or inclusion of additional hidden values to provide network. The purpose of this study was to illustrate the regularities using neural network methods. The regularities include common stock returns of IBM daily, interpretation and modification of neural network learning methods and the connect with the salient features of economic time series. Narendra and Parthasarathy (1990) used neural networks for identification and control of non-linear dynamic system. The research was conducted using static and dynamic back- propagation technique for alteration of parameters. They also discussed the use of multilayer and recurrent networks.

Werbos (1990) analysed the concept of basic backpropagation widely used in pattern recognition and fault diagnosis. He presented basic equation of backpropagation through time, which is then applied to neural network of varying degree of complexity. He took advantage of Backpropagation which is a simple and efficient method to calculate all the derivatives of a single target quantity with respect to input of large set quantities. Park et al (1991) presented the methodology of artificial neural network to predict electric load. ANN was considered as the most appropriate method to to predict future load pattern by incorporating the past temperature pattern and load data in a training set. He presented an algorithm which utilized layered perceptron artificial neural network (ANN) by combining both the regression and time series.

Kryzanowski et al (1993) developed a system that could accurately classify a company's stock movement. The model attempted to classify stocks with positive returns from the stocks with negative returns by training an ANN network which could predict future prices depending on data of previous four years. The model reduced the time needed to screen the companies and help portfolio manager to evaluate movement of stocks in a given period. The difference in results appeared due to the volume of data and shortage of time. It was found that ANN was able to find out 72% of the positive and negative returns correctly. Hill et al (1994) compares artificial neural network with statistical approach focussing on regression-based forecasting, time series forecasting, and decision making. The objective was to assess the capability of artificial neural networks for predicting and making future decisions based on the empirical results.

Connors et al (1994) researched on recurrent neural networks by filtering outliers from the data. A comparison was made between ability of least square estimated recurrent network on synthetic data and time series data. The recurrent neural networks gave best and accurate results. The superiority of recurrent networks in comparison to feedforward networks in predicting is not just due to its ability to model time series data with least errors but rather to train a model set accordingly. Further, the ability to predict accurately was dependent on the type of data. Better predictions were obtained with the help of neural network trained on filtered data in comparison to neural network trained on unfiltered data. Abhyankar et al (1997) analyse the trends (ups and downs) in stock market returns. The data of four important stock indices was tested for non-linear dependence. The study concluded that the return process is characterized by the pattern of data or some stochastic component.

Adya and Collopy (1998) analysed 48 researches carried out during 1988 to 1994 for validation and effective implementation of neural network. A comparison was made between neural network and alternative methods. Artificial neural networks were containing huge number of processing units, inter-connection between processing units, and gave results with in a faulty tolerance. In various studies, artificial neural network showed less good results than alternative models when compared. It was found out that only 11 studies were validating neural networks and were implemented successfully. Others were either validated successfully or implemented successfully without validation. Saih et al (1998) analysed the hybrid approach of rule based systems and artificial neural network of artificial intelligence for implementing trading strategies in S&P stock index. The study used reasoning neural network instead of backpropagation which yielded better and accurate results and outperformed backpropagation and perceptron models. The study also analysed other factors influencing the financial markets, including conditions of general economic, political events and trader's demand. These factors reflected the problems in forecasting the financial stock market. They found that hybrid approach helped to develop more reliable and intelligent systems to model expert thinking and making future decisions to predict the financial stock prices easier in such cases.

Atiya et al (1999) applied neural networks to solve the difficulties in prediction of flow of river Nile in Egypt. They found that neural networks help to create good results for accurate forecasting of water flows. Further, various models of neural network were compared to pre-process the input in the context of forecasted values. After performing multistep comparisons, they concluded that direct method, which is back propagation through time approach in the best method for pre-processing the data. Marcek (2000) paid attention on the introduction of the fuzzy regression model & autoregressive model and application of these models in forecasting the stock market prices of VAHOSTAV Company. ANN being a part of artificial intelligence was concluded to be the best method to identify the hidden and unlikely patterns in data. He treated this as a better way for prediction of share market prices of stocks.

Lakshminarayanan (2005) constructed a hybrid model using technical indicators like Elliot's wave theory, fuzzy logic, etc. for stock market prediction. They indicated 3 different multilayer perceptrons and generalized feed forward networks on the Amerigroup Corporation (AGP) stock's closing price. The study analyses several factors which are not generally understood and affect the behaviour of stock market. A neural network was developed with different properties and architectures to solve the issue and to get accurate predictions for stock market. The study focused on more efficient forecasting of stock prices by making sequential improvements in the model. Abraham (2005) briefed about the basic aspects of ANN modelling to resolve the problems of forecasting of stock prices. The study gave a brief insight of artificial neural networks techniques. The basic processing elements of neural networks simplified mathematical model of neuron. The neuron impulse is then computed as the weighted sum of the input signals, transformed by the transfer function.

Morariu et al (2009) discussed forecasting of time series using pattern recognition technique and neural network. The data corresponding to the evolution in time of the activity considered are processed using the methods already mentioned. Technical tools like pattern recognition and multilayer perceptron were used for making predictions. The study also applied regression techniques in case of linear systems. It was found that artificial neural network was an effective tool as it had the ability to find non-linear dependency in the input data for linear systems. Hadavandi et al (2010) presented an integrated method involving genetic fuzzy systems (GFS) and artificial neural networks (ANN)for information technology and airlines sector's stock price forecasting. They studied the factors such as political event, general economic conditions and traders' expectations which affect the stock prices with the help of stepwise regression analysis. The data is then divided into groups and analysed with the help of self-organizing map neural networks. They observed that the hybrid model improves the accuracy of stock price prediction and hence, it was concluded as the best tool for forecasting.

Aamodt (2010) focussed on forecasting the times series by application of artificial neural networks. The data used consist of records of every trade that occurred in 10 separate stocks traded on the Oslo stock exchange (OSE) from 1st January 1999 to 1st January 2009. The repetition of patterns in historical prices of stocks were analysed to predict stock price. An environment was created to test and train the artificial neural network to forecast the stock prices accurately. The study used Karl Pearson's correlation to analyse the actual prices, predicted prices and hit rates. The results indicated that few ANN's can be trained to predict with significant power. It was observed that the longer term networks seemed to out-performed the shorter term networks as network performance became less and less promising on the shorter time scales. Naeini et al (2010) predicted future stock prices using feed forward multilayer perceptron (MLP) and an Elman recurrent network. The stock data had been extracted from Tehran stock market from a period of 2000-2005. Trading of shares for 1094 companies was done during this period. The study predicted the future price for three set of share prices, i.e., high value, low value and the average value of the stock on a given day. It was concluded from the experimental results that for analysing the direction of the change in price, simple linear regression was the best technique. Further, MLP neural network was found to be more reliable and accurate as compared to other models for predicting actual prices of the stocks.

Tarsauliya et al (2010) forecasted financial data series using various techniques of artificial neural networks. The data set was comprised of daily closing price of IBM and S & P 500 stock from 1st January 1980 to 8th October 1992.The study tried to overcome the difficulty in financial predictions due to volatility and non-linearity of data. Different models of ANN such as back propagation, radial basis function are applied and to analyse predict stock prices. The models were compared for accuracy. The study concluded artificial neural network to be the best technique which has the potential to predict the financial data having volatile and non-linear nature with maximum accuracy. Khan et al (2011) proposed new methods such as artificial neural network (ANN) and artificial intelligence (AI) to predict data by relying on historical data and eliminate the traditional techniques, i.e.,technical analysis, fundamental analysis, time series analysis and statistical analysis which were more expensive and time consuming. They used ANN techniques which have the capability to differentiate between hidden and unknown patterns in the data and proved to be more effective for prediction of stock market prices. This study used backpropagation algorithm and multilayer feedforward network for prediction of stock price. The ultimate objective of any investment is to earn higher returns. In this study, the objective was achieved by training the system and varying input data with the use of historical data to provide more accurate predictions with less error.

Philip et al (2011) designed a model to analyse the foreign exchange fluctuation in real life. The study analysed the artificial neural network foreign exchange rate forecasting model (AFERFM) for prediction of foreign exchange rate. In this study, back propagation algorithm and feed forward network were used to train foreign exchange rates and multilayer perceptron network was used for forecasting. They used sigmoid function for training input data. It was concluded that AFERFM was the most efficient method for predicting foreign exchange rate with an accuracy of 81.2% whereas HFERM had an accuracy of 69.9%. Lahmiri (2011) analyzed the accuracy of backpropagation neural networks trained with different heuristic and numerical algorithms were measured for comparison purpose. The data used for the study consist of the S&P 500 daily prices from October 2003 to January 2008. It was found that numerical techniques are suitable to train BPNN than heuristic methods when the problems of S&P 500 stock market forecasting is considered.

Sharma et al (2012) analysed the important characteristics and business application of artificial neural network. The study is about developing new models which decreases run time and reduces complexity of real life problems. It emphasized on the need of artificial intelligence which is growing with the feature of parallel processing. Oancea and Ciucu (2012) asserted that neural networks helped to solve the problems of predicting exchange rate with advance techniques which approximate nonlinear functions. The study compared the performances of recurrent neural network and feed forward networks for forecasting the exchange rate of EUR/RON and USD/RON. For further analysis, the data series was normalised by removing the correlation between them and it was found that a recurrent network was more efficient in predicting the exchange rate thana feed forward network.

Simon and Raoot (2012) asserted that for improving the accuracy of a stock, a company's prospects and portfolio of financial condition should also be taken into account. The study analysed various ANN models with different techniques to train the data for improving the accuracy of stock market forecasting with minimum errors. The study compares three models, multilayer perceptron (MLP), adaptive neuro-fuzzy inference systems (ANFIS) and general growing and pruning radial basis function (GGAP-RBF). It was concluded that MLP with back propagation algorithm was the most efficient model to predict foreign exchange rate accurately. Kumar and Elango (2012) used neural network techniques multilayer perception model for forecasting of stock prices of TCS from the national stock exchange (NSE) of India beginning from 1st November 2009 to 12th December 2011. They found that for statistical evaluation and prediction of stock prices, neural network tools are the most efficient when combined with algorithms for prediction. Neural network helped the investors to get better results for trading and making future business decisions (buy or sell stocks). This study concluded multi-layer Perceptron (MLP) architecture with back propagation algorithm to be the best for prediction with greater accuracy in comparison to other neural network algorithms.

Agata and Artur (2013) presented neural networks which are used in prediction of various phenomenon's such as credit rating assessment, stock prices and stock exchange index, sorting or detection of economic entities matching signal filtering or optimization. Yadav et al (2013) focussed on basic structure, characteristics, variations and forms of neural network. Their study includes comparison of the activation functions of ANN such as threshold, piecewise linear, sigmoid and gaussian. Further, feed-forward and feedback architecture of neural network are studied. The study concluded that due to massive data in the world and the growing need of artificial intelligence, artificial neural networks when combined with the computational automata and fuzzy logic will help in developing efficient way to forecast the future. Proietti and Lutkepohl (2013) analysed whether transforming a variable will lead to any improvement in forecasting accuracy. They used Box-Cox transformation and observed improvement in the accuracy of forecasting.

Patil and Yalamalle (2014) investigated the challenging positions in prediction of stock market. The data of companies listed under LIX15 index of NSE, for duration of 36 months (1-1-2011 to 1-1-2014) have been collected. Different techniques of prediction were used for prediction of stock market to get the maximum accurate results. It was noticed that ANN techniques were very useful to predict the stock prices. Chauhan et al (2014) presented and captured complex input / output relationship in neural network. According to them ANN proved to be a better prediction model to improve the forecasting accuracy. The reasons cited by them are (i) ability of ANN to capture non-linear relations and (ii) features of fault tolerance. They have used data of BP neural network algorithm to predict the stock market by establishing a three-tier structure of the neural network, namely input layer, hidden layer and output layer. Finally, they get a better predictive model to improve forecast accuracy.

Maind and Wanker (2014) carried out research on biological nervous system like brain and its processing system using neural network. The research gave various advantages of artificial neural network over traditional approaches. ANN provided alternative better techniques over conventional technique when configured for a particular application, such as learning process for pattern recognition and data classification. The process involved the adjustment of the synaptic connections that exists between the neurons through learning in biological systems.

Parveen and Pooja (2014) gave brief review of the characteristics and application of artificial neural network. They mentioned that the parallel processing technique which can be embedded with ANN, the parallel processing technique save time and money by processing multiple queries in one go. Further, techniques such as computational automata, FPGA and fuzzy logic when combined with artificial neural can overcome drawbacks of artificial neural network technologies.

Munasinghe and Vlajic (2015) investigated factors such as data quantity and time factor and its effects on stock market data forecasts with artificial neural networks. They examined the long term and short term perspective considering time delay. The increase in quantity of data made no impact on the results of configuration of short term data but there was a delay in time for different configuration. Multilayer feedforward networks were implemented for supervised learning and for specific configuration, the models have undergone extensive by mean squared errors and statistical analysis. Grigoryan (2015) presented the hybrid models for prediction using artificial neural network. It introduced PCA-NARX prediction model based on ANN theories as a tool for financial time series forecasting. He mentioned that for accuracy of forecasting, optimal variable search played an important role. The PCA technique filtered the components depending on technical indicators and then used the filtered components as input of ANN-based technique to build the forecasting model. He analysed data of Nasdaq OMX baltic stock exchange beginning from 12th March 2012 to 30th December 2014 for total 700 daily observations.

Karlsson and Nordberg (2015) reviewed the effect of location change on predicting the stock market using artificial neural network. In their study, data from different location such as Denmark, Germany, Japan, Sweden and USA was taken and Index used OMX30 Copenhagan, DAX, Nikkei, OMX30 Stockholm and S&P500 respectively over a time period from1st January 2014 to 1st June 2014 to cross tested on other markets which affected the prediction performance. It was found that artificial neural networks performance is not dependent on the location change. The results suggested that an artificial neural network performed in the same manner on a market different from the one it was trained on. It was also observed that the ANN learns from the same market, which it predicts or does the core mechanisms of a stock market and make it possible to transfer learning between different regions. Saini et al (2016) introduced artificial neural networks for business practitioner in predicting the foreign exchange rates. They compared the performance of feed forward and recurrent neural network models used for forecasting the daily exchange rate of Indian rupee against four base currencies namely British pound, US dollar, Euro and Japanese Yen. It was clearly mentioned that ANN gave better results in predicting the rates of foreign exchange rate. They also analysed and compared the performance and results of the ANN models with different parameter values.

2.4 GENETIC ALGORITHM (GA)

Decision making and optimization techniques were revolutionized with the introduction of genetic algorithm (GA) by Holland (1975). This technique is used to find an accurate and better solution to search and optimisation of problems. Its structure is based on biological factors such as mutation, reproduction, mate selection and crossover of genetic information. In nature, the stress of particular atmosphere forces different individuals within species to compete and reproduce the most fit offspring. In genetic algorithms approach the fitness of various possible solutions is interrelated and objective is to find fittest possible solutions to produce best solution (offspring). This section presents review of research work carried out on genetic algorithm models by various authors in the context of forecasting. Tabular presentation of the research paper is given in table 2.4.1

2.4.1 SUMMARY OF REVIEW OF LITERATURE –GENETIC ALGORITHM

Authors	Year	Model used	Application
Mahfoud and Mani	1996	Genetic Algorithm- Selection, Crossover, Mutation	Optimization the domain of financial forecasting
Neely, Weller and Dittmar	1997	Genetic Programming technique- trading rules	Analysis of foreign exchange market
Thomas and Sycara	1999	GPS for data mining-trading rules	Foreign exchange market data from dollar / yen and dollar / DM
Allen and Karjalainen	1999	Genetic Algorithms-trading rules	Technical trading rule of S & P 500 index
Kim and Han	2000	Hybrid genetic model of ANN and Gas	Forecasting of stock price index
Lin, Cao, Wang and Zhang	2000	Genetic Algorithm- Selection, Crossover, Mutation-Trading Rules	Stock market prediction

Solomatine and Xue	2004	M5 model tree and Artificial Neural Network model	Flood forecasting
Abraham, Grosan, Han and Gelbukh	2005	Genetic Programming technique- Multi Expression programming	Prediction of stock indices
Solomatine and Siek	2006	Modular model including model tees – M5 tree	Approaches to build a modular model
Kwon and Moon	2007	Hybrid Neuro-Genetic System- ANN and GA	Stock forecasting
Rajabioun and Rahimi-Kian	2008	GP-based stock price models- MLP and Neuro Fuzzy Model- Trading Rules	Stock price prediction
Canillas, Sanchez and Baran	2009	Genetic Algorithm-Linear Genetic Programming	Consumer price index and soybean prices
Nair, Mohandas and Sakthivel	2010	GA Decision Tree, SVM, and Hybrid Prediction System, GA based parameter optimization,	Prediction of stock market trends
Mandziuk and Jaruszewicz	2011	Neuro Genetic (Neural Network and Genetic Algorithms)	Short term stock index prediction of Germen stock exchange
Kapoor, Dey and Khurana	2011	Genetic Algorithm- Selection, Crossover, Mutation-Trading Rules	Optimizations of technical rules
Vora	2011	Genetic Algorithm- Machine learning technique-Trading Rules	Technical analysis of components, i.e.,population, fitness function, boosting
Yusuf and Asif	2012	Traditional Time series prediction with ANN, Machine learning method	Prediction the trend of Bombay stock exchange
Naik, Ramesh, Manjula and Govardhan	2012	Genetic Algorithm- Selection, Crossover, Mutation-Trading Rules	Stock market prediction

Hegazy, Soliman and Salam	2013	Machine Learning Model- PSO and Least Square-SVM	Stock market prediction
Mousavishiri and Saeidi	2013	Genetic Algorithm with ANN, MLP, GFF, ANFIS-Trading Rules	Stock market prediction
Jakel and Sosík	2013	Multi-Agent system specification, agent candlestick pattern logical formula	Stock market prediction
Zareimoravej, Heidari, Zarei and Zarin	2013	Hybrid model using genetic theory and measure of errors	Prediction of stock prices
Chandrika, Ramesh, Anand and Cunha	2014	Genetic Algorithm, Hybrid Clustering, i.e., Fuzzy C Means and K-Medoids	Stock market prediction
Sabri and Mogadam	2014	LM Algorithms and quasi newton algorithm, Sigmoid function, linear function	Forecasting stock price
Sisodia, Kumar and Gupta	2014	Horizontal partition decision tree on based of Genetic Algorithm	Stock market prediction
Jena and Padhy	2014	Genetic Algorithm with Support Vector Mechanism (SVM)	Stock market prediction
Amin, Salehnezhad, Valipour and Nasirlu	2014	Genetic Algorithm to optimize Artificial Neural Network	Predicting of stock price index
Bonde and Khaled	2015	Hybrid Neuro Genetic Data mining technique	Stock prediction
Samant	2015	Genetic Algorithm and associative rule mining	Prediction of financial performance
Olsson and Magnusson	2016	Training an ANN using genetic algorithms	Stock forecasting
Patil, Tamhane, Dhage, Gawande and Mogal	2016	Fragment based association mining and Genetic Algorithm for optimization	Stock market prediction

2.4.2 LITERATURE REVIEWS OF GENETIC ALGORITHM MODELS

To solve the tricky problems quickly, reliably and accurately without the need of human intervention, genetic algorithm was introduced as an improved technique by the researchers. Genetic algorithms are employed to make improvement in the technique of learning algorithm and to minimize the issues in feature space. The main objective of GAs is to optimize the result of traditional /conventional and ANN models. The combination of two models is called hybridization. Generally, it is observed that models based on combination of genetic algorithm & neural network resulted better prediction of volatility of stock prices. Empirically it has been proved that hybridization is a better technique to solve the issues related to forecasting in comparison to stand alone application of models. A combined forecasting model based on GA technique reduced the error in estimation of stock prices. A review of genetic algorithms application is presented in the following subsections of this chapter.

Mahfoud and Mani (1996) showed that combining genetic algorithm system with neural network system significantly produced better result in comparison to both systems individually. In this study genetic algorithm system is compared to an established neural network system in the domain of financial forecasting, using the results from over 1600 stocks and roughly 5000 experiments. Genetic algorithm system was benchmarked a better methodology in comparison to artificial neural network system. Neely et al (1997) explored the technical trading rules related to evidence of significant returns using genetic programming techniques. They found significant improvement in the performance of models when dollar/deutschemark rules got permission to decide trades in the other markets as except to deutschemark/yen. They observed that patterns which were not apprehended by prevailing statistical models were detected by trading rules and genetic algorithm techniques.

Thomas and Sycara (1999) tried to discover trading rule based on genetic programming. The performance of the model was verified over real world exchange rate data in the doller /dm and dollar /yen market and better results were obtained from the dollar / yen market. The study analysed the aspects of system that helped to fight over-fitting specially validation methodologies and rule complexity. Allen and Karjalainen (1999) used genetic algorithm to learn technical trading rules for S&P stock and used every day prices for a period of 1928-1995. They tested their model on low transaction cost of liquid markets, including financial features, commodity and foreign exchange markets. The result showed a relationship between volatility and trading rule. Returns were lower when volatility was higher and vice versa.

Kim and Han (2000) tried to reduce the complexity in feature space and improved the learning algorithm by employing genetic algorithm. Genetic Algorithm optimized related weight between layers and threshold for feature discretization. With the help of feature discretization, they tried to minimize the complexity of the feature space and eliminate the factors which are not relevant. The result showed that genetic algorithm approach for feature discretization models increased performance for prediction of stock price in comparison to gradient descent algorithm. Lin et al (2000) presented genetic algorithm as the best technique for forecasting the prices of stock market and financial fields in real time analysis The stock data is selected from Australian Stock Exchange (ASX) beginning from 1992-2002. GA makes the possible of real time analysis in comparison to greedy algorithm which takes a lot of time to get the most profit combination. It helped the investors to solve the problematic areas for selecting the values of trading rules and get the best possible combination for investment. The objective of the study was to provide the combination of parameters which could produce the maximum profit and give reasonable trading options.

Solomatine and Xue (2004) examined the use of M5 model tree machine learning technique for forecasting flood data for the upper reach of the Huai River in China. In this study, M5 model tree technique was compared to multilayer perceptron artificial neural network (ANN). The results showed that model trees were more transparent and could quickly trained than ANN. Different M5 and ANN models were built to analyse the flood samples which were categorized into different groups. The higher accuracy of M5 trees was achieved by combining ANN and M5 tree. Abraham et al (2005) introduced a genetic program technique for the prediction of two stock indices. In this study, comparison was carried out between five different intelligent paradigms which were combined using an ensemble and two well-known optimization algorithms namely PAES and NSGA II algorithms in order to obtain the most favourable combination which can optimize the presentation of four different measures. It was found that resulting ensemble gave the best result.

Solomatine et al (2006) presented approaches to build a modular model based on different types of input (training sets) and different output's models like greedy algorithm and fuzzy combinations. The M5 opt model gave better and most accurate results on the data set, which is an improvement of greedy M5 algorithm. For effective and accurate prediction, the local models were considered over global models for decision making. The study concluded that such models are trusted more than the purely machine-learning predictors. Keogh (2006) proposed a semi supervised framework for building time series classifiers. He mentioned that time series classification requires huge amount of categorized training data which is very difficult and expensive to obtain from one source. The data was collected from various sources like video datasets, electrocardiograms and handwritten notes. The results of the experiment proved that with special considerations, the self-training classifiers with not much of labelled data gave higher effective and accurate results.

Kwon and Moon (2007) presented the combination of genetic algorithm and recurrent neural network with one hidden layer for forecasting the daily stock trading. GA optimized by adjusting neural networks weight under two dimensional crossovers and encoding. The objective of the study was to focus on the development of automatic stock trading systems based on artificial neural networks and genetic algorithms. The study showed a notable improvement on buying and holding of the stock for a particular time and further improved the results by context based ensemble. Rajabioun and Rahimi-Kian (2008) used genetic programming (GP) for mathematical modelling. The study presented stock price predictor along with mean-variance based sell / buys actions and compared the potential of GP model & ANN with Neuro-Fuzzy networks. This integration affected investor's trading on the stock prices and on investor's capital. The investors who made their trading decisions based on the future price trend of GP model proved to be most successful in the stock market. These models were found capable of predicting stock prices upto succeeding 30 days with adequate prediction error.

Canillas et al (2009) presented an advanced technique which was used in the field of genetic programming such as Linear Genetic Programming (LGP). The forecast was done on consumer price index (CPI) and price of soybean per ton for a certain period. They used LGP to forecast time series with two objectives, i.e., (i) to explain the variations of time series in the past while and (ii) to predict the future behaviour of the time series. Nair et al (2010) proposed a new system to optimize the decision tree-support vector machine (SVM) hybrid system used with genetic algorithm which helped in forecasting the stock market trends one day ahead. The prediction model applied on BSE stock market data for listed companies for the period from January2, 2007 to July 30, 2010. The accuracy was higher for GA optimized decision tree-SVM hybrid system. Both the system under consideration gave more trading profits for the investors. The study showed that the hybrid system was best fit for forecasting of stock market trends.

Mandziuk and Jaruszewicz (2011) focused on short term index prediction using neuron genetic system. The study discussed a mechanism by adding a new type of crossover to control the range of chromosomes' sizes to enhance the procedure of genetic algorithm. The qualitative observations and numerical results concluded that the choice of network's architecture and the evolutionary-based input variables selection are reasonable. They proposed neuro-genetic hybrid system to enhance the results. Kapoor et al (2011) described how genetic algorithms were used to improve the performance of trading rules and how the changes affect the quality of solution obtained in trading system. They applied methodology to State Bank of India stock data taken from National stock exchange (NSE) of India, consists of 1136 observations on closing price of stock on daily basis for the period from August 12, 2001 to December 29, 2006.The results of the analysis demonstrate that there is an increase in maximum profit by using optimum moving average lengths obtained from various GAs as compared to the popular moving average lengths obtained from financial literature. The objective of this study was to set trading rules parameter for financial time series. Vora (2011) presented a new technique to identify appropriate buy / sell signals using technical indicators identified by a genetic algorithm. To identify the trading horizon (buy/sell signals), the combination of indicators identified by genetic algorithms were tested on data obtained from National Stock Exchange (NSE) of India. Simulation showed improved profitability for the projected trading horizon.

Yusuf and Asif (2012) predicted the daily excess returns of Bombay Stock Exchange (BSE) indices subsequent to the returns of Treasury bill rates. The genetic algorithm used with artificial neural networks model to construct a model to choose the optimal topology after prediction of excess returns time series using lagged value. Naik et al (2012) proposed trading rules for stock market investments (India Cement) to get maximum benefit. Although it was a difficult task but the study suggested solutions to solve the problems that were inherent in maintaining and constructing rule-based applications for stock market through genetic algorithms. Mousavishiri and Saeidi (2013) designed a hybrid model to predict stock prices. The model was a combination of genetic algorithms and neural networks. The prediction based on this model was better during uncertain market conditions. The problems which were difficult to identify with traditional methods were identified and solved by artificial intelligence techniques such as fuzzy logic, genetic algorithm and artificial neural networks. The performance of the model was found best when neural network was combined with genetic algorithm.

Jakel and Sosik (2013) applied genetic algorithms to construct candlestick pattern logical formulas (based on simulation of trades) on daily time series data of stock prices from 2000-2011 of seven stocks listed in the US stock index Dow Jones Industrial Average (DJIA). They divided the data into 2 segments, i.e., in-sample for genetic algorithm evolution and out-of-sample for evaluation. Algorithm benchmark was analysed to evolve agents genetically to enhance their stock price forecasting ability. They gave due importance to set an error function in the forecasting process and to set a fitness function for genetic evolution of agents. Zareimoravej et al (2013) presented the prediction model based on genetic theory of rhythm patterns and a hybrid model using a measure of error (MSE). The nonlinear nature of price behaviour of stocks was analysed in the study by taking sample stocks from Tehran stock exchange from year 2002 to 2012. A combined forecasting model based on set theory and genetic algorithms reduced the errors in forecasting stock prices. The results proved that genetic algorithm model gave better results of prediction than the traditional models.

Chandrika et al (2014) determined the future prices of stocks and financial instruments accurately which helped the investors to invest further and gain profit from their investment. The process included hierarchical clustering and fuzzy C-means for clustering. From the experimental results they found that fuzzy C-means and K-medoids both achieved an accuracy of 88% when using same data, rule set and the same number of clusters but the execution time of fuzzy C-means was found greater than that of K-medoids. Sabri and Mogadam (2014) studied and found the complexity of mechanisms and price changes in food and beverage companies. This study aimed to forecast the daily stock returns of food products manufactures accepted in Tehran stock exchange. Both the neural network and ARIMA model have relative position to predict the stock prices. ANN model performed better than ARIMA in predicting stock prices by using backpropagation algorithm and quasi newton in learning function. Sisodia et al (2014) made combination of two techniques namely genetic algorithm and the horizontal partition based decision tree to enhance the capability of stock market prediction. The hybrid genetic algorithm helped to classify the data and provided better results among the close values of the stock market. The resultant predictions yielded significant profits.

Jena and Padhy (2014) applied the support vector regression (SVR) model combined with genetic algorithm. The results of combined model were better. This model of forecasting was applied to the data collected from National stock exchange of India Limited of S&P CNX Nifty, S&P BSE FMCG Index, S&P Infotech 500, S&P BSE MIDCAP Index and S&P BSE oil & gas index with 650 samples. Both the models gave better results rather than performing individually. Amin et al (2014) presented the hybrid model with genetic algorithm-neural network model to predict the volatility of stock price indices. The data had been collected through the RehavardNovin database and from Tehran stock exchange. This study showed that genetic algorithm in combination with other models creates effective models which give effective results by adding artificial intelligence for model optimization.

Bonde and Khaled (2015) used genetic algorithm for optimization of weights of neural network and trained neural network for prediction of stock prices proposing a hybrid genetic approach combined with neural network for better accuracy. The data used for the study was google (GOOG), TCS (TCS.BE), Infosys (INFY.BO), HCLTECH.NS and Wipro (WIPRO.BO) beginning from 1st January 2004 to 31st December 2014. Six attributes of each company, i.e., opening price, closing price, highest price, lowest price, volume and adjusted closing price were used for prediction. They found that results of prediction were accurate upto 70%.

Samant (2015) proposed a model for predicting the performance of stock market using a combination of genetic and association rule mining algorithm for the prediction of DJIA stock market. The data was collected from yahoo finance. As it is well known that classification is an important task to forecast accurately of an unseen instance and this process classifies new data on the basis of previously generated rules. Associative classification predicted with better accuracy than traditional classification approaches but its capability of handling the data and its relation is weak. Due to this weakness, they got motivation to construct a suitable method and building associative classifiers for numerical data. In this research, prediction accuracy was found up to 95% correct.

Olsson and Magnusson (2016) investigated whether putting more computational resources into training of artificial neural networks using genetic algorithms to avoid local minima problems over traditional algorithms, can result in higher accuracy for prediction of stock prices. This study was conducted on training data for closing prices of S&P 500 index (SNP), and the used stock is Ericsson B (ERIC B) of American stock exchange. It showed that accuracy has not increased significantly by implying more resources into training with genetic algorithm. They concluded that there should be sufficient data to compare the training algorithm for combining closing data with the other data. Patil et al (2016) developed a system for predictions of the stock market movements in the Indonesia stock exchange market which followed two main phases, one is for fragment based association mining and other focus on optimization for predictions provided by genetic algorithms. They analysed stock price movements of the companies by implementing the association rule-mining algorithm to mine rules of relationship amid movements of the stock prices from time to time. The study also examined and evaluated various factors that affect number of rules generated.

CHAPTER III
DESCRIPTIVE ANALYSIS OF TIME SERIES DATA

3.1 INTRODUCTION

To have an in-depth understanding of the behaviour of any set of data, exploratory analysis is always needed. It includes calculation and interpretation of different descriptive statistics such as (i) measure of central tendency, (ii) measure of dispersion, (iii) measure of skewness, (iv) measure of kurtosis (v) outliers (vi) inconsistencies and (vii) missing values. In addition, many more tests are needed for the data in relation to specific data in the context of specific analysis. These statistics are computed and interpreted for a data set consisting of 25 companies listed at Bombay Stock Exchange (BSE) in this chapter.

The chapter is divided in six sub sections. The first section 3.1 presents a brief introduction of the chapter followed by various definitions of the time series as given by earlier researchers in section 3.2. The section also includes a brief of review of literature in relation to the application of time series analysis using ARIMA models, ANN, Genetic algorithms with specific reference to stock market data analysis. Section 3.3 presents time series data of 25 BSE Sensex companies of Indian stock market. The next section 3.4 details various statistics along with the interpretation of these statistics. It is mainly about measure of central tendency, dispersion, skewness and kurtosis. It is followed by test of normality in section 3.5 and test for outliers in section 3.6. One of the requirements of usage of times series data analysis with ARIMA models is that time series must be stationary. The test of stationary is ADF test. The results of the ADF test are given in section 3.7 and the chapter ends with comments on utility of descriptive statistics in the context of ARIMA models.

3.2 TIME SERIES AS DEFINED

This section presents the definition of time series and time series models by researchers in the literature.

Definition 1: Time series is defined as "an ordered sequence of values of a variable at equally spaced time intervals" (Source: NIST SEMATECH, e-Handbook of statistical Methods).

Definition 2: "Time Series model for the observed data $\{X_t\}$ is a specification of the joint distribution (of possibly only mean and covariance) of a sequence of random variable $\{X_t\}$ of which $\{X_t\}$ is postulated to be a realization" (Brockwell and Davis, 2002).

Definition 3: "A time series is a collection of observations of well-defined data items obtained through repeated measurements over time" (Source: Australian Bureau of Statistics- Statistical language of time series data).

Definition 4: "An ordered sequence of values of a variable at equally spaced time intervals". (Source: Engineering statistics handbook-www.itl.nist.gov/div898/handbook /pmc/ section4/ pmc41)

Definition 5: "A time series is a sequence of numerical data points in successive order. In investing, a time series tracks the movement of the chosen data points, such as a security's price, over a specified period of time with data points recorded at regular intervals. There is no minimum or maximum amount of time that must be included, allowing the data to be gathered in a way that provides the information being sought by the investor or analyst examining the activity" (Source: www.investopedia.com/terms/t/time series).

The practical utility of time series is defined in two forms.

(i) To attain knowledge of the underlying forces and configuration that created the observed data.

(ii) To fit a model and progress to forecast, monitor or even to ensure feedback and feed forward control.

A time series reveals relationship between two variables, for instance, (i) stock price and time intervals, (ii) price level of a commodity in different years, (iii) the temperature of a place on different days and (iv) production of a commodity in different months etc. As time changes, all examples indicate the change in the values of other variable.

Chatfield (1975) mentioned many examples of time series. These are " (i) economic time series (share prices, macro-economic statistics, income datasets) (ii) physical time series (river flow data, meteorological data, pollution monitoring data) (iii) marketing time series (sales figures, advertising response data) (iv) demographic time series (population levels over time) (v) manufacturing (process output and control charts) (vi) binary processes (digital data sequences, as in switching systems and data transmission systems) and (vii) temporal point

processes (1D point processes and by extension, 2D point processes and spatial point datasets) ".
Time series models such as ARIMA, ANN and GA have large number of applications. Some of these are listed in the following.

Stock Market Analysis: Following authors analysed the time series data for forecasting stock market, ARMA-GARCH model [Him Tang et al (2003), Valenzuela et al (2008)], ANN mathematical model [Alhaj et al(2011), Bagherifard et al(2012)], multiple linear regression model [Forslund and Akesson (2013)], fuzzy ARIMA model [Emamverdi et al(2013), Xiaoguang et al(2014), Adebiyi et al(2014), Devi et al(2014)], ARMA and ARIMA model [Abdullahi and Bakari (2014), Kim et al(2015), Konarasinghe et al(2015)], ANN and ARIMA model [Ostadi and Azimi (2015), Hossain et al(2015)], FANN, ARIMA models FARIMA and FARIMAH model [Khasheia et al(2015)], Genetic algorithm [lin et al, (2000), Naik et al, (2012)], hybrid neuro genetic data mining technique [Bonde and Khaled (2015)].

Budgetary Analysis: Regression analysis and structural equation modelling (Gaffin, 1981), Statistical model of ANN (Rosas et al, 2013), LIX15 of NSE, MLP, MATLAB (Patil and Yalamalle, 2014), GA-meta-optimization technique (Branke and Elomari, 2012).

Global Warming: Regression techniques for global temperature deviation for the period 1880-2000 (Hanson et al, 2006), ANN methodology (Elgaali and Gracia, 2004), ANN-FFNN & MLP (Afzali et al, 2011), GCM predictor & Statistical downscaling model (SDSM), (Dorji et al, 2017).

Load Projection: Hybrid ARIMA-ANN model used for internet traffic data projection (Babu and Reddy, 2015), ANN models, ARMAX models, Regression model, fuzzy logic, expert system (Tsekouras et al, 2015), ANN-multi-layer perceptron (Hernandez et al, 2014), ANN-Single and multi-layer feed-forward networks, recurrent networks (Vinutha et al, 2014), Regression models-simple, multiple, quadratic and exponential, ANN- feed-forward multi-layer (Aslan et al, 2011).

Yield Forecasting: ARIMA models were applied for the yield of sugarcane. (Priya and Suresh, 2010), (Verma et al, 2015), ANN- radial based function (Alkhidir et al, 2016), ANN-Multilayer perceptron and radial based function, data envelopment analysis (DEA) (Hota,

2014), Regression models-MLR, time series models- ARIMA and exponential smoothing models, probabilistic models-markov chain models (lamba and Dhaka, 2014).

Financial Market Forecasting: ARIMA, fuzzy auto-regressive integrated moving average (FARIMA), fuzzy artificial neural network (FANN) were applied for financial market forecasting (Khasheia et al, 2015), genetic algorithm and associative rule mining (Samant, 2015), genetic algorithm (Mahfoud and Mani, 1996).

Energy Potential: Used ARIMA model for analysis the wind speed data to determine the wind energy potential (Sengupta et al, 2016). ANN- feed forward neural network with backprepogation algorithm was implemented using MATLAB toolbox (Sagbas and Karamanlioglu, 2011), data mining and artificial neural networks (Olaiya, 2012), feed-forward neural network architecture (Singh, 2016).

Process and Quality Control: ARIMA models were used for information quality procedure (Ozaki, 1977), artificial neural networks (Funes et al, 2015), ANN-multi-layer feed forward (Aminabad et al, 2013).

Commodity Price Forecasting: Used ARIMA models for forecasting the wholesale prices of CASSAVA (Kwasi and Kobina, 2014), used GA technique-linear genetic programming (Canillas et al, 2009), hybrid genetic algorithm and simulated annealing (GaSa) (Anuradha and Bohra, 2012).

Economic Forecasting: ARIMA, feed forward and recurrent neural network models were used for forecasting foreign exchange rates (Tran, 2016), (Saini et al, 2016), GPS for data mining-trading rules (Thomas and Sycara, 1999), genetic algorithm (Allen and Karjalainen, 1999).

3.3 SECTOR WISE DATA

This section presents brief information on time series data of 25 BSE Sensex companies of Indian stock market. The data under consideration is taken from Yahoo India finance for a period of 2 years from 20.01.2014 - 20.01.2016. The companies are taken from 6 different sectors as per the classification of SEBI (Security Exchange Board of India). The table 3.1 below gives the sector and name of the companies.

Table 3.1: Sectors-wise classified BSE stocks

Sector	No. of Stocks	Companies
Banking & Finance	5	HDFC (Finance), HDFC Bank, State Bank Of India, Axis Bank, ICICI Bank
Pharmaceutical	4	Cipla, Sun Pharmaceuticals, Lupin Limited, Dr. Reddy
Automobiles	3	Bajaj Auto, Hero Motor Corporation, Maruti Suzuki
Coal, Gas, Power, Energy	6	Reliance Industries, GAIL, Coal India, ONGC, NTPC, Power Grid Corporation
Steel, Ports & Infrastructure	3	Adani Ports, L&T, Tata Steel
IT & Telecommunication	4	Infosys, TCS, Wipro, Bharti Airtel
Total No. of Stocks	**25**	

3.4 DESCRIPTIVE STATISTICS PRICES OF STOCKS

Descriptive statistics help in understanding the nature of target population to a great extent. These statistics give a meaning to the entire data set. The advantage of descriptive statistics is to provide an insight in the humongous data set. Descriptive statistics include measures of central tendency or averages and measures of dispersion or spreads, and other measures as listed in section 3.1. The succeeding sub-sections present these descriptive statistics for 25 stocks. These time series encompass daily actual stock prices for a period of two years (20.01.14 to 20.01.16) which makes 523 observations for analysis. There was no missing value found in the data under consideration.

3.4.1 Analysis of measure of central tendency and measures of dispersion

Measure of central tendency or Averages are "statistical constants which enable us to comprehend in a single effort the significance of the whole" (Bowley, 1907). In simple words, it is a single value which represents the entire data. The following measures of central tendency are analysed in this research.

(i) **Arithmetic Mean**:

It is the sum of all the observations divided by the total number of observations. (Bowley, 1907)

The mean ($\bar{x}$) of n observations $x_1, x_2, x_3, \ldots x_n$ can be represented as:

$$\bar{x} = \frac{1}{n}\sum_{i=1}^{n} x_i \tag{3.1}$$

(ii) **Median:**

"Median is that value of the variate which divides the total frequency into two halves" (Griffin, 1962).

"Median is that value of the variable which divides the group into two equal parts, one part comprising all values greater and the other values less than the median" (Connor, 1932).

Median of given data can be calculated as:

(i) Arranging the series in ascending or descending order of the magnitude.

(ii) When the total number of items are odd, then the median is represented as $\frac{(n+1)}{2}$ th term. (3.2)

(iii) When the total number of items is even, then median is represented as the mean of $\frac{n}{2}$ th and $\left(\frac{n}{2}+1\right)$ th term. (3.3)

Where n = number of terms

Measure of dispersion:

"Dispersion is the measure of variation of items" (Bowley, 1907).

"Dispersion is a measure of the extent to which individual items vary" (Connor, 1932).

Measure of dispersion is used to understand the consistency of averages and it is used to compare between two or more-time series. The following measures of dispersion are analysed in this study.

(i) **Standard deviation:**

It is defined as "the square root of the arithmetic mean of the squares of the deviation of the values taken from mean" (Karl Pearson, 1920). It is also known as root mean square deviation. It is denoted by greek letter sigma: $'\sigma'$.

$$\sigma = \sqrt{\frac{\Sigma(X-\bar{X})^2}{N}} \text{ or } \sqrt{\frac{\Sigma x^2}{N}} \qquad (3.4)$$

where $x = X - \bar{X}$

X is the variable, $\bar{X}$ is the mean of the sample and N is total number of observations.

(ii) **Coefficient of variance** (C.V.) is calculated for comparing the variability of two series. Coefficient of Variance can be calculated as:

$$C_v = \frac{\sigma}{\mu} \times 100 \quad \text{(Karl Pearson, 1920)} \qquad (3.5)$$

where, σ is the standard deviation and μ is the arithmetic mean of the data.

The following table 3.2 presents the analysis of measure of central tendency (mean, median) and measure of dispersion (standard deviation and coefficient of variance) of the series under consideration.

Table 3.2: Measures of central tendency and measures of dispersion

Name of the Company	Face Value of Share	No. of Obs.	Arithmetic Mean	Median	S.D. (σ)	C.V.
Banking & Finance Sector							
HDFC (Finance)	2	523	1119.73	975.90	161.75	14.45
HDFC Bank	2	523	937.60	1151.00	138.01	14.72
SBI Bank$_1$	1	523	251.03	255.10	991.46	95.97
Axis Bank$_2$	2	523	778.42	550.00	495.26	63.62
ICICI Bank$_3$	2	523	769.19	347.80	553.22	71.92
Pharmaceutical Sector							
Cipla	2	523	578.88	630.90	116.48	20.12
Sun Pharma	1	523	807.70	826.10	132.28	16.38
Lupin Limited	2	523	1488.67	1480.00	374.13	25.13
Dr.Reddy	5	523	3230.72	3203.00	525.86	16.28
Automobiles Sector							
Bajaj Auto	10	523	2267.92	3858.00	219.26	9.67
Hero Motor Corporation	2	523	2574.94	2599.00	287.76	11.18
Maruti Suzuki	5	523	3324.11	3480.00	925.86	27.85
Coal, Gas, Power, Energy							
Reliance Industries	10	523	939.34	939.50	72.00	7.66
GAIL	10	523	389.93	384.80	52.46	13.45
Coal India	10	523	350.60	358.00	43.58	12.43
ONGC	5	523	325.21	320.10	64.54	19.85
NTPC	10	523	137.63	138.00	11.54	8.38
Power Grid	10	523	132.37	136.00	15.00	11.33
Steel, Ports & Infrastructure Sector							
Adani Ports	2	523	277.28	289.80	55.29	19.94
L&T	2	523	1524.09	1569.00	215.93	14.17
Tata Steel	10	523	371.34	368.10	102.16	27.51
IT & Telecommunication							
Infosys	5	523	2384.67	2209.00	1062.90	44.57
TCS	1	523	2462.04	2512.00	173.99	7.07
Wipro	2	523	568.47	562.00	33.50	5.89
BhartiAirtel	5	523	2462.04	355.50	173.99	7.07

₁ State Bank of India (SBI) shares have been split from the face value of its shares from Rs 10 to Rs 1 on 31.10.2014. The share prices have been adjusted by dividing 10 for the period 20.01.2014 to 30.10.2014.

₂ Axis Bank shares have been split from the face value of its shares from Rs 10 to Rs 2 on 17.07.2014. The share prices have been adjusted by dividing 5 for the period 20.01.2014 to 16.07.2014.

₃ ICICI Bank shares have been split from the face value of its shares from Rs 10 to Rs 2 on 25.11.2014. The share prices have been adjusted by dividing 5 for the period 20.01.2014 to 24.11.2014

3.4.2 Observations

Any series with a greater C.V. is said to be more volatile whereas series with a lower C.V. is said to be more consistent. As per the results obtained from the above analysis, it is found that stocks of State Bank of India are highly volatile having C.V. = 95.97 whereas stocks of Wipro are highly consistent with a C.V. = 5.89.

3.4.3 Measures of Skewness and Kurtosis,

Measure of Skewness:

Measures of dispersion tell us about the variability in a series whereas measure of skewness tells us about the dire0ction of variation. Skewness measures the lack of symmetry. It also gives an idea about the shape of the curve of a given data set.

Skewness is defined as:

$$g_1 = \frac{m_3}{m_2^{3/2}}, \tag{3.6}$$

where,

$$m_3 = \frac{\sum_{i=0}^{n}(x-\bar{x})^3}{n} \quad \text{and} \quad m_2 = \frac{\sum_{i=0}^{n}(x-\bar{x})^2}{n},$$

$\bar{x}$ is the mean, n is the sample size, m_3 is the third moment of the data set and m_2 is second moment (variance).

Measure of kurtosis:

A measure to check whether the data is heavy-tailed or light-tailed relative to a normal distribution is known as kurtosis. Heavy-tailed data sets are known as heavy due to presence of outliers in the data whereas data set without outliers is known as light –tailed. Increasing kurtosis is associated with the "movement of probability mass from the shoulders of a distribution into its centre and tails." (Balanda and MacGillivray, 1988)

Excess kurtosis is an important consideration while observing historical returns from a stock. The kurtosis of a normal distribution is equal to 3. If the coefficient is above the "normal level", it is more likely that the future returns of that particular stock will be either extremely large or extremely small. The excess kurtosis is generally used when the kurtosis of a normal distribution is zero. (Westfall, 2014)

Kurtosis is represented as:

$$a_4 = \frac{m_4}{m_2^2} \qquad (3.7)$$

And excess kurtosis (Westfall, 2014) is represented as:

$$g_2 = a_4 - 3 \qquad (3.8)$$

where,

$$m_4 = \frac{\sum_{i=0}^{n}(x-\bar{x})^4}{n} \quad \text{and} \quad m_2 = \frac{\sum_{i=0}^{n}(x-\bar{x})^2}{n},$$

$\bar{x}$ is the mean and n is the sample size, m_4 is the fourth moment of the data set and m_2 is the variance, i.e., the square of the standard deviation.

It shows that "higher kurtosis means more of the variance is the result of infrequent extreme deviations, as opposed to frequent modestly sized deviations".

The reference standard is a normal distribution, which has a kurtosis of 3. In token of this, often the **excess kurtosis** is presented: excess kurtosis is simply **kurtosis − 3**. For example, the "kurtosis" reported by Excel is actually the excess kurtosis.

a) A normal distribution has kurtosis equal to 3 and excess kurtosis equal to 0. Any distribution with kurtosis ≈3 (excess kurtosis ≈0) is called **mesokurtic.**

b) A distribution with kurtosis <3 (excess kurtosis <0) is called **platykurtic**. The tails of platykurtickutosis are shorter and thinner and central peak is the lowest and broadest of all other kurtosis.

c) A distribution with kurtosis > 3 (excess kurtosis > 0) is called **leptokurtic**. When compared to a normal distribution, its tails are longer and fatter, and often its central peak is higher and sharper.

"Kurtosis as a statistical measure has significant importance for the investors, because it represents the possibility of the price of stocks to change significantly (up and down from current level). Obtaining information about the shape of distribution is an important step for model of pricing risky assets where distribution and estimates of volatility are used as inputs" (Ivanovski et al, 2015).

The following table presents these statistics for the stock price data of select companies.

3.4.4 Test Statistics of Skewness, and Kurtosis:

Table 3.3: Measures of Skewness and Kurtosis

Name of the Company	Face Value of Share	No. of Obs	Skewness	Kurtosis
HDFC (Finance)	2	523	0.45	0.87
HDFC Bank	2	523	-0.59	-0.88
SBI Bank	1	523	0.63	-1.41
Axis Bank	2	523	1.36	0.29
ICICI Bank	2	523	0.44	-1.62
Cipla	2	523	0.67	1.16
Sun Pharmaceuticals	1	523	-0.08	0.39
Lupin Limited	2	523	0.22	1.33
Dr. Reddy	5	523	0.37	-0.68
Bajaj Auto	10	523	-0.15	-1.15
Hero Motor Corporation	2	523	-0.13	-0.07
Maruti Suzuki	5	523	0.31	1.03
Reliance Industries	10	523	0.22	0.52
GAIL	10	523	-0.05	-0.47
Coal India	10	523	0.59	0.10
ONGC	5	523	0.11	1.01
NTPC	10	523	-0.04	-0.35
Power Grid	10	523	1.19	0.59
Adani Ports	2	523	-0.83	-0.18
L and T	2	523	-0.80	0.01
Tata Steel	10	523	0.18	1.04
Infosys	5	523	0.04	-1.49
TCS	1	523	-0.65	-0.56
Wipro	2	523	0.89	1.28
Bharti Airtel	5	523	0.89	1.28

A test statistic is a standard value which is calculated from a sample of data for testing a hypothesis. It is used to calculate the critical values, i.e., p-values for a given data set and to reject the null hypothesis. In short, a test statistic measures how closely the sample data and null hypothesis are related. Generally, when a test statistic becomes too large or too small, the p-value becomes too small which leads to rejection of the null hypothesis.

Test- Statistics of Skewness:

Test statistics: $Z_{g1} = G_1/SES$ (3.9)

where,

g_1 is the measure of skewness (as calculated in sub section 3.4.2) and SES is standard error of skewness, which is calculated as:

where $SES = \sqrt{\dfrac{6n(n-1)}{(n-2)(n+1)(n+3)}}$ (3.10)

where n is value of data set. (Cramer, 1997)

Critical Value of Zg_1 and interpretation:

The critical value of Z_{g1} is approximately 2. It is a two-tailed test of skewness (which is $\neq 0$) at 0.05 significance level.

a)   If $Z_{g1} < -2$, the population is likely to be skewed negatively.

b)   If Z_{g1} is between -2 and $+2$, the population might be symmetric or it might be skewed in either direction.

c)   If $Z_{g1} > 2$, the population is very likely to be skewed positively.

Meaning of this test statistics and the amount of skewness are different. "The amount of skewness tells us how highly skewed the sample is: the bigger the number, the bigger the skew. The test statistic tells us whether the whole population is probably skewed, but not by how much: the bigger the number, the higher the probability" (Cramer 1997).

The table 3.4 presents the values of skewness and test statistics of skewness.

Table 3.4: Test statistics of Skewness

Name of the Company	Face Value of Share	No. of Observation	Skewness	SES	Test- statistic
Banking & Finance Sector					
HDFC (Finance)	2	523	0.45	0.10	4.21
HDFC Bank	2	523	-0.59	0.10	-5.52
State Bank Of India	1	523	0.63	0.10	5.89
Axis Bank	2	523	1.36	0.10	12.73
ICICI Bank	2	523	0.44	0.10	4.11
Pharmaceutical Sector					
Cipla	2	523	0.67	0.10	6.27
Sun Pharmaceuticals	1	523	-0.08	0.10	-0.74
Lupin Limited	2	523	0.22	0.10	2.05
Dr.Reddy	5	523	0.37	0.10	3.46
Automobiles Sector					
Bajaj Auto	10	523	-0.15	0.10	-1.40
Hero Motor Corporation	2	523	-0.13	0.10	-1.21
Maruti Suzuki	5	523	0.31	0.10	2.90
Coal, Gas, Power, Energy					
Reliance Industries	10	523	0.22	0.10	2.05
GAIL	10	523	-0.05	0.10	-0.46
Coal India	10	523	0.59	0.10	5.52
ONGC	5	523	0.11	0.10	1.02
NTPC	10	523	-0.04	0.10	-0.37
Power Grid Corporation	10	523	1.19	0.10	11.14
Steel, Ports and Infrastructure					
Adani Ports	2	523	-0.83	0.10	-7.77
L and T	2	523	-0.80	0.10	-7.49
Tata Steel	10	523	0.18	0.10	1.68
IT and Telecommunication					
Infosys	5	523	0.04	0.10	0.37
TCS	1	523	-0.65	0.10	-6.08
Wipro	2	523	0.89	0.10	8.33
BhartiAirtel	5	523	0.89	0.10	8.33

Observation:

The following observations are recorded from the results presented in table 3.4

I. $Z_{g1} < -2$ for 3 stocks namely, HDFC Bank, Adani Ports, and TCS. Hence, the stock prices of these stocks are very likely to be skewed negatively.

II. Z_{g1} is between -2 and +2 in case of Sun Pharmaceuticals, Bajaj Auto, Hero Motor Corporation, GAIL, ONGC, NTPC, Tata Steel and Infosys. Therefore, no accurate conclusion can be drawn about the skewness of the prices of these stocks, as it might be symmetric or it might be skewed in either direction.

III. $Z_{g1} > -2$ for HDFC (Finance), State Bank of India, Axis Bank, ICICI Bank, Cipla, Lupin Limited, Dr.Reddy, Maruti Suzuki, Reliance Industries, Power Grid Corporation, Wipro and BhartiAirtel. Hence, the prices of these stocks are very likely to be skewed positively.

Test Statistics of Kurtosis:

To get the test statistic for kurtosis, divide the sample excess kurtosis by the standard error of kurtosis. It tells us how many standard errors, the sample excess kurtosis has from zero. Test statistics for kurtosis is denoted as:

$$Z_{g_2} = \frac{g_2}{SEK} \quad (3.11)$$

where, g_2 is excess kurtosis, SEK stands for standard error of kurtosis, SES is Standard Error of Skewness (derived in above sub-section). (Cramer, 1979)

$$SEK = 2 \, (SES) \sqrt{\frac{n^2 - 1}{(n-3)(n+5)}} \quad (3.12)$$

Where "n" stands for number of observations of a data set

Critical Value of z_{g_2}:

The critical value of Z_{g2} is approximately 2. It is a two-tailed test of excess kurtosis (which is $\neq 0$) at 0.05 significance level (Cramer, 1979).

a) If $z_{g_2} < -2$, the population is very likely to have negative excess kurtosis.

b) If z_{g_2} is between -2 and $+2$, the excess kurtosis might be positive, negative, or zero.

c) If $z_{g_2} > +2$, the population is very likely to have positive excess kurtosis

The table 3.5 presents the values of kurtosis, excess kurtosis, SEK and test statistic of kurtosis for the stock prices of select companies.

Table 3.5: Descriptive analysis- Kurtosis and Test statistic of kurtosis

Name of the Company	Face Value of Share	No. of Observation	Kurtosis	Excess Kurtosis	SEK	Test-Statistic
Banking & Finance Sector							
HDFC (Finance)	2	523	0.87	-2.13	0.21	-9.99
HDFC Bank	2	523	-0.88	-3.88	0.21	-18.19
State Bank Of India	1	523	-1.41	-4.41	0.21	-20.68
Axis Bank	2	523	0.29	-2.71	0.21	-12.71
ICICI Bank	2	523	-1.62	-4.62	0.21	-21.66
Pharmaceutical Sector							
Cipla	2	523	1.16	-1.84	0.21	-8.63
Sun Pharma	1	523	0.39	-2.61	0.21	-12.24
Lupin Limited	2	523	1.33	-1.67	0.21	-7.83
Dr.Reddy	5	523	-0.68	-3.68	0.21	-17.26
Automobiles Sector							
Bajaj Auto	10	523	-1.15	-4.15	0.21	-19.46
Hero Motor	2	523	-0.07	-3.07	0.21	-14.39
Maruti Suzuki	5	523	1.03	-1.97	0.21	-9.24
Coal, Gas, Power, Energy							
Reliance Industries	10	523	0.52	-2.48	0.21	-11.63
GAIL	10	523	-0.47	-3.47	0.21	-16.27
Coal India	10	523	0.10	-2.90	0.21	-13.60
ONGC	5	523	1.01	-1.99	0.21	-9.33
NTPC	10	523	-0.35	-3.35	0.21	-15.71
Power Grid	10	523	0.59	-2.41	0.21	-11.30
Steel, Ports and Infrastructure							
Adani Ports	2	523	-0.18	-3.18	0.21	-14.91
L and T	2	523	0.01	-2.99	0.21	-14.02
Tata Steel	10	523	1.04	-1.96	0.21	-9.19

IT and Telecommunication							
Infosys	5	523	-1.49	-4.49	0.21	-21.05
TCS	1	523	-0.56	-3.56	0.21	-16.69
Wipro	2	523	1.28	-1.72	0.21	-8.06
BhartiAirtel	5	523	1.28	-1.72	0.21	-8.06

Observation:

It is observed from the above table that the value of z_{g_2} is < -2 for all the stocks. Therefore, the stock prices of these stocks are likely to have negative excess kurtosis (kurtosis < 3, platykurtic).

The test statistics are compared with chi square distribution with degree of freedom as 2. The null hypothesis is rejected if the computed test statistics of kurtosis exceeds the critical values.

The critical values can be used from the below table for chi-square distribution:

Table 3.6 – Chi square distribution values:

Significance level α	Critical value (p)
0.10	4.61
0.05	5.99
0.01	9.21

Jarque –Bera Test (JB):

This is a test done to check the normality of the data set. It is computed with the help of values obtained from Skewness and Kurtosis.

The Jarque-Bera test statistic is represented as:

$$JB = n \left[\frac{S^2}{6} + \frac{EK^2}{24} \right] \quad (3.13)$$

where, S= Skewness and EK = Excess Kurtosis (which is K - 3)

The following table 3.7 presents the analysis of test statistic of kurtosis.

Table 3.7: Analysis of Jarque-Bera Test Statistics

Name of the Company	No. of Obs.	Jarque-Bera> Critical Value (9.21)	Jarque-Bera< Critical Value (9.21)	Probability > significance Level (0.01)	Probability < significance level (0.01)
Banking & Finance Sector					
HDFC (Finance)	523	20.91	-	-	0.000
HDFC Bank	523	24.71	-	-	0.000
State Bank Of India	523	51.97	-	-	0.000
Axis Bank	523	41.86	-	-	0.000
ICICI Bank	523	61.53	-	-	0.000
Pharmaceutical Sector					
Cipla	523	39.11	-	-	0.000
Sun Pharmaceuticals	523	-	3.45	0.178	-
Lupin Limited	523	39.60	-	-	0.000
Dr.Reddy	523	12.92	-	-	0.002
Automobiles Sector					
Bajaj Auto	523	29.38	-	-	0.000
Hero Motor Corporation	523	-	0.51	0.776	-
Maruti Suzuki	523	25.21	-	-	0.000
Coal, Gas, Power, Energy					
Reliance Industries	523	-	6.95	0.031	-
GAIL	523	-	4.87	0.088	-
Coal India	523	-	7.80	0.020	-
ONGC	523	22.49	-	-	0.000
NTPC	523	-	2.70	0.259	-
Power Grid Corporation	523	38.44	-	-	0.000
Steel, Ports& Infrastructure Sector					
Adani Ports	523	15.83	-	-	0.000
L&T	523	14.03	-	-	0.001
Tata Steel	523	24.28	-	-	0.000
IT & Telecommunication					
Infosys	523	48.41	-	-	0.000
TCS	523	16.04	-	-	0.000
Wipro	523	52.96	-	-	0.000
BhartiAirtel	523	53.13	-	-	0.000

Observation:

Jarque-Bera test is done to check the normality of the data set.

a) It is found that the stocks of the following 19 companies, namely, HDFC (Finance), HDFC Bank, State Bank of India, Axis Bank, ICICI Bank, Cipla, Lupin Limited, Dr Reddy, Bajaj Auto, Maruti Suzuki, ONGC, Power Grid, Adani Port, L&T, Tata steel, Infosys, TCS, Wipro and BhartiAirtel are exceeding the critical value of 9.21 for significance level (0.01). Therefore, it is concluded that the daily return of these companies do not follow a normal distribution whereas the stocks of other 6 companies have value less than the critical value of 9.21 at significance level (0.01).

b) The p-value for the 6 companies, namely, , i.e., Sun Pharmaceuticals, Hero Motor Corporation, Reliance Industries, GAIL, Coal India and NTPC is greater than the usual significance level of 0.01. According to the results, we observe that there is no evidence to reject H_0 for the daily returns of the stocks whereas for other 19 companies, p value < 0.001 that means the H_1 alternate hypothesis is accepted and H_0 is rejected.

3.5 OUTLIER TEST

In a random sample of population, an outlier is known as an observation which lies at an irregular distance from other values. This test is done to characterize normal observations so that abnormal observations can be figured out before conducting any analysis.

Box plot construction:

Box plot is a very useful graphical display which is constructed to describe the data behaviour in the middle and ends of the distribution. It uses median, the lower and the upper quartiles generally known as 25th and 75th percentiles. Interquartile (IQ) range is calculated as:

$$IQ = Q3 - Q1 \qquad (3.14)$$

where, Q1 is first quartile and Q3 is the third quartile.

Box plots with fences:

A box plot is fenced to identify the median by drawing a box between the upper and lower quartiles. The below mentioned fences are used to identify the extreme values in the tails of the distribution:

(i) Lower inner fence : (Q1 - 1.5) x IQ
(ii) Upper inner fence : (Q3 + 1.5) x IQ

(iii) Lower outer fence : $(Q1 - 3) \times IQ$
(iv) Upper outer fence : $(Q3 + 3) \times IQ$

The results obtained from the above methodology of the select companies with no outlier are presented below graphically:

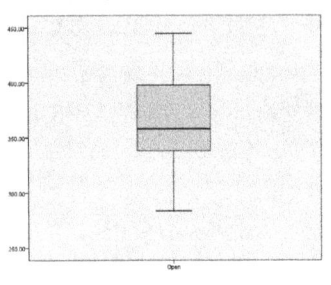

Airtel Limited

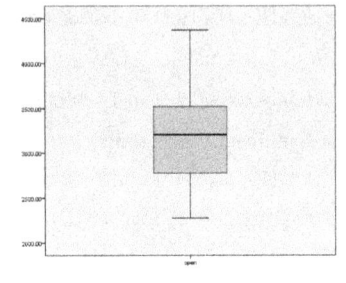

Dr. Reddy Limited

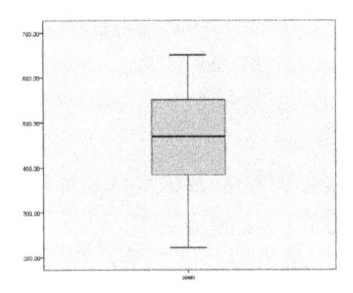

Axis Bank Ltd.

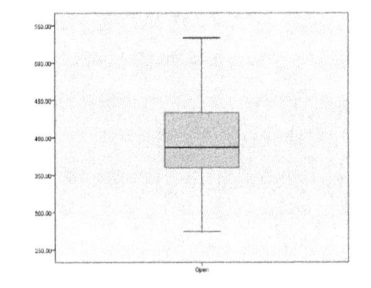

GAIL (India) Ltd.

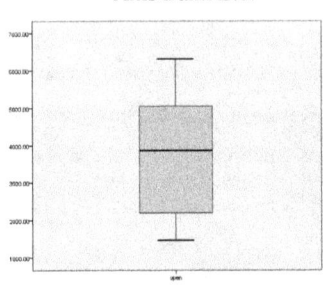

Bajaj Auto Ltd.

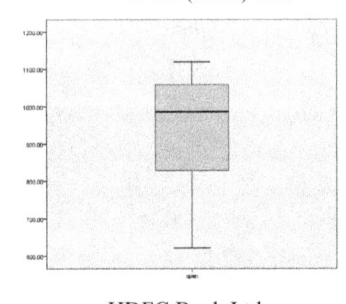

HDFC Bank Ltd.

Cipla Ltd.

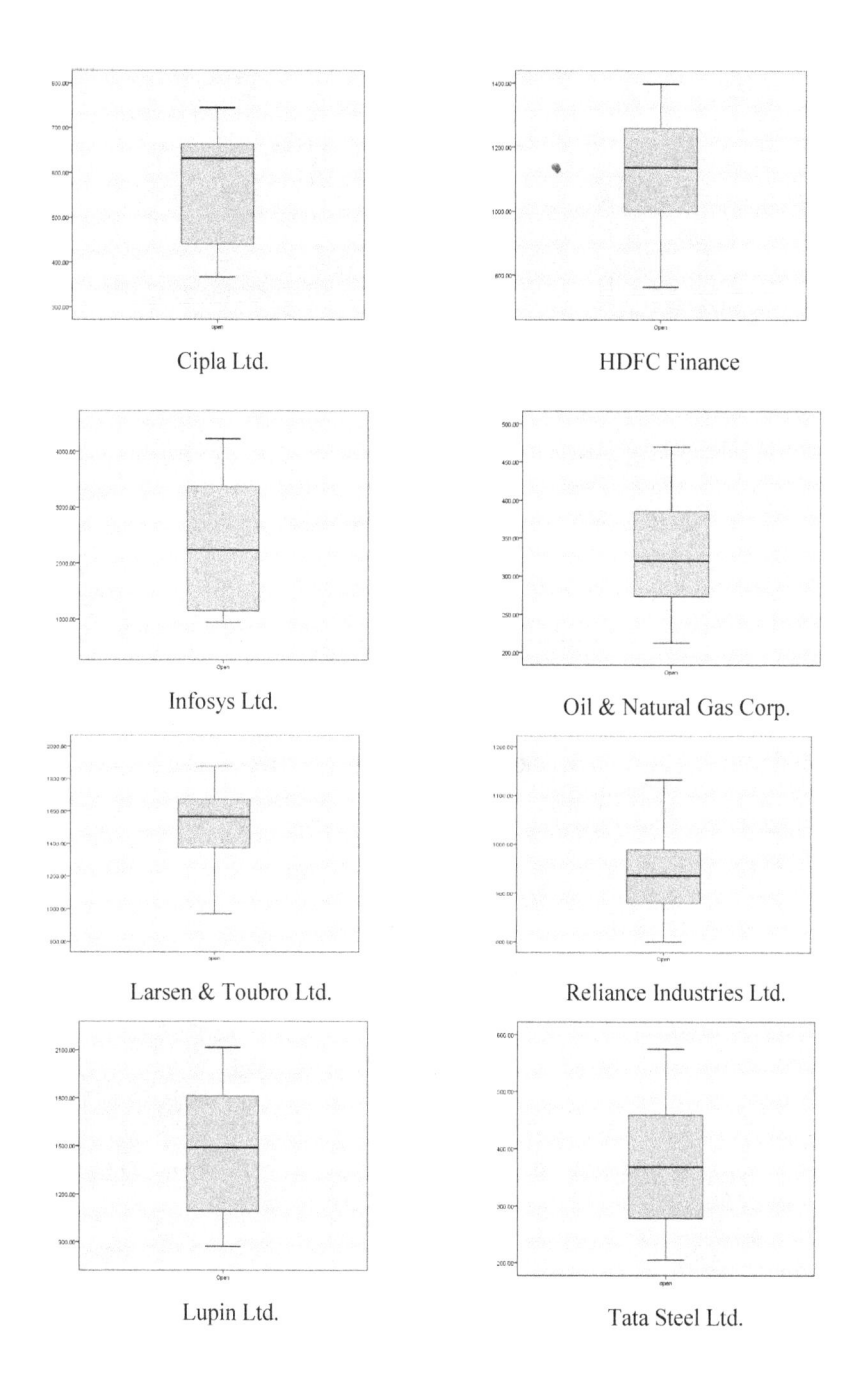

HDFC Finance

Infosys Ltd.

Oil & Natural Gas Corp.

Larsen & Toubro Ltd.

Reliance Industries Ltd.

Lupin Ltd.

Tata Steel Ltd.

NTPC Ltd.   ICICI Bank Ltd.

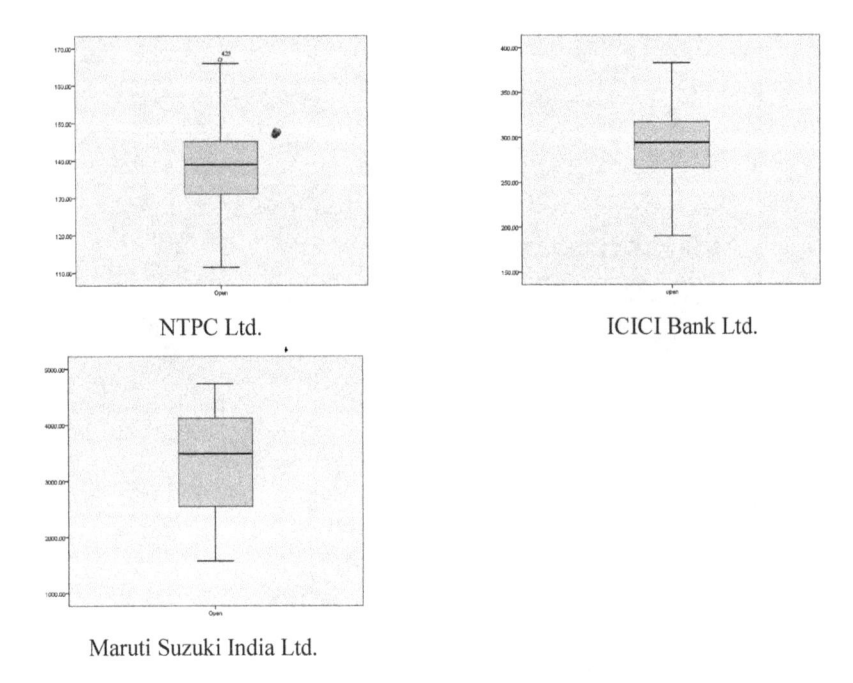

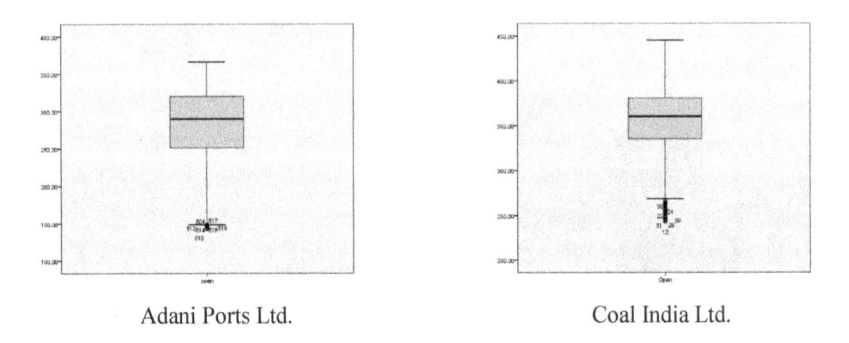

Maruti Suzuki India Ltd.

Figure 3.1- Graphical representation of the companies with no outliers:

The results of the select companies with outlier are presented below graphically:

Adani Ports Ltd.   Coal India Ltd.

Hero Motor Corp.   Sun pharmaceutical Ltd.

Power Grid Corporation   Wipro Ltd.

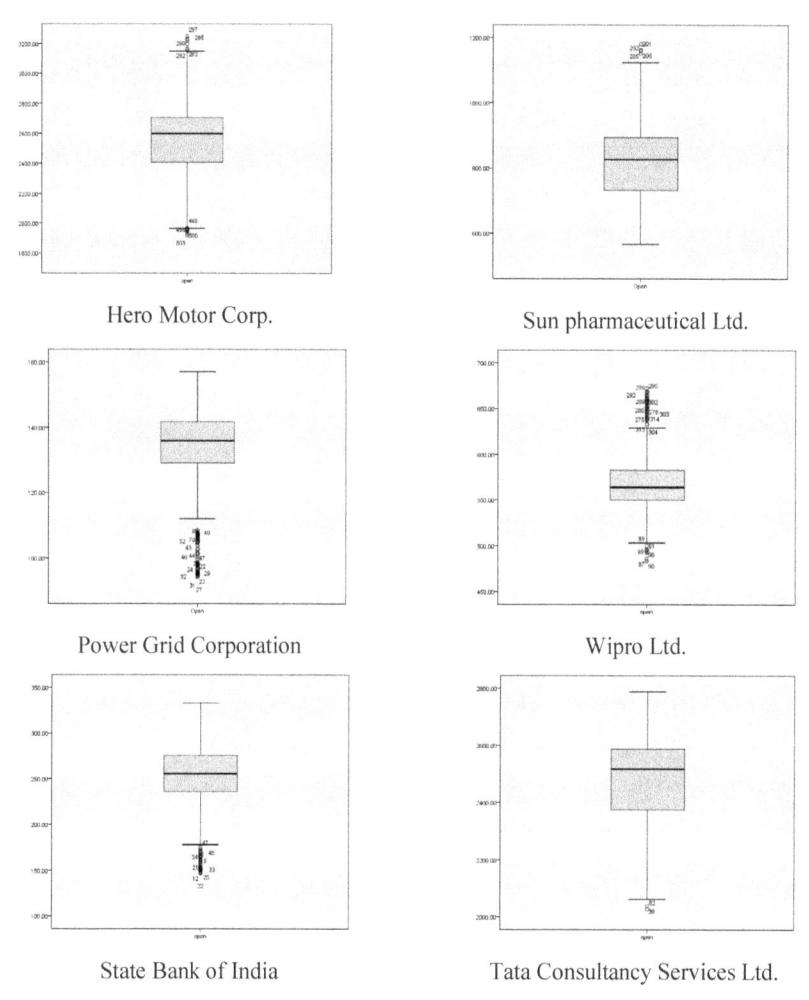

State Bank of India   Tata Consultancy Services Ltd.

Figure 3.2: Graphical representation of companies having outliers

Observation:

In statistics, an outliner is considered to be a bad data as it is distinct from all other observation in a population. Data set without outliers is considered to make better predictions as outliers make statistical analyses difficult. The outlier test is applied on the stocks of 25 companies. It is observed that 17 companies are not having any outlier in the data whereas rest 8 companies (as detailed in the table) are having outliers in their data set.

Table 3.8 - Results of the companies having outliers in the data

Name of the Company	No. of Observation	No. of Outliers	Reference No of outlier
State Bank Of India	523	10	12,22,25,21,33,34,35,47,48,49
Sun Pharmaceuticals	523	4	201,202,205,206
Hero Motor Corporation	523	9	498,499,500,503,290,292,293,295,297
Coal India	523	7	38,24,22,29,30.31,12
Power Grid Corporation	523	16	6,48,52,70,43,46,44,47,20,22,24,29, 32,23,27,31
Adani Ports	523	7	504,517,512,514,518,516,515
TCS	523	2	83,39
Wipro	523	18	292,295,296,289,302,280,278,303,275,315,304,315,89,91,99,98,87,90

3.6 STATIONARITY CHECK

Stationarity of the series is the pre-requisite for the application of ARIMA Model to develop a forecasting model. In this study, Augmented Dickey-Fuller test is used to check the stationarity of the considered stocks.

Consider the simplest arithmetic regression model.

$$y_t = \emptyset y_{t-1} + \epsilon_t \qquad (3.15)$$

where, $\emptyset$ is the coefficient of autoregression, ϵ_t is the random error at t and y_t is the actual value.

The Augmented Dickey Fuller test statistic is mathematically represented as:

$$DF = \frac{\tau}{SE\,\tau} \qquad (3.16)$$

If the test statistic is less than critical value, then the null hypothesis is rejected and no unit root is present.

The simplest approach to test for a unit root begins with the above model

Hypothesis:

H_0: There is a unit root for the series.

H_1: There is no unit root for the series which means the series is stationary.

Entire dataset is checked for stationarity by using software XLStat. Here observed value of tau (τ) and p-value of 0.05 significance level is considered for analyzing the results. In the instant case, τ value is more than the critical value so H_0 is rejected and alternate hypothesis is favoured. The series is differenced for first level and it is observed that it becomes stationary, however in anticipation for better results it is differenced at second level too. It is observed that the results of second difference are highly negative than the first order and the original values. For example, for stocks of HDFC Bank, the original value is -2.229, the first order value is -7.715 and the second order value is -14.052. The second differential value is highly negative which shows that the data under consideration is moving towards stationarity. The results are better when data is stationary however results will be compared with the actual values in the next chapters.

The results of the Augmented Dickey-Fuller (ADF) Test performed at various levels are detailed in the table below:

Table 3.9- Results of Augmented Dickey-Fuller (ADF) Test at different levels

Name of the Company	Tau (Observed Value)	P-Value	First Diff. of Observed Value	First Diff. of P-Value	Second Diff of Observed Value	Second Diff. of P-Value
Banking & Finance						
HDFC (Finance)	-2.029	0.580	-8.207	< 0.0001	-13.707	< 0.0001
HDFC Bank	-2.229	0.463	-7.715	< 0.0001	-14.052	< 0.0001
State Bank Of India	-0.992	0.939	-7.211	< 0.0001	-13.605	< 0.0001
Axis Bank	-2.191	0.485	-7.541	< 0.0001	-13.488	< 0.0001
ICICI Bank	-1.933	0.633	-7.788	< 0.0001	-13.595	< 0.0001
Pharmaceutical Sector						
Cipla	-1.444	0.844	-8.139	< 0.0001	-12.550	< 0.0001
Sun Pharmaceuticals	-2.164	0.501	-7.984	< 0.0001	-13.421	< 0.0001
Lupin Limited	-2.369	0.386	-7.956	< 0.0001	-11.794	< 0.0001
Dr.Reddy	-3.130	0.097	-7.703	< 0.0001	-13.396	< 0.0001

Automobile Sector					
Bajaj Auto	-2.695	0.232	-9.200	< 0.0001	-14.571	< 0.0001
Hero Motor Corporation	-1.059	0.930	-8.095	< 0.0001	-12.415	< 0.0001
Maruti Suzuki	-3.055	0.114	-9.011	< 0.0001	-13.780	< 0.0001
Coal, Gas, Power, Energy					
Reliance Industries	-2.503	0.319	-8.141	< 0.0001	-13.350	< 0.0001
GAIL	-2.384	0.379	-7.621	< 0.0001	-12.131	< 0.0001
Coal India	-1.841	0.680	-8.904	< 0.0001	-13.207	< 0.0001
ONGC	-2.359	0.391	-8.978	< 0.0001	-13.258	< 0.0001
NTPC	-2.450	0.345	-7.327	< 0.0001	-14.191	< 0.0001
Power Grid Corporation	-1.712	0.743	-8.566	< 0.0001	-13.672	< 0.0001
Adani Ports	-2.288	0.429	-9.017	< 0.0001	-13.585	< 0.0001
L&T	-1.917	0.637	-7.048	< 0.0001	-11.794	< 0.0001
Tata Steel	-2.153	0.508	-8.382	< 0.0001	-13.124	< 0.0001
IT & Communication					
Infosys	-2.512	0.314	-7.833	< 0.0001	-14.047	< 0.0001
TCS	-2.165	0.500	-8.549	< 0.0001	-13.357	< 0.0001
Wipro	-2.530	0.306	-7.930	< 0.0001	-13.267	< 0.0001
BhartiAirtel	-1.407	0.855	-8.476	< 0.0001	-14.315	< 0.0001

Observation:

According to the results obtained,

a) The computed p-value is lower than the significance level, $\alpha = 0.05$, one should reject the null hypothesis H_0 and accept the alternative hypothesis H_1.

b) The risk to reject the null hypothesis H_0 (when it is true) is lower than 0.01%.

c) The p-value (one-tailed) $<\alpha$, i.e., $0.001 < 0.05$.

Time Series data of all the companies are observed stationary at first difference. However, in anticipation of better results the data are further differenced at second level. The results of ADF test performed at different levels indicate that all series are stationery with first difference and second difference as well. The time series data under consideration is now ready for fitting ARIMA models.

3.7 UTILITY OF DESCRIPTIVE STATISTICS

Descriptive statistics as mentioned earlier is used to get familiar with the basic nature of the data sets of stock prices of selected companies. Each descriptive study reduces the large amount of data into a simpler summary. Some of the advantages are listed below:

a) It summarizes the data and makes it meaningful and easy to understand.
b) It is a simple tool that converts results into graphical representations like distribution of frequency and overall averages.
c) It computes standard deviation, which shows the variability in a data set.
d) It is used to avoid building of complex research models.
e) It is a good way to learn about various statistics.
f) Instead of drawing conclusions, it deals single variables.
g) It opens opportunities for further research by identifying unusual patterns.

These statistics will be linked to the accuracy measures of different forecasting models used in the subsequent chapters of this dissertation.

CHAPTER IV
ANALYSIS OF STOCK PRICES DATA WITH ARIMA MODEL

4.1 INTRODUCTION

Stock price prediction will always remain an interesting area for the investors, traders and researchers to explore. It has attracted the interest of researchers to develop better predictive models every now and then. From the subject point of view, stock prices predictions are an important topic of the subjects such as finance and economics. The financial institutions and individual investors need an effective strategy to forecast and take decision based on these forecasts on daily basis. The stock price prediction is regarded as one of the most difficult task to achieve due to complex nature of stock markets [(Pai and Lin, 2005), (Wang et al, 2012), (Wei, 2013)] and investment risk of the stock market. This remains an inspiring aspect for research scholars to evolve with new predictive models or improve the existing ones (Atsalakis et al, 2011).

Till date, various models and techniques had been used to predict stock prices. Among these ARIMA models are the most popular statistical algorithms. As it is often reported in the literature, forecasting can be done on the basis of two different viewpoints, i.e., (i) using statistical techniques, (ii) and using artificial intelligence technique (Wang et al, 2012). ARIMA models are known to be very efficient for forecasting particularly for short-term prediction in the field of financial time series and even the more popular than ANNs techniques in many cases, ((Kyungjoo et al, 2007), (Merh et al, 2010)).Other popular statistical models used in forecasting are regression method, exponential smoothing, generalized autoregressive conditional Heteroscedasticity (GARCH). Few related works that is based on ARIMA models for forecasting financial time series includes (Verma et al, 2015), (Uma Devi et al, 2013), (Kwasi and Kobina, 2014), (Manoj and Edward, 2016), (Abdullahi and Bakari, 2014), (Ozaki, 2016), (Adebiyi et al, 2014), (Diem Ngo et al, 2013), (Rangan and Titida, 2006), (Meyler et al, 1998), (Tabachnick and Fidell, 2001).

This chapter presents extensive process of building ARIMA models for short-term stock price prediction. The results obtained from the real-life data establishes the potential strength of ARIMA models to provide stockholders short-term prediction that could support investment decision making processes.

Section 4.1 presents the introduction of the chapter followed by the review of literature in section 4.2. Section 4.3 describes briefly about ARIMA models, whereas section 4.4 presents general rules laid for non-seasonal Box-Jenkins model identification procedures. Section 4.5 presents the methodology used in this study to carry forward the research and simultaneously section 4.6 illustrates the development processes of the experiments, its results obtained and the interpretation for normal time series stock data, i.e., Sun Pharmaceutical and finally, section 4.7 discusses about the process of the experiments, its results obtained, and interpretation for non- normal time series stock, i.e., Lupin Limited.

4.2 BRIEF OVERVIEW OF SOME RELATED LITERATURE

Ozaki (1977) ascertained that AIC is a powerful tool in identification of different ARIMA models. He used MAICE (minimum AIC estimation) procedure, which selects a model by using Akaike's Information Criterion (AIC) for determining the best ARIMA Models. He obtained that MAICE procedure produces almost results similar to five ARIMA models ((1, d, 0), (2, d, 0), (0, d, 1), (0, d, 2) and (1, d, 1)) of Box-Jenkins.

Rangsan and Titida (2006) developed various ARIMA models for forecasting oil palm prices of Thailand for a period of 5 years from 2000 to 2004. The criteria for choosing best ARIMA model was minimum of mean absolute percentage error (MAPE). They found ARIMA (2,1,0) for the farm price model, ARIMA (1,0,1) for whole sale price, and ARIMA (3,0,0) for pure oil price as the best model in their respective categories. Valenzuela et al (2008) suggested the use of hybrid ARIMA–ANN models for better accuracy than ARMA models which had been prominent by used in linear models of forecasting of time series. They used hybridization of intelligent techniques such as Evolutionary Algorithms, Artificial Neural Networks and Fuzzy systems.

Abdullahi and Bakari (2014) examined the trend or pattern of Nigerian stock market for a period of 1985-2008. They examined the tendency of the Nigerian capital market by applying various ARIMA models. They concluded that ARIMA (2, 1, 2) model performed better on the basis of least MAPE and MAE.

Adebiyi et al (2014) carried out research for prediction of stock prices using ARIMA models on historical stock data collected from Nigeria Stock Exchange and New York Stock Exchange. They found that proposed method of forecasting on short-term basis satisfactorily in comparison to existing techniques for stock price prediction. The results compete reasonably well with emerging forecasting techniques in short-term prediction with the result obtained from ARIMA models.

Mondal et al (2014) analysed 56 time series of Indian stocks from different sectors to determine the accuracy of forecasting methods using ARIMA models. They also mentioned that results obtained in the study were accurate up to 85% of ARIMA models.

Xiaoguang et al (2014) analysed the shares of China Merchants Bank for opening prices (04.01.2013 –18.10.2013) and to predict the next five days (21.10.2013 – 25.10.2013) stock opening price data using ARIMA models-SAS system and concluded it to be very efficient and suitable model for short-term stock predictions.

Konarasinghe et al (2015) focused on the forecasting of Sri Lankan share market returns using ARIMA models. The stock price series were tested with partial autocorrelation functions and autocorrelation functions for stationarity of time series. The total market returns, sector returns and individual company returns were forecasted. They have used mean square error, mean absolute deviation, Anderson-Darling test and residual plots for model validation.

Jadhav et al (2015) analysed the historical data of six years for Indian stock market using six different models on monthly closing stock indices of Sensex and concluded that ARIMA model helped in predicting fairly accurate values of the future stock indices. Out of the initial six different models, they choose ARIMA (1,0,1) as the best model based on the fact that it satisfies all the conditions for the "goodness of fit unlike the rest".

Ngan (2016) analysed foreign exchange rate actual data for three years from 2013 to 2015 of commercial joint stock banks in Vietnam to forecast foreign exchange rate between Vietnam Dong and United State Dollar (VND/USD) in successive 12 months of 2016 using ARIMA Models. Their results proved ARIMA models, to be most suitable for estimating foreign exchange rate in short-term period.

Manoj and Edward (2016) developed and applied ARIMA models on the Indian sectorial stock prices in their sector specific study of 6 sectors namely automobiles, banking, healthcare, information technology, oil & gas and power for daily actual data of 9 years from

February 2007 to April 2015 with 1996 observations to forecast stock prices. They performed sector-specific study for forecasting and suggested that (1, 1, 0) to be the most suitable ARIMA model in comparison to others.

4.3 ARIMA MODEL

Methodology for forecasting of financial time series data known as ARIMA models was introduced in 1970 by Box and Jenkins. Therefore, it is known as Box-Jenkins methodology. The building of ARIMA models for prediction is based on certain set of activities such as (i) identification (ii) estimation (iii) diagnostics checking and (iv) finally forecasting of the results (Ngo et al, 2013). It is one of the leading method used for forecasting in financial time series ((Pai and Lin, 2005), (Devi et al, 2013), (Abdullahi and Bakari, 2014)). ARIMA models have shown efficient capability to generate short-term forecasts. It is treated as one of the best model for short-term prediction (Meyler et al, 1998).

In ARIMA Models future value of the variables is a linear combination of past values and past errors. Mathematically it is represented as:

$$y_t = \Phi_0 + \Phi_1 y_{t-1} + \Phi_2 y_{t-2} + \ldots + \Phi_p y_{t-p} + \epsilon_t - \theta_1 \epsilon_{t-1} - \theta_2 \epsilon_{t-2} - \ldots - \theta_q \epsilon_{t-q} \qquad (4.1)$$

where actual values of the data are denoted as y_t, coefficients are denoted as Φ_i and θ_j. The random errors are denoted by ϵ_i and degree of auto regressive and moving averages are represented by integer's *p* and *q*. (Ayodele et al, 2014).

4.3.1 Autoregressive (AR) and its Basic Concepts

In autoregressive model the series is regressed on to past values of itself. Therefore, future value of a variable is assumed to be a linear combination of past observation and a random error together with a constant.

An autoregressive (AR) Model of order p, , i.e., AR (p) model can be expressed with the following equations.

$$y_i = \emptyset_0 + \emptyset_1 y_{i-1} + \emptyset_2 y_{i-2} + \ldots + \emptyset_p y_{i-p} + \epsilon_i \qquad (4.2)$$

Here y_i and ϵ_i are actual values and random errors (or random shock) at time '*i*'.

Φ_I (*I = 1-p)* are model parameters and '$\emptyset$' is a constant term. The Integer *p* is known as the order of the model.

Some of the properties of the autoregressive process when mean, variance and autocorrelation are in stationary AR *(p)* processes are listed in the following.

Property 1: Mean of stationary AR(*p*) process

$$\mu = \frac{\emptyset_0}{\sum_{j=1}^{p} \emptyset_j} \qquad (4.3)$$

Property 2: Variance of the stationary AR (1) process

$$var(y_i) = \frac{\sigma^2}{1 - \emptyset_1^2} \qquad (4.4)$$

Property 3: Lag '*h*' autocorrelation of a stationary AR (1) process

$$\rho_h = \emptyset_1^h \qquad (4.5)$$

Property 4: In general for any stationary AR(*p*) process, the auto covariance at lag *k* > 0 is given by:

$$y_k = \emptyset_1 Y_{k-1} + \emptyset_2 Y_{k-2} + \cdots + \emptyset_p Y_{k-p} \qquad (4.6)$$

Similarly the autocorrelation at lag *k* > 0 can be calculated by

$$\rho_k = \emptyset_1 \rho_{k-1} + \emptyset_2 \rho_{k-2} + \cdots + \emptyset_p \rho_{k-p} \qquad (4.7)$$

Where, $Y_h = Y_{-h}$ and $\rho_h = \rho_{-h}$ if *h* < 0, and $\rho_0 = 1$

These equations are known as the **Yule-Walker equations**.

Property 5: On adding 'σ^2' to the sum these equations hold true for *k* = 0 and are equivalent to:

$$y_0 = \emptyset_1 y_1 + \emptyset_2 y_2 + .. + \emptyset_p y_p + \sigma^2 \qquad (4.8)$$

Property 6: This property holds true for AR (2) stationary process:

$$\rho_0 = 1^{p1} = \frac{\emptyset_1}{1 - \emptyset_2 \rho_k} = \emptyset_1 \rho_{k-1} + \emptyset_2 \rho_{k-2} \text{ for } k > 1 \qquad (4.9)$$

Property 7: The variance of the y_i in a AR (2) stationary process depicted as:

$$var(y_i) = \frac{1 - \emptyset_2}{1 + \emptyset_2} \cdot \frac{\sigma^2}{(1 - \emptyset_2)^2 - \emptyset_1^2} \qquad (4.10)$$

4.3.2 Moving Average (MA) Models and its Basic Concepts

Moving average (MA) models suggest that the time series can be expressed as a function of previous forecasting errors (or noise) 'ϵ_i'. Therefore, MA model's prediction is based on the errors made in the past, so one can learn from the errors made in the past to improve later predictions. (It means it learns from its own mistake).

A moving average (MA) model of order q, or an MA (q) model can be expressed with the following equation:

$$y_i = \mu + \epsilon_i + \theta_1 \epsilon_{i-1} + \cdots + \theta_q \epsilon_{i-q} \tag{4.11}$$

Here y_i and ϵ_i are actual values and random errors (or random shock) at time 'i'. The value of 'y' at time '$i+1$' is a linear function of past errors. Mean of the sample data is depicted by the symbol 'μ'. It is assumed that the error terms are independently distributed with a normal distribution having mean = 0 and constant variance = σ^2. Φ_I ($I = 1$-p) are model parameters and 'μ' is a constant term. The Integer q is known as the order of the model.

Property 1: The mean of an MA (q) process is μ.

Property 2: The variance of an MA (q) process is defined as:

$$var(y_i) = \sigma^2 (1 + \theta_1^2 + \cdots + \theta_q^2) \tag{4.12}$$

Property 3: The autocorrelation function of an MA (1) process is presented as:

$$\rho_1 = \frac{\theta_2}{1+\theta_1^2} \rho_h = 0 \text{ for } h > 1 \tag{4.13}$$

Property 4: The autocorrelation function of an MA (2) process is presented as:

$$\rho_2 = \frac{\theta_1 + \theta_1\theta_2}{1+\theta_1^2\theta_2^2} = \frac{\theta_2}{1+\theta_1^2\theta_2^2} \rho_h = 0 \text{ for } h > 2 \tag{4.14}$$

Property 5: The autocorrelation function of an MA(q) process is defined as:

$$\rho_h = \frac{\theta_h + \sum_{j=q}^{q-h} \theta_j \theta_{j+h}}{1+\sum_{j=1}^{q} \theta_j^2} \tag{4.15}$$

for $h \leq q$ and $\rho_h = 0 = 0$ for $h > q$

Property 6: The PACF of an MA(1) process is presented by the equation as follows:

$$\pi_k = \frac{-(-\theta_1)^k}{1+\sum_{i=1}^{k}\theta_1^{2i}} \pi_{k,k-j} = \frac{-(-\theta_1)^j}{1+\sum_{i=1}^{j}\theta_1^{2i}} \cdot \pi_k \tag{4.16}$$

4.3.3 Autoregressive Moving Average (ARMA) models and its Basic Concepts

A Model which contains all important features of a given time series data is always treated as the best model. Sometimes, autoregressive (AR) model or moving average (MA) model alone does not work out. In such cases a combination of both the models, i.e., autoregressive of order 'p' and moving average of order 'q' is applied to get the desired results. The combination of these two models is known as ARMA model. The mathematical of an ARMA (p, q) model is presented by the following equation.

$$y_i = \emptyset_0 + \emptyset_1 Y_{i-1} + \emptyset_2 Y_{i-2} + \cdots + \emptyset_p Y_{k-p} + \epsilon_i + \theta_1 \epsilon_{i-1} + \cdots + \theta_q \epsilon_{i-q}$$

Or

$$y_i = \emptyset_0 + \sum_{j=1}^{p} \emptyset_j Y_{i-j} + \in_i + \sum_{j=1}^{q} \emptyset_j \in_{i-j} \qquad (4.17)$$

If a time series $z_1,\ldots,z_n$ has an ARMA(p, q) process and zero mean (where $z_i = y_i - \mu$), than it can be defined as ARMA(p, q) by removing the constant term (, i.e., φ_0) and saying that $y_1, \ldots, y_n$ has an ARMA(p, q) process with mean μ.

4.3.4 Autoregressive Integrated Moving Average (ARIMA) models.

The components of this model are consisting of three parts: an Autoregressive (AR) part, a moving Average (MA) part and 'I' the differencing part. This model is particularly referred to as the ARIMA (p, d, p) model (Box-Jenkins). Here 'p' is the order of the Autoregressive part, 'd' is the order of differencing and 'q' is the order of the moving average part. For instance, an ARIMA (2, 1, 2) model means, that it contains 2 Autoregressive (p) parameters and 2 moving Average (q) parameters and it is differenced once to attain the stationarity of the time series data.

If d = 0, the model becomes ARMA, and is considered as a linear stationary model.

If d > 0, the model becomes ARIMA and is considered as a linear non-stationary model. (Refer equation 4.1, page no.82).

If the time series under investigation is non-stationary, it is suggested to take the difference of the series with itself 'd' times to make it stationary. Further, ARMA model is applied on to the differenced part (Abdhuli and Bakari, 2014).

4.4 General process of forecasting using ARIMA models as per Box-Jenkins methodology

ARIMA forecasting processes consists of four steps/stages as mentioned below.

(i)   Model Identification
(ii)   Model Parameter Estimation
(iii) Diagnostic Checking
(iv)   Forecasting

Box-Jenkins methodology requires that time series values must be stationary and invertible before one recognizes any pattern in the data and attempt to fit any of the ARIMA model. The graph of autocorrelation function (ACF) reflects about the nature of time series data whether it is stationary or non-stationary over the time. The time series values are considered stationary if the graph of autocorrelation function (ACF) cuts off or dies down very quickly.

On the contrary, it is treated as non-stationary if the graph of autocorrelation function either cuts off or dies down gradually. Some of the examples of the graphs are listed below:

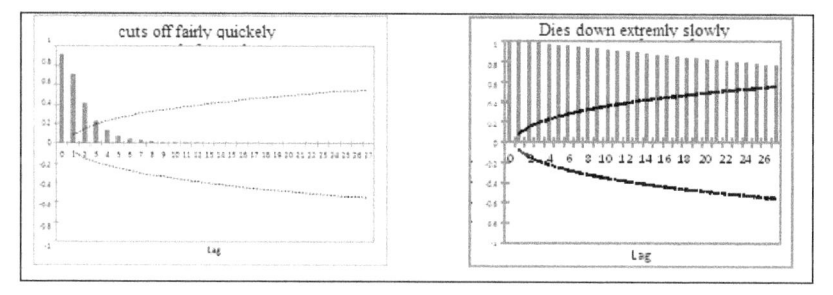

Fig: 4.1 "The ACF (PACF) cuts off fairly quickly versus dies down extremely slowly"(Bowerman,o'connell and Koehler, p. 413)

One can converts the non- stationary time series to stationary time series by calculating the first difference or second or third differences of the original data if the data values are non-seasonal and non-stationary. (Ngo, 2013) as under

The differences of time series data introduced a new variable Z_t. The series Z_t will be the first difference of Y_t and is calculated as follows:

First Difference: $Z_t = Y_t - Y_{t-1}$ **Where $t = 2,3,....., n$** (4.18)

On finding the first difference if the mean of the time series is not constant than Z_t is recalculated as the difference of the first difference as follows:

Second Difference: $Z_t = (Y_t - Y_{t-1}) - (Y_{t-1} - Y_{t-2})$ **where $t = 3,4,....., n$** (4.19)

A series which has been made stationary by applying the appropriate differencing has zero mean and it is considered as a deterministic component of the series. The data is presented as derivation from the mean to concentrate on the random behaviour of the series.

4.4.1 Types of Models or Model Identification

On observing the sample autocorrelation function (ACF) and partial autocorrelation function (PACF) of the original time series time series $y_1, y_2, ..., y_n$ or the transformed time series (z_t's), it can be ascertained whether series are stationary or non-stationary and the models to be fitted are called theoretical non-seasonal Box-Jenkins models.

Non-seasonal theoretical Box-Jenkins models are categorized in three categories, i.e., (i) autoregressive (AR) model of order p (ii) moving average (MA) model of order q and (iii) combined autoregressive- moving average (ARMA) model of order (p, q). However, when the ACF cuts off quickly after lag q and the PACF cuts off quickly after lag p, for such a condition there is no theoretical Box-Jenkins model. These conditions are summarized in the table as follows:

Table 4.1 Theoretical Box-Jenkins model

Model	ACF	PACF
Moving average of order q $Z_t = \delta + a_t - \theta_1 a_{t-1} - \theta_2 a_{t-2} - \ldots - \theta_q a_{t-q}$	Cuts off after lag q	Dies down
Autoregressive of order p $Z_t = \delta + \varphi_1 z_{t-1} + \varphi_2 z_{t-2} + \ldots + \varphi_p z_{t-p} + a_t$	Dies down	Cuts off after lag q
Mixed autoregressive-moving average of order (p , q) $Z_t = \delta + \Phi_1 z_{t-1} + \Phi_2 z_{t-2} + \ldots + \Phi_p z_{t-p} + a_t - \theta_1 a_{t-1} - \theta_2 a_{t-2} - \ldots - \theta_q a_{t-q}$	Dies down	Dies down

Some of the examples displaying the different behaviours of autocorrelation function and partial autocorrelation function are depicted below

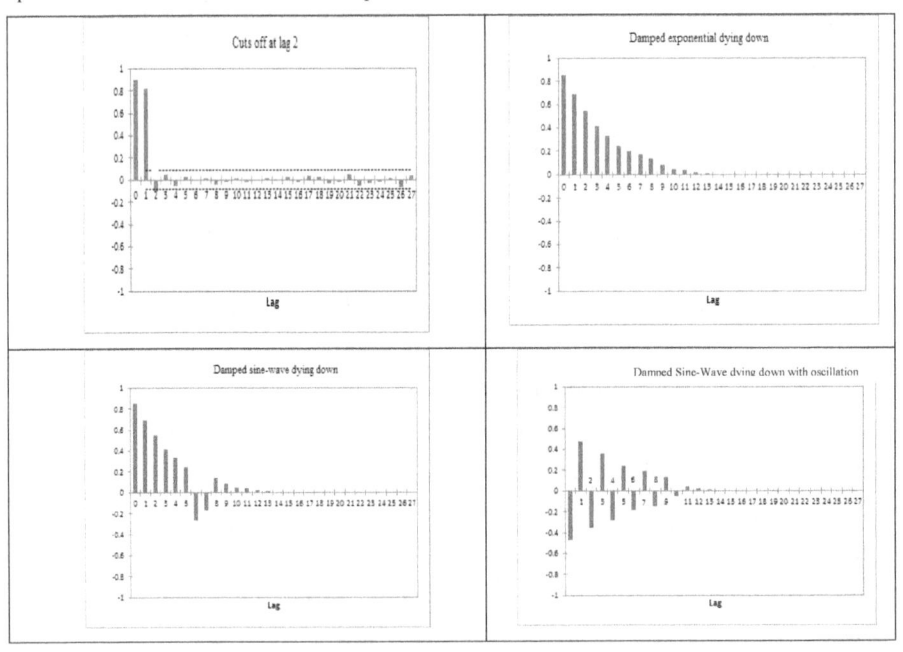

Fig: 4.2 The ACF and PACF Behaviours (Bowerman, o'connell and Koehler, p. 412)

It is suggested to follow the subsequent general rules laid out in this text to identify the best model if the ACF or PACF is cutting off more abruptly.

4.4.2 Model Parameter Estimations

"Stationarity is the first condition of a Box-Jenkins model. It should be invertible also. Invertible means recent observations are more heavily weighted than more remote observations; the parameters ($\emptyset_1, \emptyset_2, ..., \emptyset_p, \theta_1, \theta_2, ..., \theta_q$) used in the model decline from the most recent observations down to the further past observations". (Bowerman et al, 2010). The *t*-values and approximate *p*-values test the following hypothesis.

"Let θ be any particular parameter in a Box-Jenkins model.

$H_0 : \theta = 0$ versus $H_1 : \theta \neq 0$

We can reject null hypothesis H_0 if and only if either of the following conditions holds:

1. $|t| > t_{\alpha/2}^{(n-n_p)}$ where n_p is the number of parameters in the model.
2. P – value < α (Bowerman et al, 2010)".

If the null hypothesis is rejected at the smaller significant level α, it indicates very strongly that the observed parameter is very important for the model. To decide the best model we compare the results based on Akaike's Information Criterion (AIC), and Schwarz's Bayesian Criterion (SBC) etc. The best model has smaller standard errors.

4.4.3 DIAGNOSTICS CHECKING

The key role of diagnostic checking is to ascertain the adequacy of the ARIMA models fitted to the data. A model is adequate if it extracts all the relevant information from the data. The unexplained part of the data, i.e., residual should be very small. The parts of the data which are not explained by the model should be as small as possible and residuals should not have systematic or predictable patterns.

As per Box-Jenkins methodology diagnostics testing includes all essential statistical properties of the error terms, i.e., normality and weak white noise assumptions.

Residual of an estimated model should demonstrate white noise behaviour. If this assumption is not true then there is a scope to extract some more important information from modelling process. Two methods used for diagnostic checking are mentioned below.

- Graphical method:
    (i) Plots of residuals to check the systematic pattern.

(ii) Use the SACF and SPACF (relate to identification step) of the residuals.
By examining the autocorrelations and partial autocorrelation graphs of the residuals adequacy of the models can be ascertained. If the spikes are exceeding two standard errors, it is an indication of an adequate model.

- Testing method: Autocorrelation Tests (Q-test)

To test the adequacy of an overall model, the null and alternative hypotheses are:

H_0: The model is adequate or the model does not exhibit lack of fit.

H_a: The model is inadequate or the model exhibit lack of fit.

Test statistics to test H_0 is given as under:

$$\text{The Ljung – Box Statistic: } Q = n(n+2)\sum_{k=1}^{m}\frac{r_k^2}{(n-k)} \qquad (4.22)$$

Where

n = length of time series or number of observations used to fit ARIMA models.

$\hat{r}$ = estimated auto correlation of the residual series of lag 'k'.

m = number of lags being tested.

d = degree of non-seasonal differencing used to transform the original time series value into stationary. If it is included in the building of ARIMA model than 'n' of equation (4.22) will be replaced by n' where n'=n-d. (Bowerman, O'Connell and Koehler, p. 459).

α = Significance level

Critical Region: The Box-Ljung test rejects the null hypothesis if

$$Q > \chi^2_{(1-\alpha, h)}$$

Where $\chi^2_{(1-\alpha, h)}$ is the chi-square distribution table value with h degree of freedom and $h = m-p-q$. One can also use level of significance or *p-values* calculated for a given value of χ^2 to test H_0.

If the p-value is greater than α it can be recommended that the model is adequate.

Weakness of Q-test:

Q-test is only asymptotically valid. In case of small and medium size samples it may perform poorly. Diagnostic test based on autocorrelation test can only diagnose and reveal the under parameterized model but will not reveal the over parameterized model. Modifications have been incorporated in the literature for Ljung-Box test are available in the form of McLeod-Li test, Monti's test, etc.

4.4.4 Forecasting Stock Prices of Select Indian Companies-An Empirical Evidence

This section deals with the brief interpretation of time series data of 25 BSE Sensex companies of Indian stock market. The data under consideration is taken from Yahoo India finance for a period of 2 years from 20.01.2014 - 20.01.2016. All 25 stocks are analysed for normality test. In this research, we have taken 2 companies from pharmaceutical sector for the detailed analysis (due to space constraints). It contains both types of distribution, i.e., normal distribution and non-normal distribution. The stocks of Lupin Limited follow non-normal distribution while stocks of Sun Pharmaceuticals follow normal distribution. With the help of Jarque Bera test statistic, we accept the normality hypothesis for Sun Pharmaceutical and reject the normality hypothesis for Lupin Limited.

In all 500 observations are used for fitting various ARIMA models and rest 23 observations are used to test the data. The data is comprised of four variables, namely: open price, low price, high price and close price respectively. In the research, open price of the data represents the price of the index to be forecasted. Open price for the forecast is selected because in stock market everyone is interested to know about the ups and downs of the prices of the next day with respect to the prices of the previous day.

In this segment the data will be examined to check for the most appropriate class of ARIMA processes by selecting the order of non-seasonal models applied. During forecasting processes certain errors are committed. These forecasting errors are the difference between the actual value and the forecast value for the corresponding period. These can be calculated as '$E_t = A_t - F_t$' where 'E' is the forecast error at period 't'. 'A' is the actual value at period 't' and 'F' is the forecast for period 't'. Some of the measures of forecasting accuracy used for the analysis are listed below.

Table 4.2: Measures of error for forecasting accuracy

Mean absolute error (MAE)	$\Sigma E_t / N$
Mean absolute percentage error (MAPE)	$\Sigma E_t / A_t / N$
Percent Mean Absolute error Deviation (PMAD)	$\Sigma E_t / \Sigma A_t$
Mean squared Error (MSE)	$\Sigma E_t^2 / N$
Root Mean squared Error (RMSE)	$\sqrt{\Sigma E_t^2 / N}$

To validate the forecast, the data is divided into two parts. The first part of the data is used for fitting ARIMA models and the other part of the data is used for judging the goodness of fit statistics for the different models.

The method used in the study to develop ARIMA models for stock price prediction is explained in detail underneath:

(i) To check the basic nature of the data, whether it is stationary or not, the graphical analysis is done with software, Microsoft Excel.

(ii) To check the presence of unit root in the data, Augmented Dickey Fuller test is applied.

(iii) The data under consideration is found non-stationary and it is made stationary by taking first difference and second difference of the series simultaneously.

(iv) ARIMA models are fitted taking p = [0,1,2], q = [0,1,2] and d= [0,1,2], where p + q is less than or equal to 3. This is how 12 ARIMA models are tested on the time series data.

(v) Interpretation of goodness of fit statistics and graphical analysis is done by analysing behaviours (spikes) of ACF and PACF to identify the best ARIMA model autocorrelogram (ACF) and partial-autocorrelogram (PACF) graphs to identify the best fit ARIMA model.

(vi) To determine the best ARIMA model among various fitted models, the following criterions were used in this study for each stock data:

(i)   Degree of freedom:

In statistics, the number of degrees of freedom is the number of values in the final calculation of a statistic that are free to vary. The number of independent ways by which a dynamic system can move, without violating any constraint imposed on it, is called number of degrees of freedom

(ii)   The sum of squares due to error:

"This statistic measures the total deviation of the response values from the fit to the response values. It is also called the summed square of residuals and is usually labelled as *SSE*.

$$\text{SSE} = \sum_{i=1}^{n} w_i (y_i - \hat{y}_i)^2 \qquad (4.23)$$

SSE **value closer to 0** indicates that the model has a smaller random error component, and the fit will be more useful for prediction".

(Source:*http://in.mathworks.com/help/curvefit/evaluating-goodness-of-fit.html? requested Domain www.mathworks.com)*

(iii) **Mean Square Error**

"MSE is the mean square error or the residual mean square. Mathematically it is represented as:

$$\text{MSE} = \frac{SSE}{v} \quad (4.24)$$

MSE value closer to 0 indicates a fit that is more useful for prediction".(source:http://in.mathworks.com/help/curvefit/evaluating-goodness-of-fit.html?requestedDomain=www.mathworks.com)

(iv) **Root Mean Squared Error**

"RMSE is also known as the fit standard error and the standard error of the regression. It is an estimate of the standard deviation of the random component in the data, and is defined as:

$$\text{RMSE} = s = \sqrt{MSE} \quad (4.25)$$

Where MSE is the mean square error or the residual mean square
Value of SSE closer to 0 indicates a fit that is more useful for prediction".(source:http://in.mathworks.com/help/curvefit/evaluating-goodness-of-fit.html?requestedDomain=www.mathworks.com)

(v) **White Noise Variance and its processes**

"White noise the sequence $\{\varrho_t\}$, consisting of independent (or uncorrelated) random variables with mean 0 and variance σ^2 is called white noise. It is a second order stationary series with $y_0 = \sigma 2$ and $y_k = 0$, k 6= 0.

Covariance stationary processes for time series, 'y_t' are as follows:
1. $E(y_t) = \mu$ for all t
2. $Var(y\ t) = \sigma 2$ for all t, $\sigma 2 < \infty$
3. $Cov(y_t, y_{t-\tau}) = \gamma(\tau)$ for all t and τ".

(source: http://www.statslab.cam.ac.uk/~rrw1/timeseries/t.pdf)

(vi) **Mean Absolute Percentage Error (MAPE):**

"MAPE is a measure to calculate, how much a dependent series varies from its model-predicted level. It is independent of the units used and can therefore be used to compare series with different units.

It expresses the accuracy as a percentage of the error and is easier to understand than any other statistics. MAPE can be calculated by the following equation.

$$\frac{\sum |(y_t - \hat{y}_t)/y_t|}{n} \times 100 \quad (y_t \neq 0) \quad (4.26)$$

where y_t equals the actual value, $\hat{y}_t$ equals the fitted value, and n equals the number of observations."*(Source: http://support.minitab.com/en-us/minitab/17/topic-library/modeling-statistics/time-series/time-series-models/what-are-mape-mad-and-msd/)*

(vii) Final Prediction Error

"Akaike's Final Prediction Error (FPE) criterion provides a measure of model quality by simulating the situation where the model is tested on a different data set. As per Akaike's theory, the most accurate model has the smallest FPE.

Mathematically it is defined as follows:

$$\text{FPE (P)} = \sigma^2(p)\left(1 + \frac{p+1}{N}\right)\left(1 - \frac{p+1}{N}\right)^{-1} \quad (4.27)$$

It is an estimate of the one step ahead prediction error variance model of order p, where $0^2(p)$ is the estimated residual variance of the model and N is the number of observations

OR

If you use the same data set for both model estimation and validation, the fit always improves as you increase the model order and, therefore, the flexibility of the model structure.

Akaike's Final Prediction Error (FPE) is defined by the following equation:

$$\text{FPE} = \det\left(\frac{1}{N}\sum_1^N e(t,\theta_N)\left(e(t,\theta_N)\right)^T\right)\left(\frac{1+d/N}{1-d/N}\right) \quad (4.28)$$

where:

N is the number of values in the estimation data set.

$e(t)$ is a ny-by-1 vector of prediction errors.

θ_N represents the estimated parameters and d is the number of estimated parameters.

If number of parameters exceeds the number of samples, FPE is not computed when model estimation is performed (model. Report FPE is empty). The FPE command returns NaN".*(source- //in.mathworks.com/help/ident/ref/fpe.html*

(viii) Akaike Information criterion

"**AIC** is a measure of the relative quality of **statistical** models for a given set of data. It estimates the quality of each model, relative to each of the other models. Hence, **AIC** provides a means for model selection.

The new procedure of order determination developed by Akaike (1972 and 1973), is a promising one. Akaike's Information Criterion (AIC) is defined as follows:

AIC = (-2) loge (maximum likelihood) + 2 (number of free parameters)

AIC measures both the fit of a model and the unreliability of a model. Akaike (1973) introduced the MAICE (minimum AIC estimation) procedure which selects the model whose structure with its associated parameter values gives the minimum of AIC.

AIC and BIC hold the same interpretation in terms of model comparison. That is, the larger difference in either AIC or BIC indicates stronger evidence for one model over the other (the lower the better)".

(source:https://en.wikipedia.org/wiki/Akaike_information_criterion)

(ix) Correction of Akaike's Information criterion

"AICc is AIC with a correction for finite sample sizes. The formula for AICc depends upon the statistical model. Assuming that the model is univariate, linear, and has normally distributed residuals (conditional upon regressors), the formula for AICc can be defined as follows:

$$\text{AICc} = \text{AIC} + \frac{2k(k+1)}{n-k-1} \qquad (4.29)$$

where n denotes the sample size and k denotes the number of parameters".*(source-https://en.wikipedia.org/wiki/Akaike_information_criterion)*

(x) Schwarz Bayesian information Criterion

"Bayesian information criterion (BIC) or Schwarz (SBC, SBIC) is a criterion for model selection among a finite set of models; the model with the lowest BIC is preferred. It is based, in part, on the likelihood function and it is closely related to the Akaike information criterion (AIC).

When fitting models, it is possible to increase the likelihood by adding parameters, but it may result in over-fitting. Both BIC and AIC resolve this problem by introducing a penalty term for the number of parameters in the model; the penalty term is larger in BIC than in AIC".
(source-https://en.wikipedia.org/wiki/Bayesian _in formation criterion)

4.5 DEVELOPMENT PROCESSES AND RESULTS OF ARIMA MODELS

In the subsequent section, actual experimental process to build various ARIMA models is carried out by using software Microsoft Excel and software XLStat. Various experiments are conducted by applying different ARIMA models and results are calculated on the basis of goodness of fit statistics and other accuracy measures as stated above. The graphical representation of the stock prices of Sun Pharmaceutical following normal distribution is illustrated below.

4.5 EXPERIMENTAL PROCESS AND RESULTS OF SUN PHARMACEUTICAL (NORMAL DISTRIBUTION)

4.6.1 Graphical Analysis

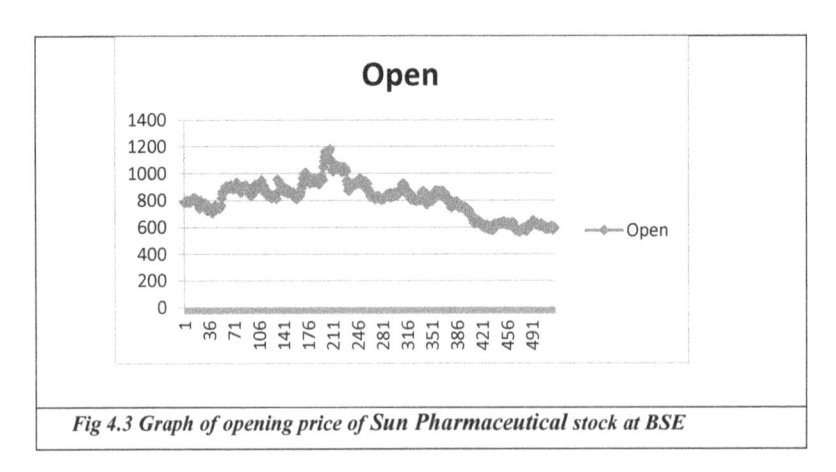

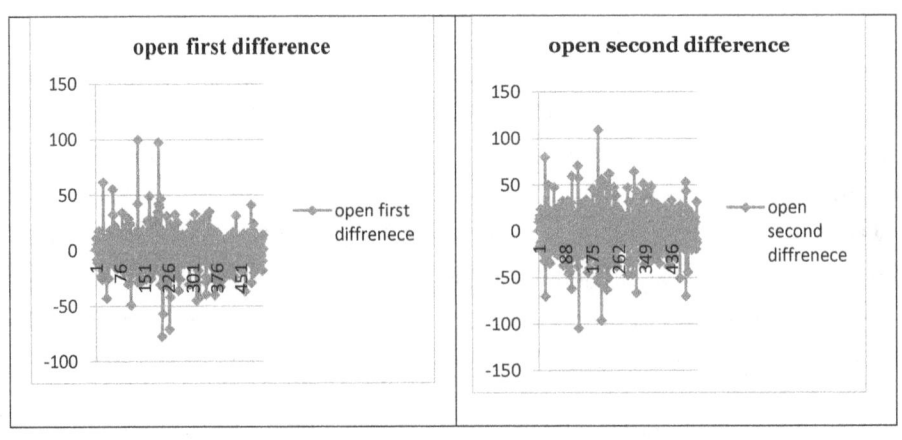

Fig 4.3 Graph of opening price of Sun Pharmaceutical stock at BSE

Fig 4.4 Graph of First Difference of opening price of Sun Pharmaceutical stock at BSE	Fig 4.5 Graph of Second Difference of opening price of Pharmaceutical stock at BSE

Table 4.3: Augmented Dickey-Fuller Statistics

	Original	First Difference	Second Difference
Tau (Observed value)	-2.164	-7.991	-13.443
Tau (Critical value)	-0.907	-0.907	-0.907
p-value (one-tailed)	0.501	< 0.0001	< 0.0001
Alpha	0.05	0.05	0.05

Table 4.4: Various statistics of ARIMA models at First Difference for opening price of Sun Pharmaceutical stock at BSE

Model	(0,1,0)	(1,1,0)	(0,1,1)	(2,1,0)	(0,1,2)	(1,1,1)	(2,1,2)	(1,1,2)	(2,1,1)
SSE	282477.8	1187400	150181.9	188472.8	149673.4	149656	149573.8	149529.5	149596.1
MSE	568.3658	2389.134	302.177	379.2209	301.1538	301.1187	300.9532	300.8643	300.9982
RMSE	23.84042	48.87877	17.38324	19.47359	17.35378	17.35277	17.348	17.34544	17.3493
WN Variance	568.3658	2389.134	302.177	379.2209	301.1538	301.1187	300.9532	300.8643	300.9982
MAPE(Diff)	99.80871	239.597	208.8889	210.873	199.8472	199.5004	199.1988	200.2772	199.3024
MAPE	472.244	424.9271	104.4784	266.6475	115.111	115.3711	113.6292	124.2316	114.1899
-2Log(Like.)		5276.762	4255.009	4362.214	4253.212	4253.143	4252.788	4252.765	4252.9
FPE	568.3658	2398.768	302.177	382.2853	301.1538	302.3329	303.3852	302.0774	303.4305
AIC		5280.762	4259.009	4368.214	4259.212	4259.143	4262.788	4260.765	4260.9
AICC		5280.786	4259.033	4368.263	4259.26	4259.192	4262.91	4260.846	4260.982
SBC		5289.179	4267.426	4380.84	4271.837	4271.769	4283.831	4277.599	4277.735

Model	(0,2,0)	(1,2,0)	(0,2,1)	(1,2,1)	(2,2,1)	(1,2,2)	(2,2,2)	(2,2,0)	(0,2,2)
SSE	2750243	1300588	835999.6	487188.9	341204.3	217577.5	189161.8	762418.2	282999.1
MSE	5556.046	2627.45	1688.888	984.22	689.3017	439.5506	382.145	1540.239	571.7153
RMSE	74.53889	51.25866	41.09608	31.37228	26.25456	20.96546	19.54853	39.24588	23.91057
WN Variance	5556.046	2627.45	1688.888	984.22	689.3017	439.5506	382.145	1540.239	571.7153
MAPE(Diff)	190.6844	2653.282	10859.3	17791.13	29278.78	25881.24	27066.65	2723.486	21290.68
MAPE	1122.049	531.6326	424.0333	325.0355	306.4595	210.1273	208.3362	506.2749	101.8827
-		5303.011	5089.709	4823.951	4649.223	4436.932	4369.274	5039.705	4564.772

2Log(Like.)									
FPE	5556.046	2638.087	1688.888	988.2046	694.8944	441.3301	385.2455	1552.736	571.7153
AIC		5307.011	5093.709	4829.951	4657.223	4444.932	4379.274	5045.705	4570.772
AICC		5307.035	5093.734	4830	4657.305	4445.014	4379.397	5045.754	4570.82
SBC		5315.42	5102.119	4842.564	4674.041	4461.751	4400.297	5058.319	4583.385

Table 4.5: ARIMA models at Second Difference for opening price of Sun Pharmaceutical stock at BSE

Table 4.6: Descriptive Statistics of opening price of Sun Pharmaceutical stock at BSE

Model	Minimum	Maximum	Mean	Std. deviation
(0,1,0)	-77.300	99.650	-0.331	17.366
(1,1,0)	-77.300	99.650	-0.331	17.366
(0,1,1)	-77.300	99.650	-0.331	17.366
(2,1,0)	-77.300	99.650	-0.331	17.366
(0,1,2)	-77.300	99.650	-0.331	17.366
(1,1,1)	-77.300	99.650	-0.331	17.366

(2,1,2)	-77.300	99.650	-0.331	17.366
(1,1,2)	-77.300	99.650	-0.331	17.366
(2,1,1)	-77.300	99.650	-0.331	17.366
(0,2,0)	-104.500	109.000	-0.016	23.824
(1,2,0)	-104.500	109.000	-0.016	23.824
(0,2,1)	-104.500	109.000	-0.016	23.824
(1,2,1)	-104.500	109.000	-0.016	23.824
(2,2,1)	-104.500	109.000	-0.016	23.824
(1,2,2)	-104.500	109.000	-0.016	23.824
(2,2,2)	-104.500	109.000	-0.016	23.824
(2,2,0)	-104.500	109.000	-0.016	23.824
(0,2,2)	-104.500	109.000	-0.016	23.824

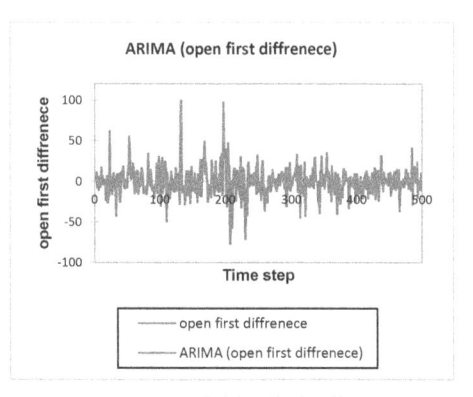

ARIMA-1D(0,1,0)

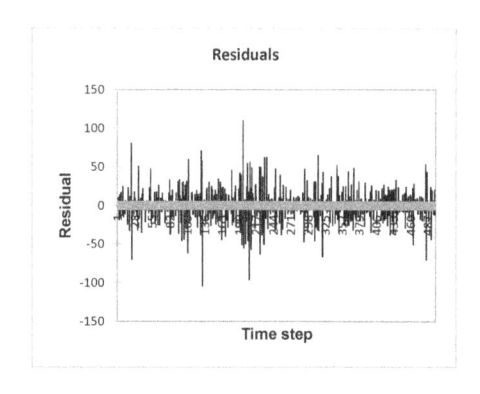

ARIMA-1D(0,1,0)

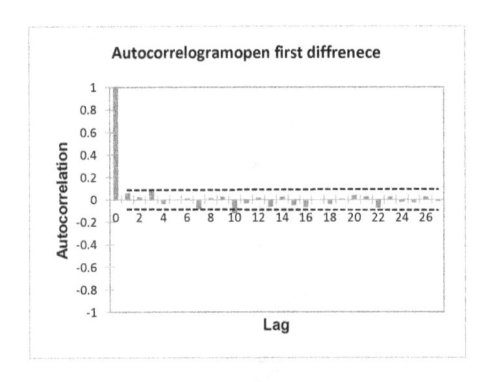

ARIMA-1D(0,1,0)

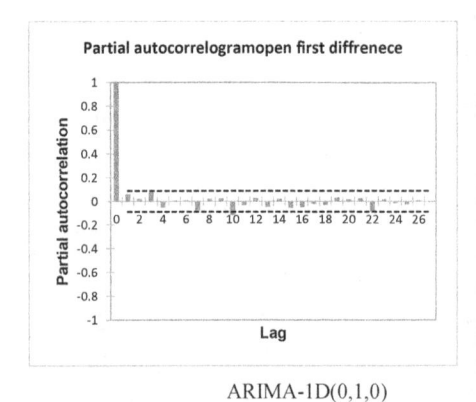

ARIMA-1D(0,1,0)

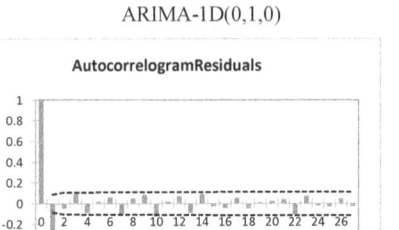

ARIMA-1D(0,1,0)

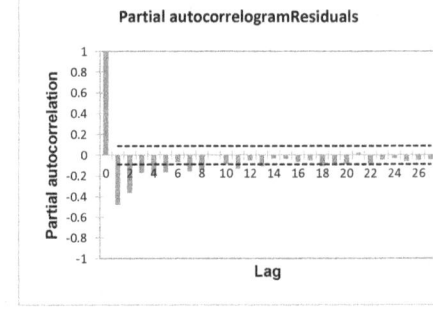

ARIMA-1D(0,1,0)

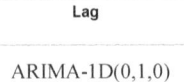

Fig 4.6: The correlogram of Sun Pharmaceutical Stock Price At [p=0 d=1 q=0]

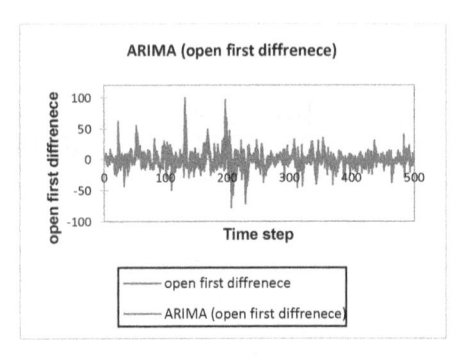

ARIMA-1D(1,1,0)

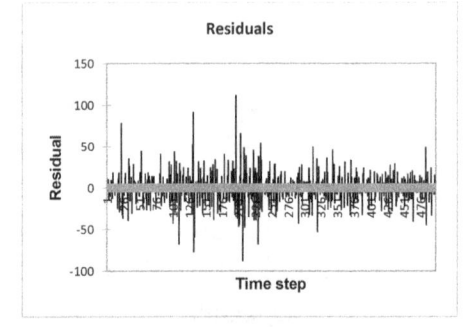

ARIMA-1D(1,1,0)

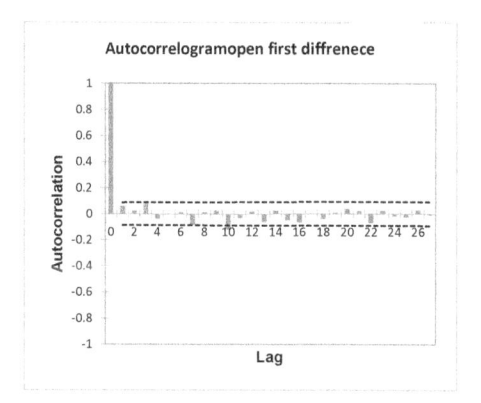

ARIMA-1D(1,1,0) 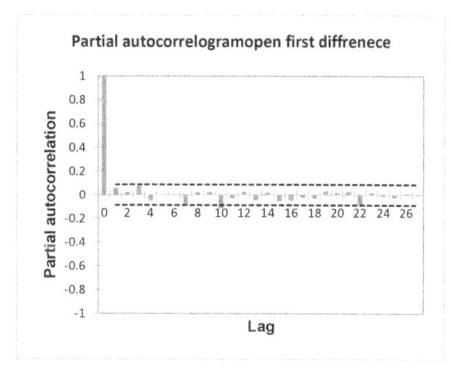 ARIMA-1D(1,1,0)

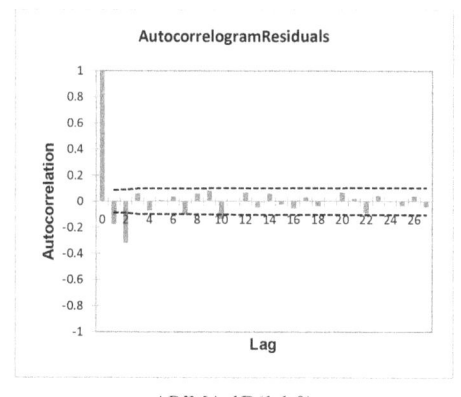

ARIMA-1D(1,1,0) 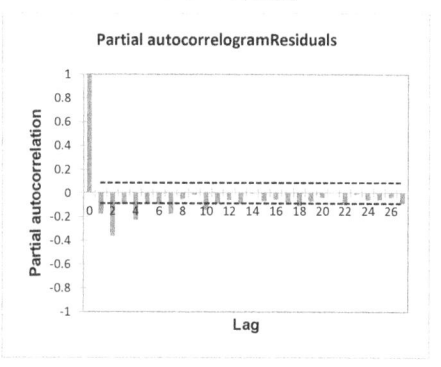 ARIMA-1D(1,1,0)

Fig 4.7: The correlogram of Sun Pharmaceutical Stock Price At [p=1 d=1 q=0]

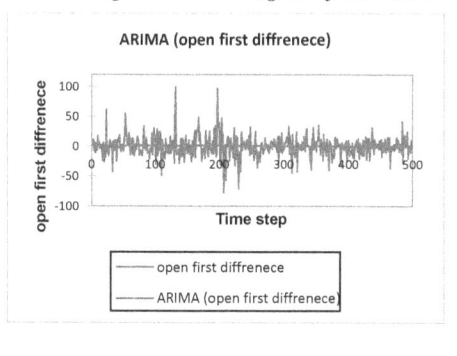

ARIMA-1D(0,1,1) 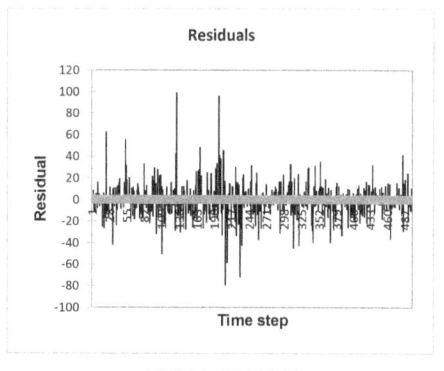 ARIMA-1D(0,1,1)

ARIMA-1D(0,1,1)　　　　　　　　　　ARIMA-1D(0,1,1)

ARIMA-1D(0,1,1)　　　　　　　　　　ARIMA-1D(0,1,1)

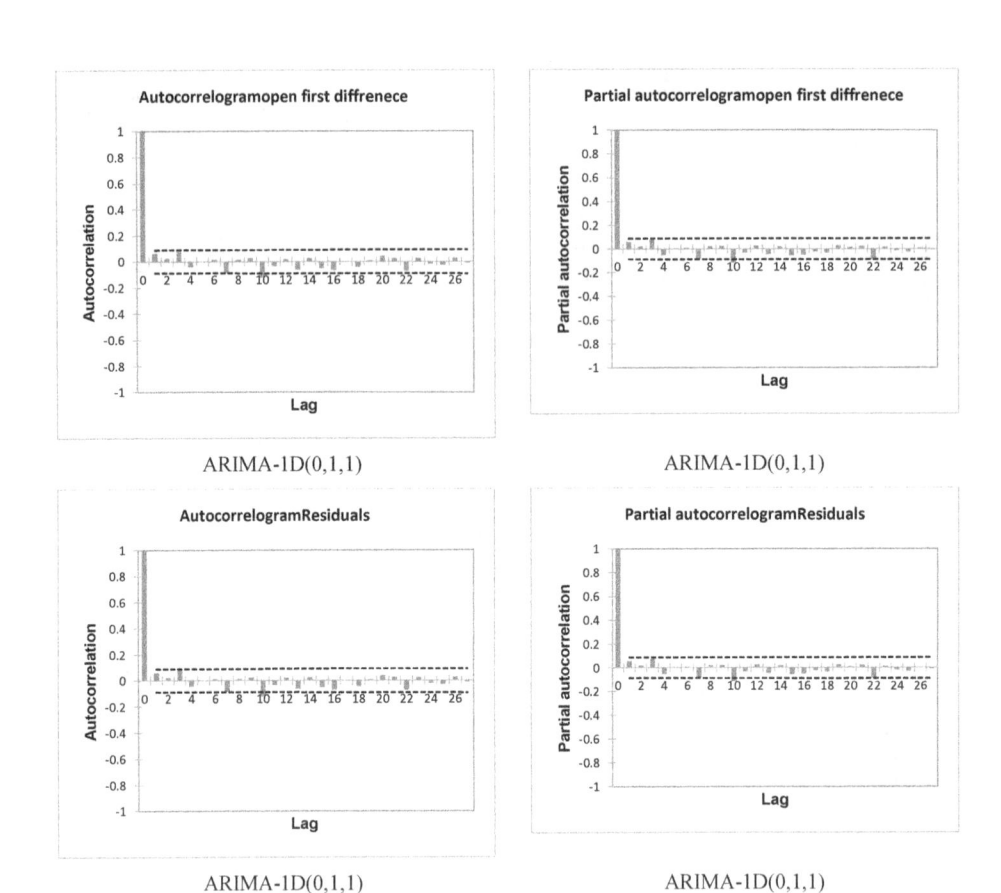

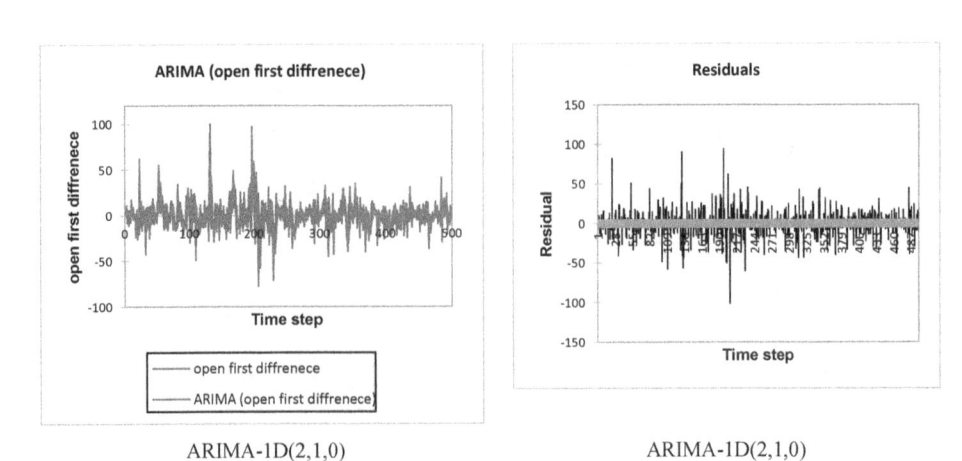

Fig 4.8: The correlogram of Sun Pharmaceutical Stock Price At [p=0 d=1 q=1]

ARIMA-1D(2,1,0)　　　　　　　　　　ARIMA-1D(2,1,0)

ARIMA-1D(2,1,0)   ARIMA-1D(2,1,0)

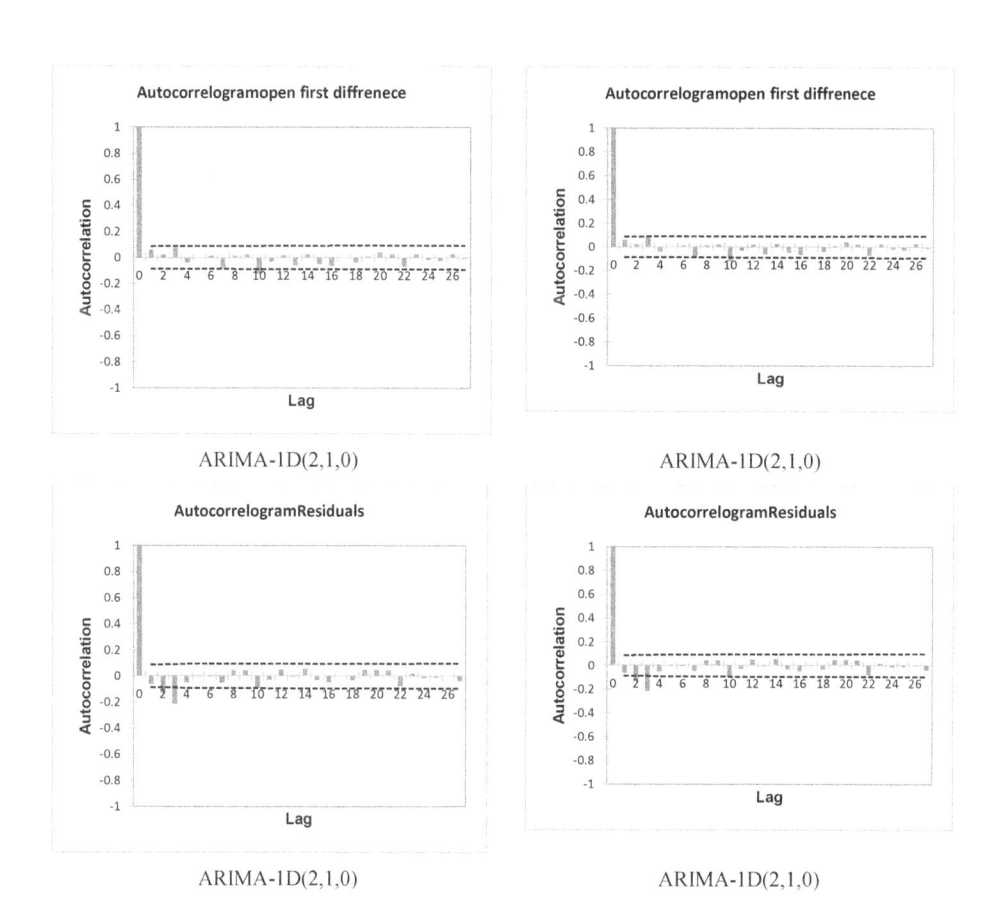

ARIMA-1D(2,1,0)   ARIMA-1D(2,1,0)

Fig 4.9: The correlogram of Sun Pharmaceutical Stock Price At [p=2 d=1 q=0]

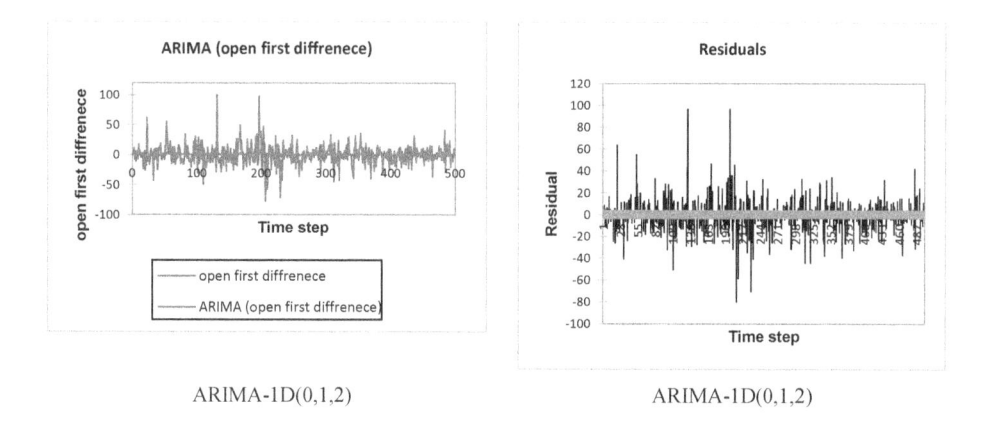

ARIMA-1D(0,1,2)   ARIMA-1D(0,1,2)

ARIMA-1D(0,1,2)   ARIMA-1D(0,1,2)

ARIMA-1D(0,1,2)   ARIMA-1D(0,1,2)

Fig 4.10: The correlogram of Sun Pharmaceutical Stock Price At [p=0 d=1 q=2]

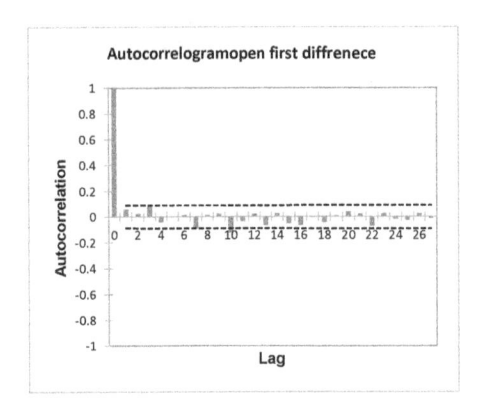

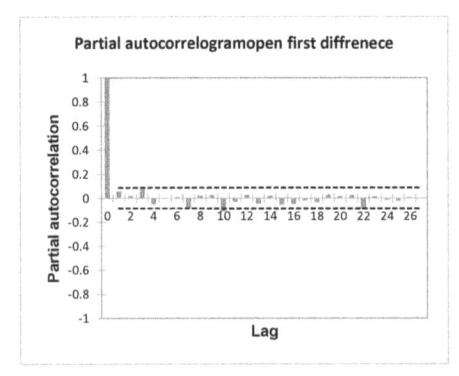

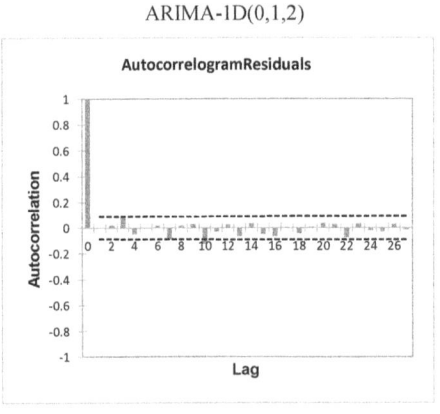

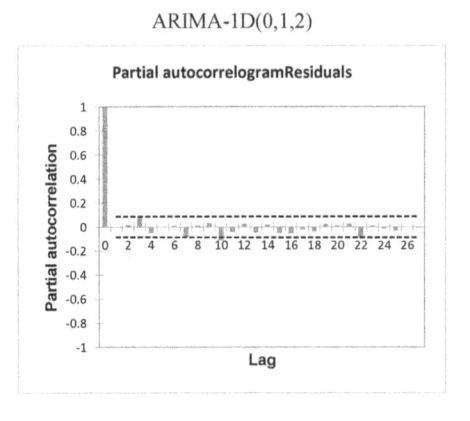

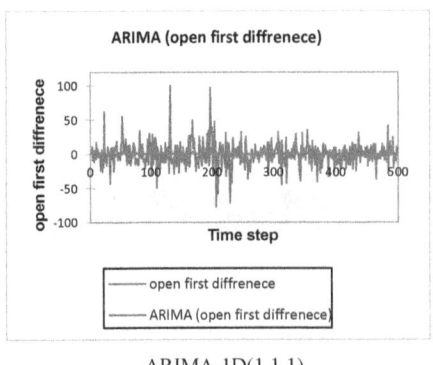

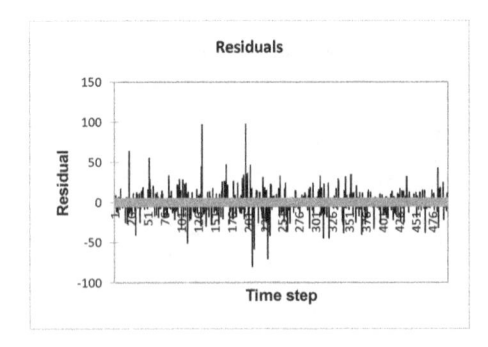

ARIMA-1D(1,1,1)   ARIMA-1D(1,1,1)

ARIMA-1D(1,1,1)   ARIMA-1D(1,1,1)

ARIMA-1D(1,1,1)   ARIMA-1D(1,1,1)

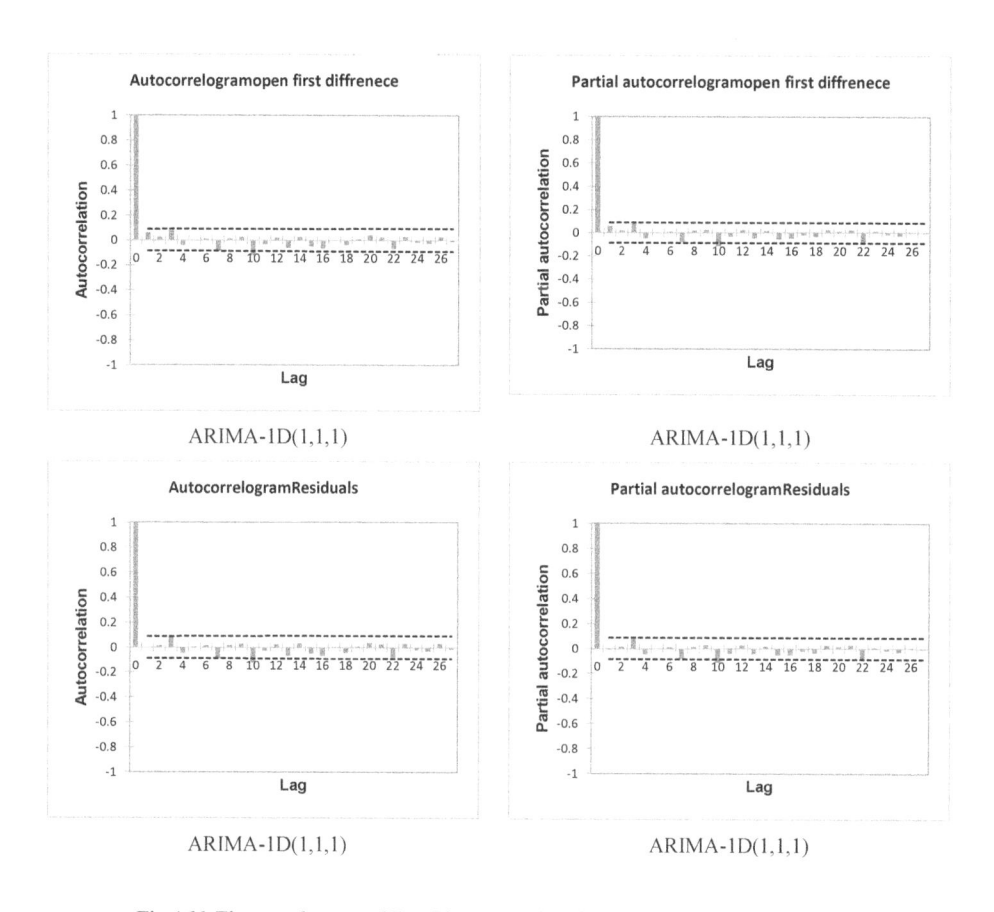

Fig 4.11: The correlogram of Sun Pharmaceutical Stock Price At [p=1 d=1 q=1]

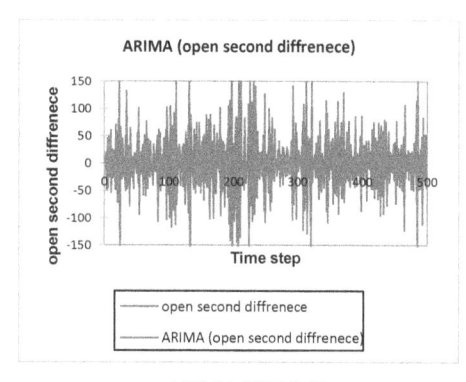

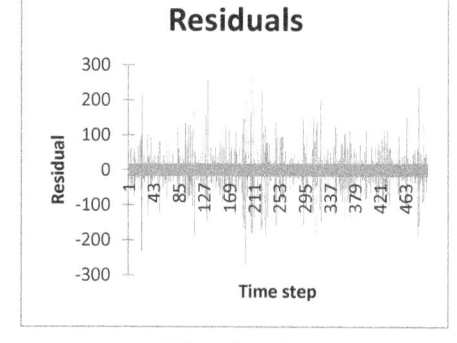

ARIMA-2D(0,2,0)   ARIMA-2D(0,2,0)

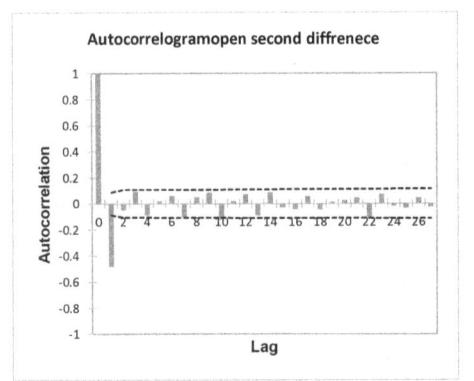

ARIMA-2D(0,2,0) 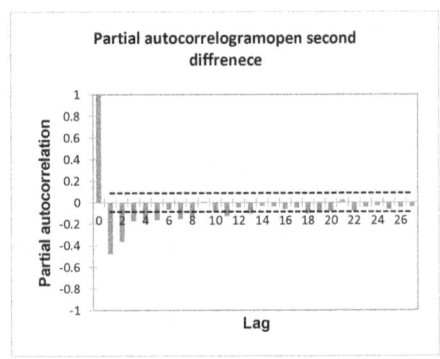   ARIMA-2D(0,2,0)

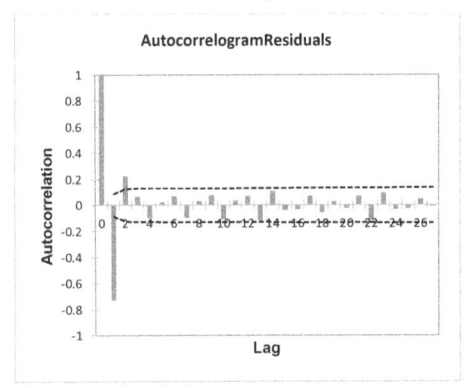

ARIMA-2D(0,2,0) 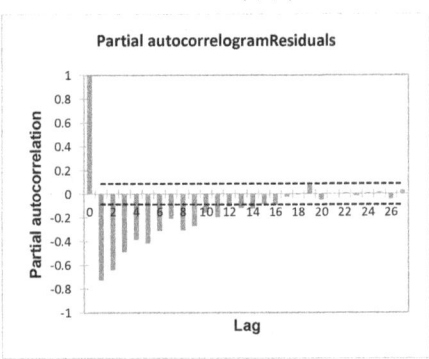   ARIMA-2D(0,2,0)

Fig 4.12: The correlogram of Sun Pharmaceutical Stock Price At [p=0 d=2 q=0]

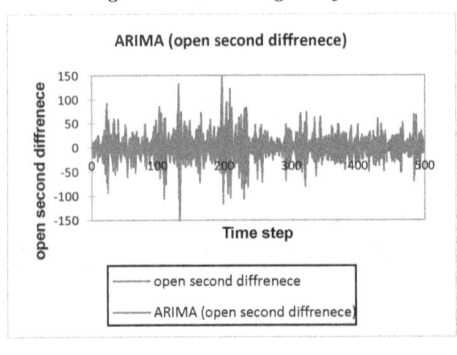

ARIMA-2D(1,2,0) 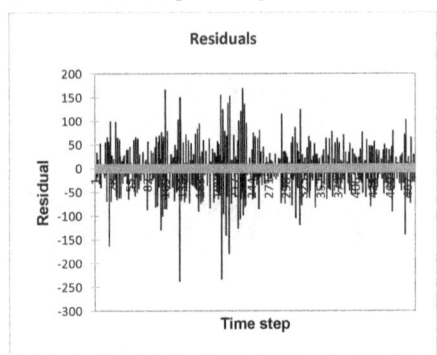   ARIMA-2D(1,2,0)

ARIMA-2D(1,2,0)   ARIMA-2D(1,2,0)

ARIMA-2D(1,2,0)   ARIMA-2D(1,2,0)

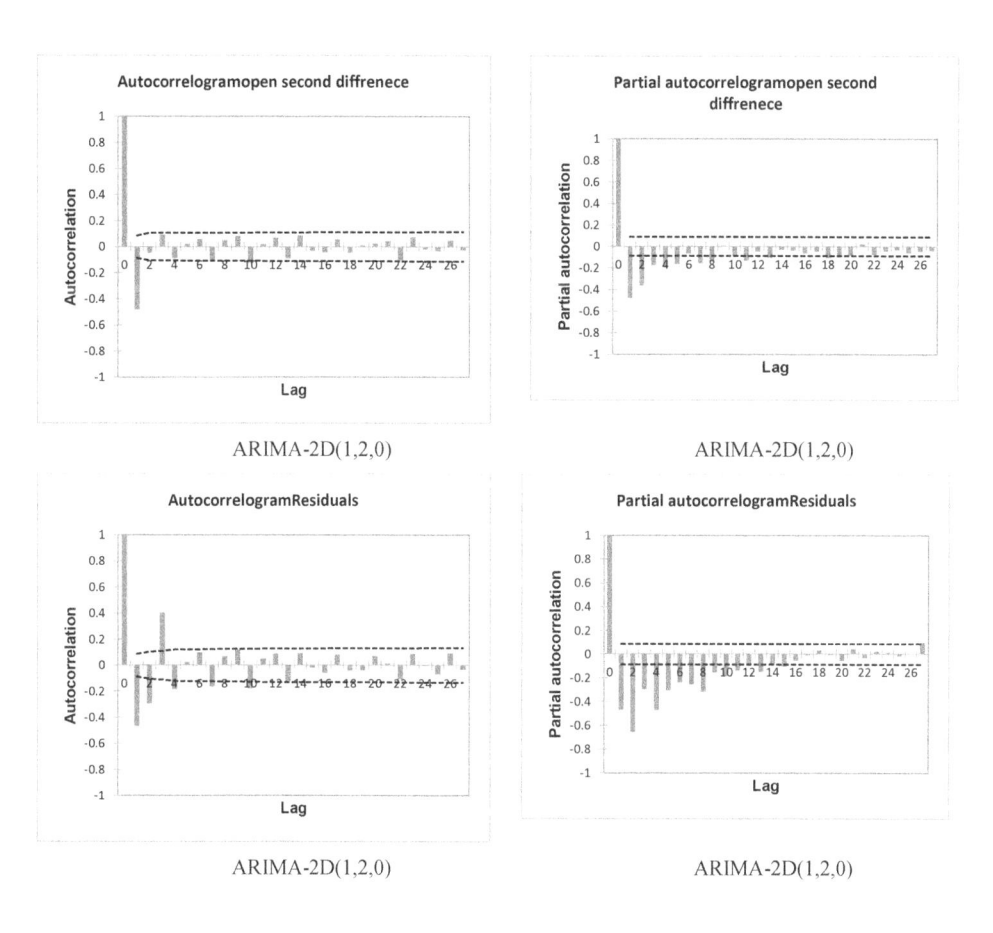

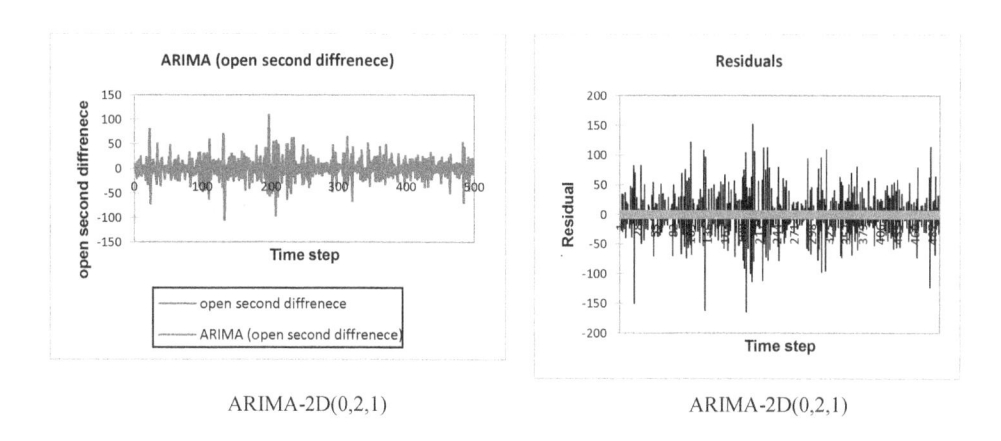

Fig 4.13: The correlogram of Sun Pharmaceutical Stock Price At [p=1 d=2 q=0]

ARIMA-2D(0,2,1)   ARIMA-2D(0,2,1)

ARIMA-2D(0,2,1) ARIMA-2D(0,2,1)

ARIMA-2D(0,2,1) ARIMA-2D(0,2,1)

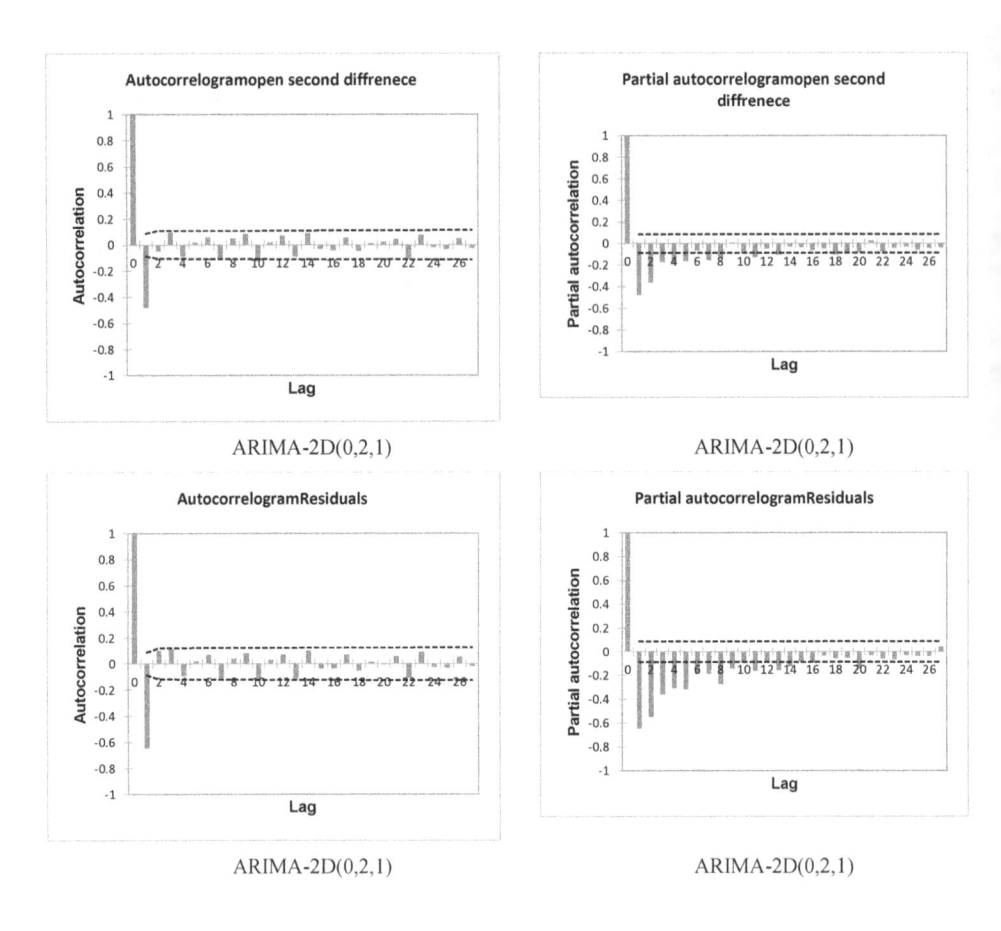

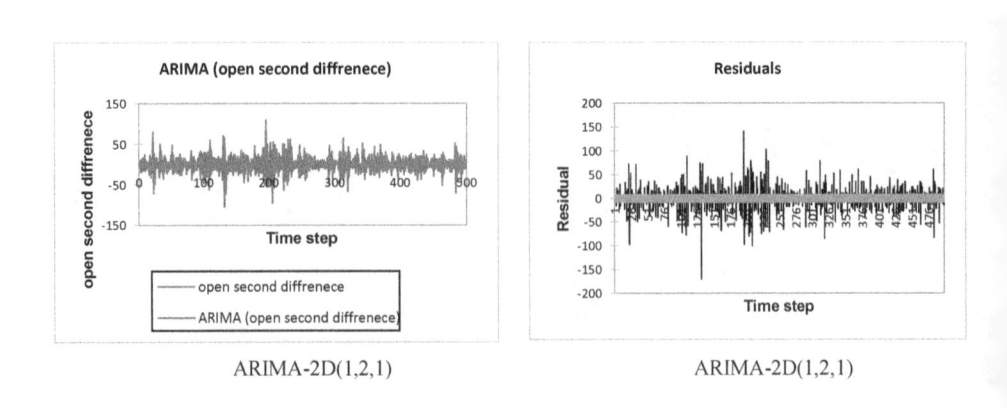

Fig 4.14: The correlogram of Sun Pharmaceutical Stock Price At [p=0 d=2 q=1]

ARIMA-2D(1,2,1) ARIMA-2D(1,2,1)

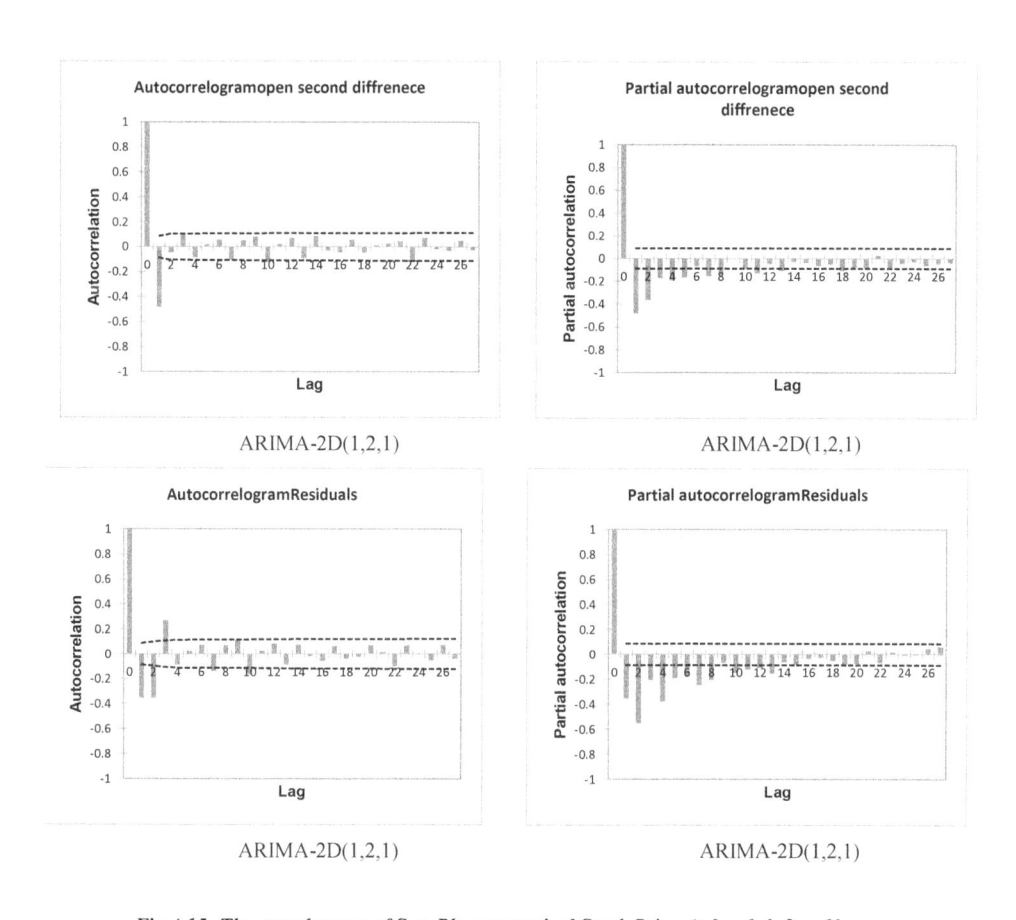

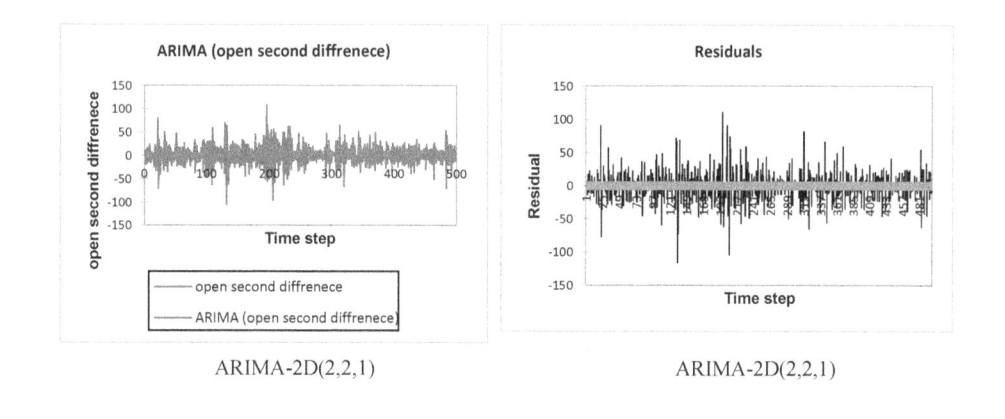

Fig 4.15: The correlogram of Sun Pharmaceutical Stock Price At [p=1 d=2 q=1]

ARIMA-2D(2,2,1)   ARIMA-2D(2,2,1)

ARIMA-2D(2,2,1)   ARIMA-2D(2,2,1)

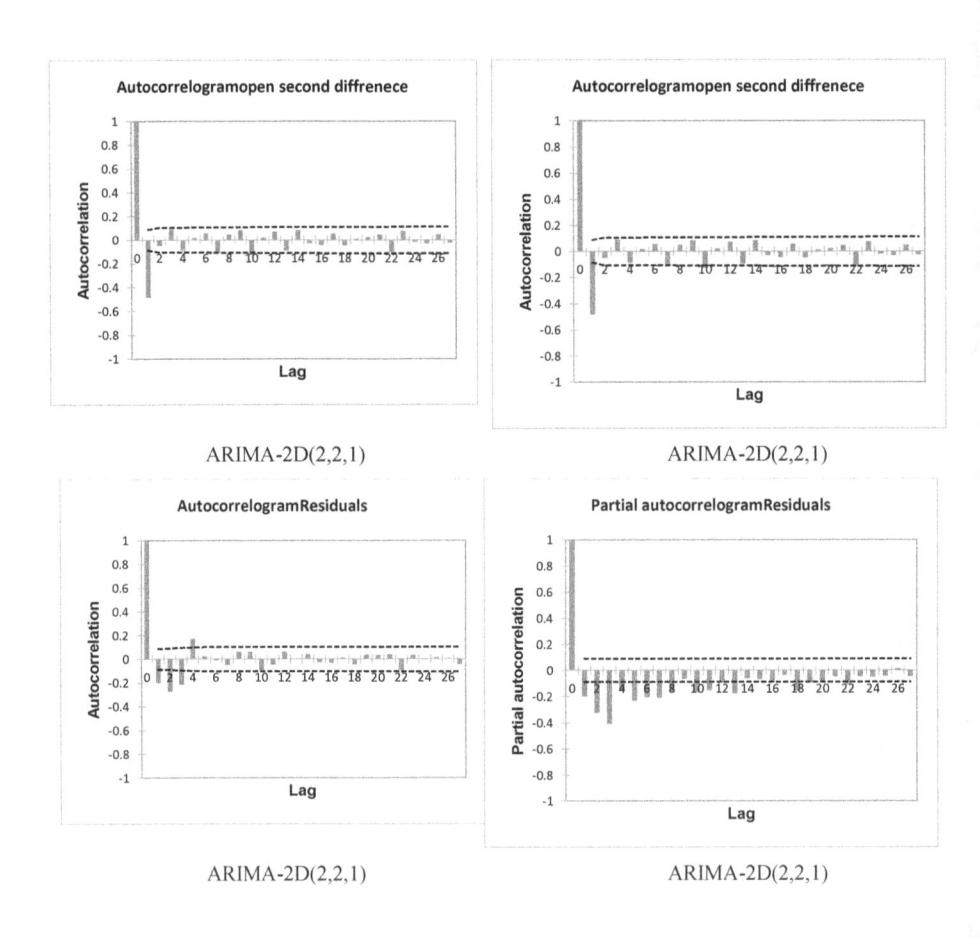

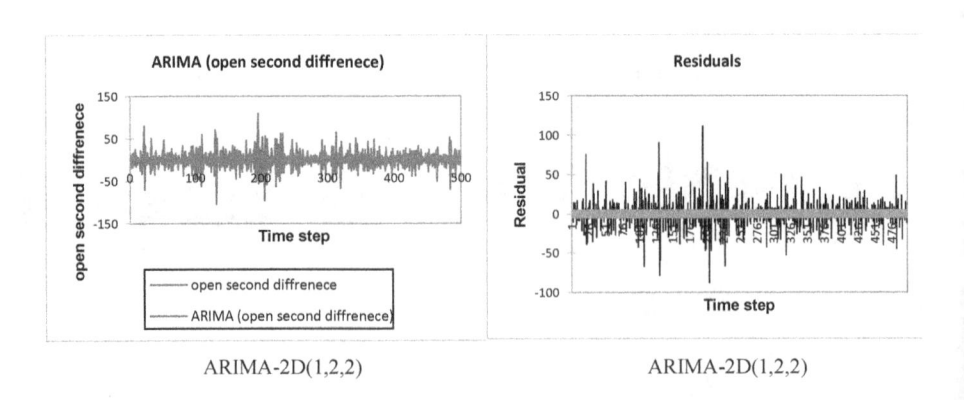

ARIMA-2D(2,2,1)   ARIMA-2D(2,2,1)

Fig 4.16: The correlogram of Sun Pharmaceutical Stock Price At [p=2 d=2 q=1]

ARIMA-2D(1,2,2)   ARIMA-2D(1,2,2)

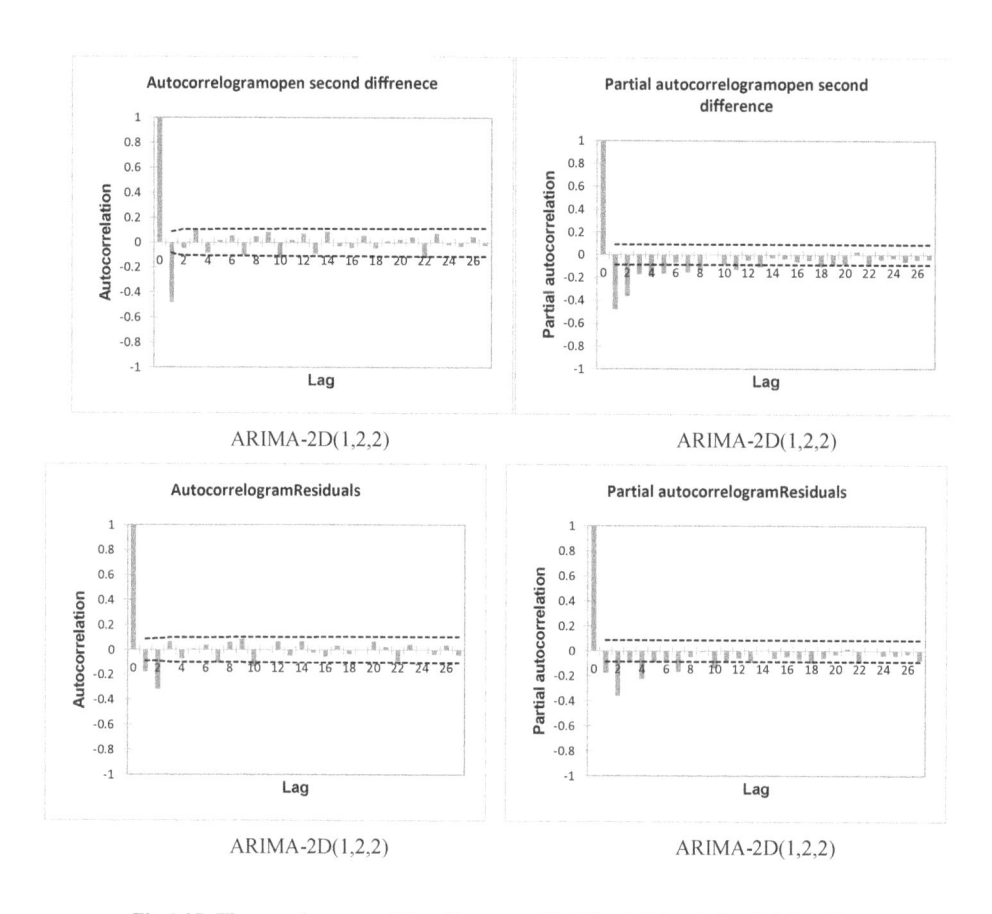

Fig 4.17: The correlogram of Sun Pharmaceutical Stock Price At [p=1 d=2 q=2]

4.6.2 Illustration and interpretation of the experimental results of Sun Pharmaceutical

Table 4.7: ARIMA Models at First Difference for opening price of Sun Pharmaceutical stock at BSE

Model	(0,1,0)	(1,1,0)	(0,1,1)	(2,1,0)	(0,1,2)	(1,1,1)	(2,1,2)	(1,1,2)	(2,1,1)
SSE	282477.8	118740.0	150181.9	188472.8	149673.4	149656	149573.8	**149529.5**	149596.1
MSE	568.3658	2389.134	302.177	379.2209	301.1538	301.1187	300.9532	**300.8643**	300.9982
RMSE	23.8404	48.8787	17.3832	19.4735	17.3537	17.3527	17.348	**17.3454**	17.3493

	2	7	4	9	8	7		4	
WN Variance	568.3658	2389.134	302.177	379.2209	301.1538	301.1187	300.9532	**300.8643**	300.9982
MAPE(Diff)	**99.80871**	239.597	208.8889	210.873	199.8472	199.5004	199.1988	200.2772	199.3024
MAPE	472.244	424.9271	**104.4784**	266.6475	115.111	115.3711	113.6292	124.2316	114.1899
-2Log(Like.)		5276.762	4255.009	4362.214	4253.212	4253.143	4252.788	**4252.765**	4252.9
FPE	568.3658	2398.768	302.177	382.2853	**301.1538**	302.3329	303.3852	302.0774	303.4305
AIC		5280.762	**4259.009**	4368.214	4259.212	4259.143	4262.788	4260.765	4260.9
AICC		5280.786	**4259.033**	4368.263	4259.26	4259.192	4262.91	4260.846	4260.982
SBC		5289.179	**4267.426**	4380.84	4271.837	4271.769	4283.831	4277.599	4277.735

Table 4.8: ARIMA Models at Second Difference for opening price of Sun Pharmaceutical stock at BSE

Model	(0,2,0)	(1,2,0)	(0,2,1)	(1,2,1)	(2,2,1)	(1,2,2)	(2,2,2)	(2,2,0)	(0,2,2)
SSE	2750243	1300588	835999.6	487188.9	341204.3	217577.5	**189161.8**	762418.2	282999.1
MSE	5556.046	2627.45	1688.888	984.22	689.3017	439.5506	**382.145**	1540.239	571.7153
RMSE	74.53889	51.25866	41.09608	31.37228	26.25456	20.96546	**19.54853**	39.24588	23.91057
WN Variance	5556.046	2627.45	1688.888	984.22	689.3017	439.5506	**382.145**	1540.239	571.7153
MAPE(Diff)	190.6844	2653.282	10859.3	17791.13	29278.78	25881.24	27066.65	2723.486	21290.68
MAPE	1122.049	531.6326	424.0333	325.0355	306.4595	210.1273	208.3362	506.2749	**101.8827**
-2Log(Like.)		5303.011	5089.709	4823.951	4649.223	4436.932	**4369.274**	5039.705	4564.772
FPE	5556.046	2638.087	1688.888	988.2046	694.8944	441.3301	**385.2455**	1552.736	571.7153
AIC		5307.01	5093.70	4829.95	4657.22	4444.93	**4379.27**	5045.70	4570.77

111

		1	9	1	3	2	4	5	2
AICC		5307.035	5093.734	4830	4657.305	4445.014	**4379.397**	5045.754	4570.82
SBC		5315.42	5102.119	4842.564	4674.041	4461.751	**4400.297**	5058.319	4583.385

Analysis of results of time series data of Sun Pharmaceutical (for normal distribution) at first difference based on the statistics of goodness of fit / accuracy using ARIMA models:

i) **Some of Squares due to Error**

Different ARIMA models are compared for SSE values. It is found that **ARIMA (1,1,2)** has the **lowest SSE value 149529.50** in comparison to ARIMA (0,1,0) having SSE value 282477.80, ARIMA (1,1,0) having value 1187400, ARIMA (0,1,1) having value 150181.90, ARIMA (2,1,0) having value 188472.80 and ARIMA (0,1,2) having value 149673.40, ARIMA (1,1,1) having value 149656, ARIMA (2,1,2) having value 149573.80 and ARIMA (2,1,1) having value 149596.10 respectively.

ii) **Mean Squared Error**

MSE values of different ARIMA models are compared. It is observed that **ARIMA (1,1,2)** has the **lowest MSE value 300.86** in comparison to ARIMA (0,1,0) having value 569.36, ARIMA (1,1,0) having value 2389.13, ARIMA (0,1,1) having value 302.17, ARIMA (2,1,0) having value 379.22, ARIMA (0,1,2) having value 301.15, ARIMA (1,1,1) having value 301.11, ARIMA (2,1,2) having value 300.95 and ARIMA (2,1,1) having value 300.99 respectively.

iii) **Root Mean Squared Error**

Different ARIMA models are compared for RMSE values. It is found that **ARIMA (1,1,2)** has **lowest RMSE value 17.34** in comparison to ARIMA (0,1,0) having value 23.84, ARIMA (1,1,0) having value 48.87, ARIMA (0,1,1) having value 17.38, ARIMA (2,1,0) having value 19.47, ARIMA (0,1,2) having value 17.35, ARIMA (1,1,1) having value 17.35, ARIMA (2,1,2) having value 17.34 and ARIMA (2,1,1) having value 17.34 respectively.

iv) White Noise Variance

WN variance values are analysed for different ARIMA models. It is observed that **ARIMA (1,1,2)** has **lowest WN variance value 300.86** in comparison to ARIMA (0,1,0) having value 569.36, ARIMA (1,1,0) having value 2389.13, ARIMA (0,1,1) having value 302.17, ARIMA (2,1,0) having value 379.22 and ARIMA (0,1,2) having value 301.15, ARIMA (1,1,1) having value 301.11, ARIMA (2,1,2) having value 300.95 and ARIMA (2,1,1) having value 300.99 respectively.

v) Mean Absolute Percentage Error

Different ARIMA models are compared for MAPE values. It is found that **ARIMA (0,1,1)** has **lowest MAPE value 104.47** in comparison to ARIMA (0,1,0) having value 472.24, ARIMA (1,1,0) having value 424.92, ARIMA (2,1,0) having value 266.64, ARIMA (0,1,2) having value 115.11, ARIMA (1,1,1) having value 115.37, ARIMA (2,1,2) having value 113.62, ARIMA (1,1,2) having value 124.23 and ARIMA (2,1,1) having value 114.18 respectively.

vi) Final Prediction Error

FPE values are analysed for different ARIMA models. It is observed that **ARIMA (0,1,2)** has **lowest FPE value 301.15** in comparison to ARIMA (0,1,0) having value 568.36, ARIMA (1,1,0) having value 2398.76, ARIMA (0,1,1) having value 302.17, ARIMA (2,1,0) having value 382.28, ARIMA (1,1,1) having value 302.33, ARIMA (2,1,2) having value 303.38, ARIMA (1,1,2) having value 302.07 and ARIMA (2,1,1) having value 303.43 respectively.

vii) Akaike Information Criterion

Different ARIMA models are compared for AIC value. It is found that **ARIMA (0,1,1)** has **lowest AIC value 4259.09** in comparison to ARIMA (1,1,0) having value 5280.76, ARIMA (2,1,0) having value 4368.21, ARIMA (0,1,2) having value 4259.21 ARIMA (1,1,1) having value 4259.14, ARIMA (2,1,2) having value 4262.78, ARIMA (1,1,2) having value 4260.76 and ARIMA (2,1,1) having value 4260.90 respectively.

viii) Correction of AIC

AICC value are analysed for different ARIMA models. It is observed that **ARIMA (0,1,1)** has **lowest AICC value 4259.03** in comparison to ARIMA (1,1,0) having value 5280.78, ARIMA (2,1,0) having value 4368.26, ARIMA (0,1,2) having value 4259.26 ARIMA (1,1,1) having value 4259.19, ARIMA (2,1,2) having value 4262.91, ARIMA (1,1,2) having value 4260.84 and ARIMA (2,1,1) having value 4260.98 respectively.

ix) Schwarz Bayesian Information Criterion

Different ARIMA models are compared for SBC value. It is found that **ARIMA (0,1,1)** has **lowest SBC value 4267.42** in comparison to ARIMA (1,1,0) having value 5289.17, ARIMA (2,1,0) having value 4380.84, ARIMA (0,1,2) having value 4271.83, ARIMA (1,1,1) having value 4271.76, ARIMA (2,1,2) having value 4283.83, ARIMA (1,1,2) having value 4277.59 and ARIMA (2,1,1) having value 4277.73 respectively.

Analysis of results of time series data of Sun Pharmaceutical (for normal distribution) at second difference based on the statistics of goodness of fit / accuracy using ARIMA model:

i) Some of Squares due to Error

Different ARIMA models are compared for SSE values. It is found that **ARIMA (2,2,2)** has **lowest SSE value 189161.8** in comparison to ARIMA (0,2,0) having value 2750243, ARIMA (1,2,0) having value 1300588, ARIMA (0,2,1) having value 835999.60, ARIMA (1,2,1) having value 487188.90, ARIMA (2,2,1) having value 341204.30, ARIMA (1,2,2) having value 217577.50, ARIMA (2,2,0) having value 762418.20 and ARIMA (0,2,2) having value 282999 respectively.

ii) Mean Squared Error

MSE value is analysed for different ARIMA models. It is observed that **ARIMA (2,2,2)** has **lowest MSE value 382.145** in comparison to ARIMA (0,2,0) having value 5556.04, ARIMA (1,2,0) having value 2627.45, ARIMA (0,2,1) having value 1688.88, ARIMA (1,2,1) having value 984.22, ARIMA (2,2,1) having value 689.30, ARIMA (1,2,2) having value 439.55, ARIMA (2,2,0) having value 1540.23 and ARIMA (0,2,2) having value 571.71 respectively.

iii) Root Mean Squared Error

Different ARIMA models are compared for RMSE value. It is found that **ARIMA (2,2,2)** has **lowest RMSE value 19.54** in comparison to ARIMA (0,2,0) having value 74.53, ARIMA (1,2,0) having value 51.25, ARIMA (0,2,1) having value 41.09, ARIMA (1,2,1)having value 31.37, ARIMA (2,2,1) having value 26.25, ARIMA (1,2,2) having value 20.96, ARIMA (2,2,0) having value 39.24 and ARIMA (0,2,2) having value 23.91 respectively.

iv) White Noise Variance

WN variance value is compared for different ARIMA models. It is observed that **ARIMA (2,2,2)** has **lowest WN variance value 382.145** in comparison to ARIMA (0,2,0) having value 5556.04, ARIMA (1,2,0) having value 2627.45, ARIMA (0,2,1) having value 1688.88, ARIMA (1,2,1) having value 984.22, ARIMA (2,2,1) having value 689.30, ARIMA (1,2,2) having value 439.55, ARIMA (2,2,0) having value 1540.23 and ARIMA (0,2,2) having value 571.71 respectively.

v) Mean Absolute Percentage Error

Different ARIMA models are compared for MAPE value. It is found that **ARIMA (0,2,2)** has **lowest MAPE value 101.88** in comparison to ARIMA (0,2,0) having value 1122.04, ARIMA (1,2,0) having value 531.63, ARIMA (0,2,1) having value 424.03, ARIMA (1,2,1) having value 325.03, ARIMA (2,2,1) having value 306.45, ARIMA (1,2,2) having value 210.12, ARIMA (2,2,2) having value 208.33 and ARIMA (2,2,0) having value 506.27 respectively.

vi) Final Prediction Error

FPE value is analyzed for different ARIMA models. It is observed that **ARIMA (2,2,2)** has **lowest FPE value 385.24** in comparison to ARIMA (0,2,0) having value 5556.04, ARIMA (1,2,0) having value 2638.08, ARIMA (0,2,1) having value 1688.88, ARIMA (1,2,1) having value 988.20, ARIMA (2,2,1) having value 694.89, ARIMA (1,2,2) having value 441.33, ARIMA (2,2,0) having value 1552.73 and ARIMA (0,2,2) having value 571.71 respectively.

vii) Akaike Information Criterion

Different ARIMA models are compared for AIC value. It is found that **ARIMA (2,2,2)** has **lowest AIC value 4379.274** in comparison to ARIMA (1,2,0) having value 5307.01, ARIMA (0,2,1) having value 5093.70, ARIMA (1,2,1) having value 4829.95, ARIMA (2,2,1) having value 4657.22, ARIMA (1,2,2) having value 4444.93, ARIMA (2,2,0) having value 5045.70 and ARIMA (0,2,2) having value 4570.77 respectively.

viii) Correction of AIC

AICC value is analysed for different ARIMA models. It is observed that **ARIMA (2,2,2)** has **lowest AICC value 4379.39** in comparison to ARIMA (1,2,0) having value 5307.03,

ARIMA (0,2,1) having value 5093.70, ARIMA (1,2,1) having value 4830.00, ARIMA (2,2,1) having value 4657.30, ARIMA (1,2,2) having value 4445.01, ARIMA (2,2,0) having value 5045.75 and ARIMA (0,2,2) having value 4570.80 respectively.

ix) Schwarz Bayesian Information Criterion

Different ARIMA models are compared for SBC value. It is found that **ARIMA (2,2,2)** has **lowest SBC value 4400.29** in comparison to ARIMA (1,2,0) having value 5315.42, ARIMA (0,2,1) having value 5102.11, ARIMA (1,2,1) having value 4842.56, ARIMA (2,2,1) having value 4674.04, ARIMA (1,2,2) having value 4461.75, ARIMA (2,2,0) having value 5058.31 and ARIMA (0,2,2) having value 4583.38 respectively.

Comparison between first and second difference results of analysed ARIMA models:

All statistics of goodness of fitness are compared for first and second difference of time series data detailed as under:

i) Some of Squares due to Error

SSE value is compared for both the orders. It is found that SSE value obtained from first differencing **(149529.50)** is lowest for **ARIMA model (1,1,2)** in comparison to SSE value for second differencing (189161.80) of ARIMA model (2,2,2). Thus, **ARIMA model (1,1,2)** is considered best model for prediction of stock prices amongst 18 models of ARIMA on the basis of SSE analysis.

ii) Mean Squared Error

On comparison of the orders of differencing, it is found that MSE value obtained on first differencing **(300.86)** was lowest for **ARIMA model (1,1,2)** in comparison to MSE value obtained on second differencing (382.14) of ARIMA model (2,2,2). Thus, **ARIMA model (1,1,2)** is considered best model for prediction of stock prices amongst 18 ARIMA models on the basis of MSE analysis.

iii) Root Mean Squared Error

RMSE value is compared for both the orders and it is found that RMSE value obtained from first differencing (17.34) was lowest for ARIMA model (1,1,2) in comparison to RMSE value for second differencing (19.54) of ARIMA model (2,2,2). Thus, **ARIMA model (1,1,2)** is considered best model for prediction of stock prices amongst 18 different models of ARIMA on the basis of RMSE analysis.

iv) White Noise Variance

On comparison of the orders of differencing, it is found that WN variance value obtained on first differencing **(300.86)** was lowest for **ARIMA model (1,1,2)** in comparison to WN variance value for second differencing (382.14) of ARIMA model (2,2,2). Thus, **ARIMA model (1,1,2)** is considered best model for prediction of stock prices amongst 18 different models of ARIMA on the basis of WN analysis.

v) Mean Absolute Percentage Error

MAPE value is compared for both the orders and it is found that MAPE value obtained from second differencing **(101.88)** was lowest for **ARIMA model (0,2,2)** in comparison to MAPE value for first differencing (104.48) of ARIMA model (0,1,1). Thus, **ARIMA model (0,2,2)** is considered best model for prediction of stock prices amongst 18 different models of ARIMA on the basis of MAPE analysis.

vi) Final Prediction Error

On comparison of the orders of differencing, it is found that FPE value obtained on first differencing **(301.15)** was lowest for **ARIMA model (0,1,2)** in comparison to FPE value for second differencing (385.24) of ARIMA model (2,2,2). Thus, **ARIMA model (0,1,2)** is considered best model for prediction of stock prices amongst 18 different models of ARIMA on the basis of FPE analysis.

vii) Akaike Information Criterion

AIC value is compared for both the orders and it is found that AIC value obtained from first differencing **(4259.00)** was lowest for **ARIMA model (0,1,1)** in comparison to AIC value for second differencing (4379.27) of ARIMA model (2,2,2). Thus, **ARIMA model (0,1,1)** is considered best model for prediction of stock prices amongst 18 different models of ARIMA on the basis of AIC analysis.

viii) Correction of AIC

On comparison of the orders of differencing, it is found that AICC value obtained on first differencing **(4259.03)** was lowest for **ARIMA model (0,1,1)** in comparison to AICC value for second differencing(4379.39) of ARIMA model (2,2,2). Thus, **ARIMA model (0,1,1)** is considered best model for prediction of stock prices amongst 18 different models of ARIMA on the basis of AICC analysis.

ix) Schwarz Bayesian Information Criterion

SBC value is compared for both the orders and it is found that SBC value obtained from first differencing **(4267.42)** is lowest for **ARIMA model (0,1,1)** in comparison to SBC value for second differencing (4400.29) of ARIMA model (2,2,2). Thus, **ARIMA model (0,1,1)** is considered best model for prediction of stock prices amongst 18 different models of ARIMA on the basis of SBC analysis.

Appraisal of experiment:

Out of eighteen applied models, the best fit model is selected for the final analysis on the basis of maximum number of votes for lowest value of each statistics for goodness of fit. ARIMA (1,1,2) at first difference earned five votes having lowest value of each for SSE, MSE, RMSE, White Noise and -2 log like respectively in comparison to four votes of ARIMA model (0,0,1). Thus, **ARIMA (1, 1, 2)** came out to be the best model amongst different ARIMA models.

Similarly, results of other five stocks where time series data is normally distributed is observed and it is found that ARIMA (1,1,1,) model is best fit for Coal India, Hero Motor Corp and Reliance Industries. ARIMA (0,1,1) model for Gail and ARIMA 1 (0,1,2) model for NTPC gave best results amongst different ARIMA models for stock prices of select companies under consideration.

4.7 Experimental Process and Results of Lupin Limited (Non- Normal Distribution)
4.7.1 Graphical Analysis:

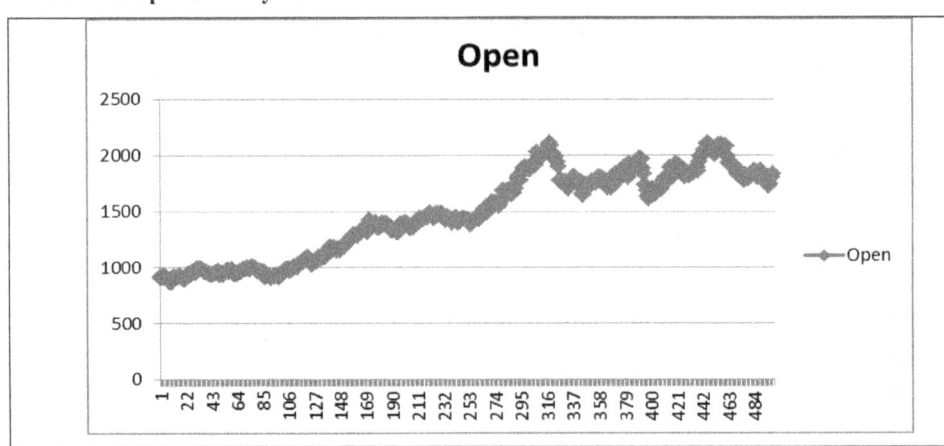

Figure 4.18 Graph of opening price of Lupin stock at BSE

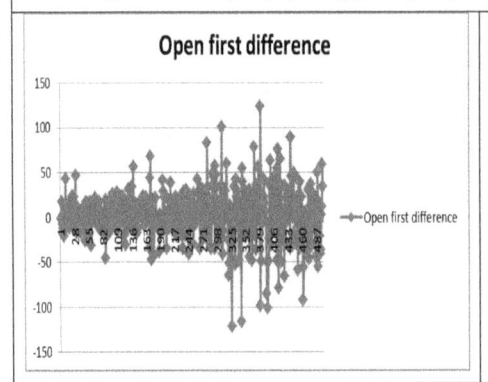

Fig 4.19: Graph of First Difference of opening price of Lupin stock at BSE

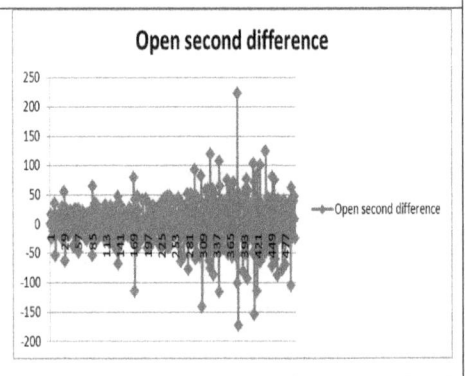

Fig 4.20: Graph of Second Difference of opening price of Lupin stock at BSE

Table 4.9: Dickey-Fuller Statistics

Dickey-Fuller test			
	Original	First Difference	Second Difference
Tau (Observed value)	-2.369	-7.956	-11.794
Tau (Critical value)	-0.907	-0.894	-0.884
p-value (one-tailed)	0.386	< 0.0001	< 0.0001
Alpha (α)	0.05	0.05	0.05

Table 4.10: Various statistics of ARIMA models at First Difference for opening price of Lupin Limited

Model	(0,1,0)	(1,1,0)	(0,1,1)	(2,1,0)	(0,1,2)	(1,1,1)	(2,1,1)	(2,1,2)	(1,1,2)
SSE	723377.5	555176.7	374520	500994.5	374111.6	374115.8	374102.1	374120	556139.7
MSE	1455.488	1117.056	753.5614	1008.037	752.7396	752.7482	752.7206	752.7565	1123.515
RMSE	38.15086	33.42238	27.45107	31.7496	27.4361	27.43626	27.43575	27.43641	33.51887
WN Variance	1455.488	1117.056	753.5614	1008.037	752.7396	752.7482	752.7206	752.7565	1123.515
MAPE(Diff)	100.0708	184.4901	167.404	221.5482	163.2159	163.2988	163.0418	163.4484	83.62179
MAPE	328.0666	267.3117	107.0687	245.5596	109.2576	109.3478	108.9857	109.6582	176.8039
-2Log(Like.)		4898.859	4709.166	4848.026	4708.556	4708.56	4708.55	4708.551	4901.536
FPE	1455.488	1121.56	753.5614	1016.183	752.7396	755.7834	758.8032	758.8393	1128.063
AIC		4902.859	4713.166	4854.026	4714.556	4714.56	4716.55	4718.551	4909.536
AICC		4902.883	4713.191	4854.075	4714.605	4714.609	4716.632	4718.673	4909.617
SBC		4911.276	4721.583	4866.652	4727.182	4727.186	4733.385	4739.594	4926.354

Table 4.11: ARIMA Model at Second Difference for opening price of Lupin Limited

Model	(0,2,0)	(1,2,0)	(0,2,1)	(1,2,1)	(2,2,1)	(1,2,2)	(0.2.2)	(2,2,0)	(2,2,2)
SSE	7108483	3090853	2143479	1209045	952965	556140	724636	2101332	503348

MSE	14360.6	6244.15	4330.26	2442.51	1925.18	1123.52	1463.91	4245.12	1016.87
RMSE	119.836	79.0199	65.8047	49.4218	43.8769	33.5189	38.2611	65.1546	31.8883
WN Variance	14360.6	6244.15	4330.26	2442.51	1925.18	1123.52	1463.91	4245.12	1016.87
MAPE(Diff)	100.131	147.35	88.3428	110.469	107.614	83.6218	77.4709	140.6	83.9244
MAPE	843.83	566.903	377.609	287.57	235.011	176.804	106.02	521.352	203.924
-2Log(Like.)		5731.58	5555.78	5273.92	5157.34	4901.54	5030.27	5541.34	4853.28
FPE	14360.6	6269.43	4330.26	2452.4	1940.8	1128.06	1463.91	4279.56	1025.12
AIC		5735.58	5559.78	5279.92	5165.34	4909.54	5036.27	5547.34	4863.28
AICC		5735.61	5559.81	5279.97	5165.42	4909.62	5036.32	5547.39	4863.4
SBC		5743.99	5568.19	5292.54	5182.16	4926.35	5048.88	5559.96	4884.3

Table 4.12: Descriptive Statistics of opening price of Lupin stock at BSE

Model	Minimum	Maximum	Mean	Std. deviation
(0,1,0)	-121.600	124.000	1.855	27.451
(1,1,0)	-121.600	124.000	1.855	27.451
(0,1,1)	-121.600	124.000	1.855	27.451
(2,1,0)	-121.600	124.000	1.855	27.451
(0,1,2)	-121.600	124.000	1.855	27.451
(1,1,1)	-121.600	124.000	1.855	27.451
(2,1,1)	-121.600	124.000	1.855	27.451
(2,1,2)	-121.600	124.000	1.855	27.451
(1,1,2)	-121.600	124.000	1.855	27.451
(0,2,0)	-172.950	222.000	0.071	38.189
(1,2,0)	-172.950	222.000	0.071	38.189
(0,2,1)	-172.950	222.000	0.071	38.189
(1,2,1)	-172.950	222.000	0.071	38.189
(2,2,1)	-172.950	222.000	0.071	38.189
(1,2,2)	-172.950	222.000	0.071	38.189
(0,2,2)	-172.950	222.000	0.071	38.189
(2,2,0)	-172.950	222.000	0.071	38.189
(2,2,2)	-172.950	222.000	0.071	38.189

ARIMA-1D(0,1,0)   ARIMA-1D(0,1,0)

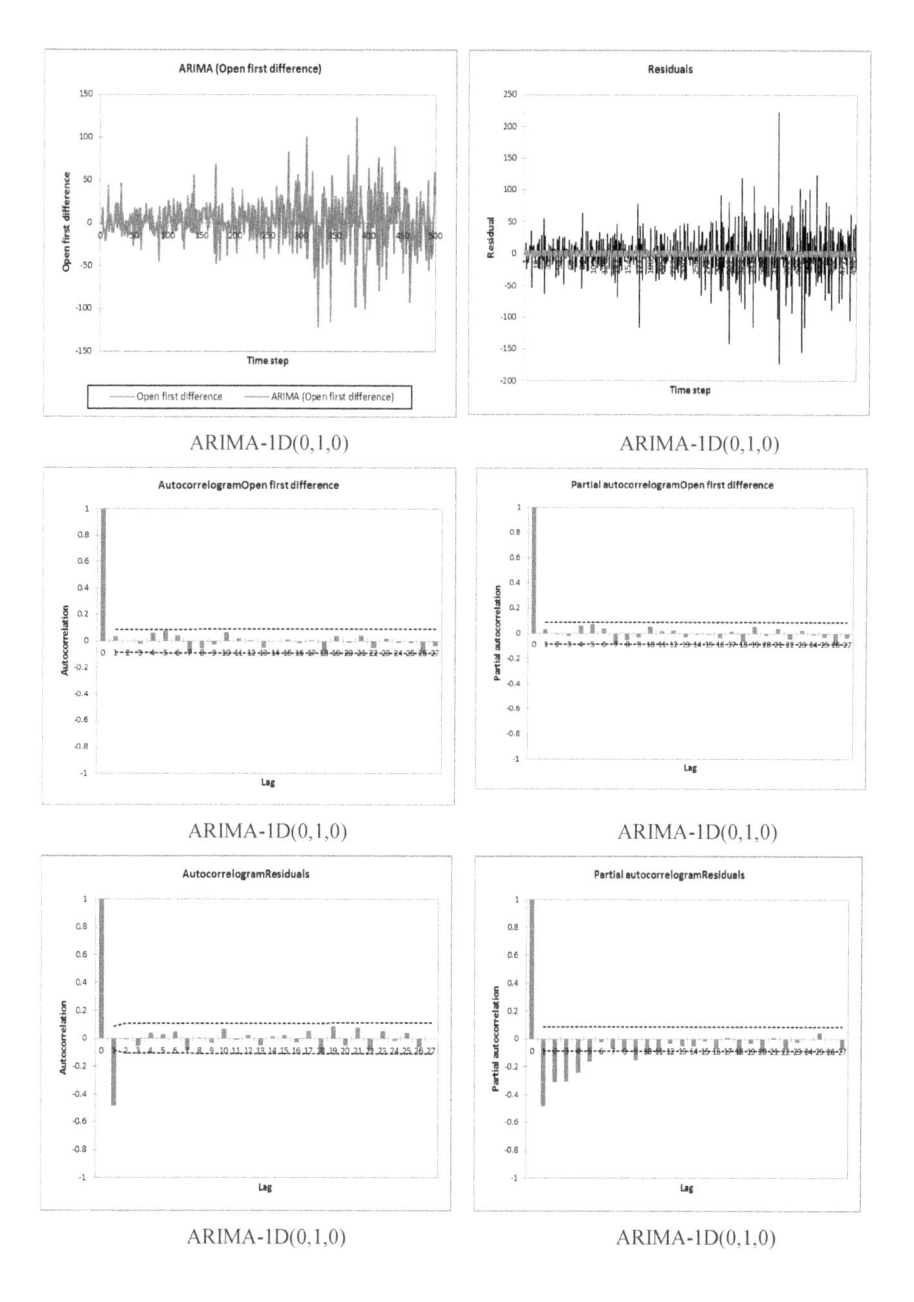

ARIMA-1D(0,1,0)   ARIMA-1D(0,1,0)

ARIMA-1D(0,1,0)   ARIMA-1D(0,1,0)

Fig 4.21: The correlogram of LUPIN Stock Price At [p=0 d=1 q=0]

ARIMA-1D(1,1,0)   ARIMA-1D(1,1,0)

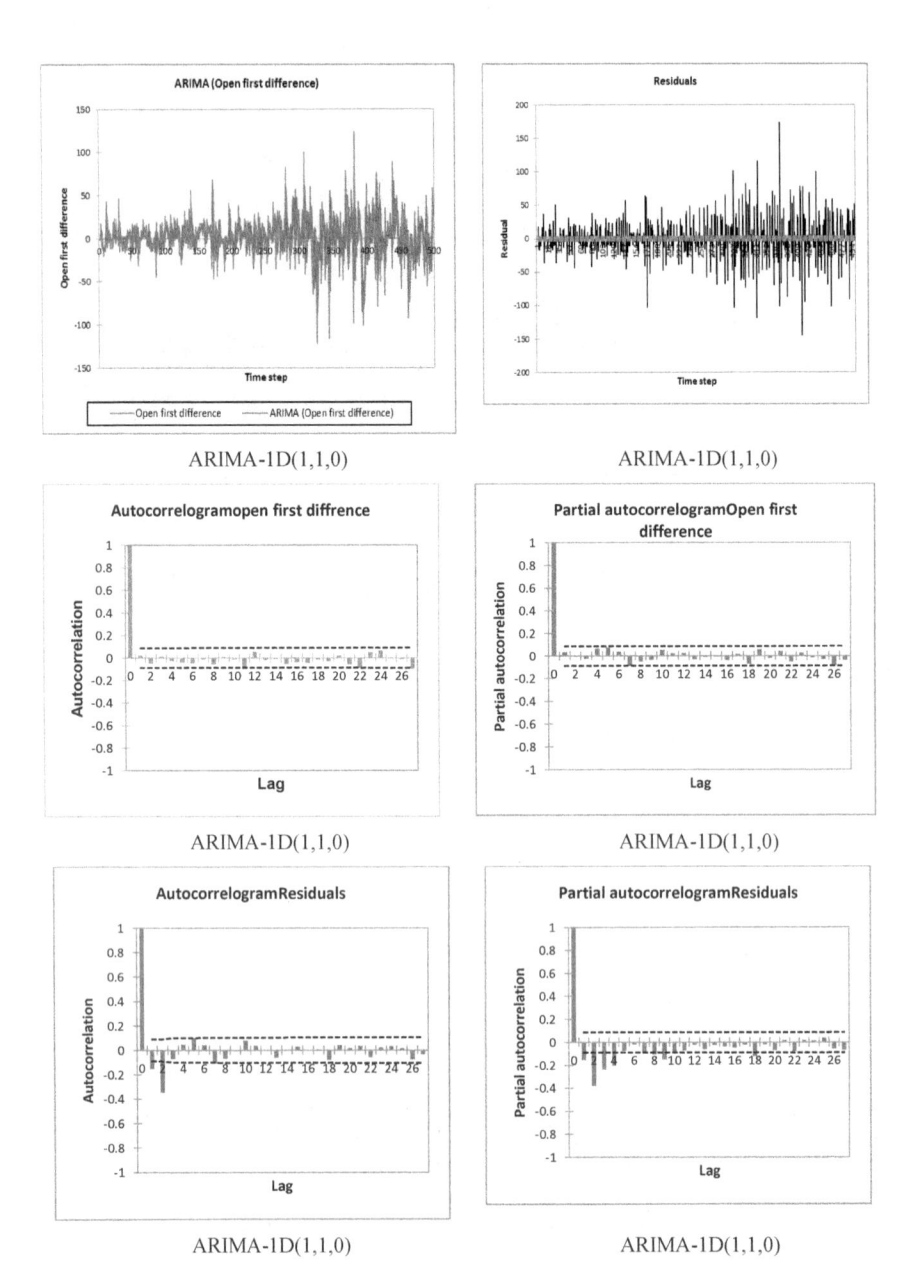

ARIMA-1D(1,1,0)   ARIMA-1D(1,1,0)

ARIMA-1D(1,1,0)   ARIMA-1D(1,1,0)

Fig 4.22: The correlogram of LUPIN Stock Price At [p=1 d=1 q=0]

ARIMA-1D(0,1,1) ARIMA-1D(0,1,1)

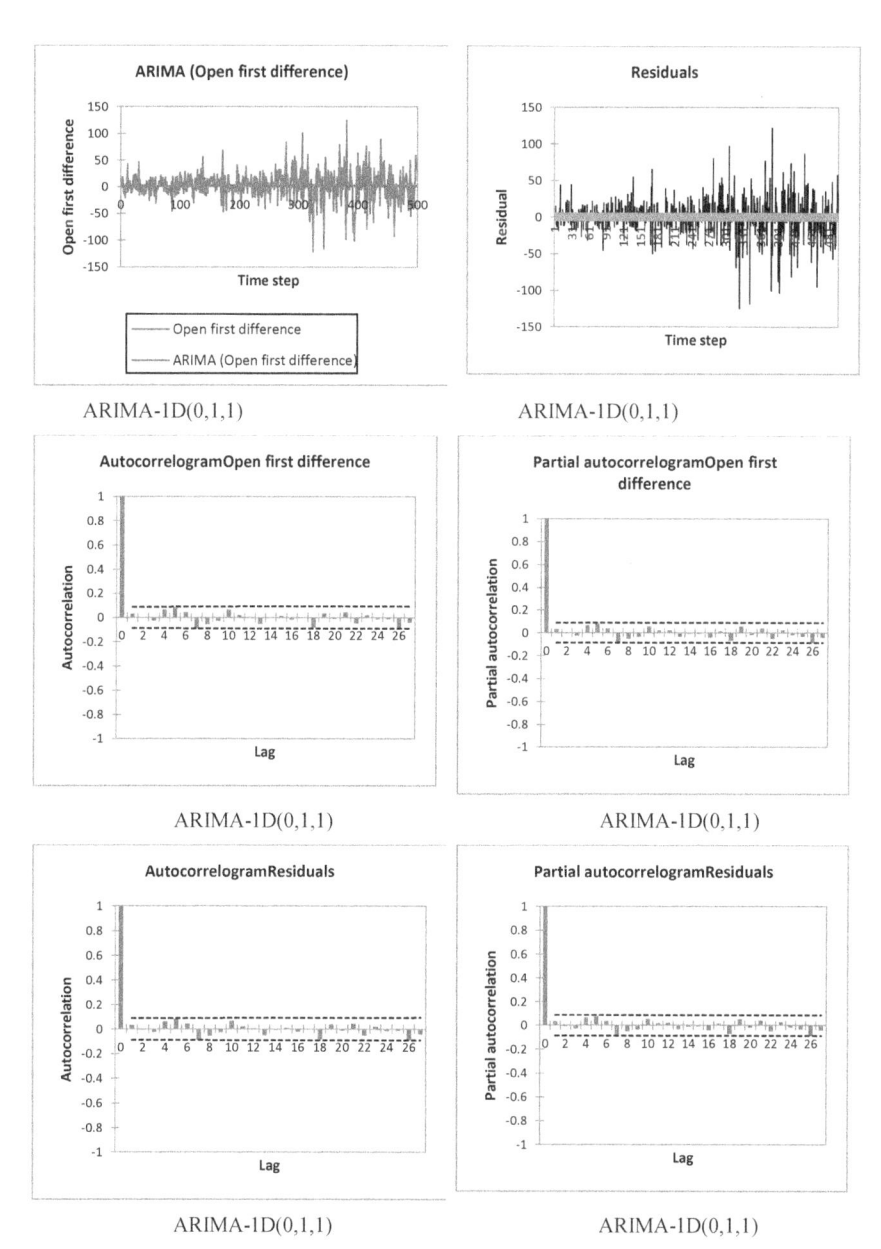

ARIMA-1D(0,1,1) ARIMA-1D(0,1,1)

ARIMA-1D(0,1,1) ARIMA-1D(0,1,1)

Fig 4.23: The correlogram of LUPIN Stock Price At [p=0 d=1 q=1]

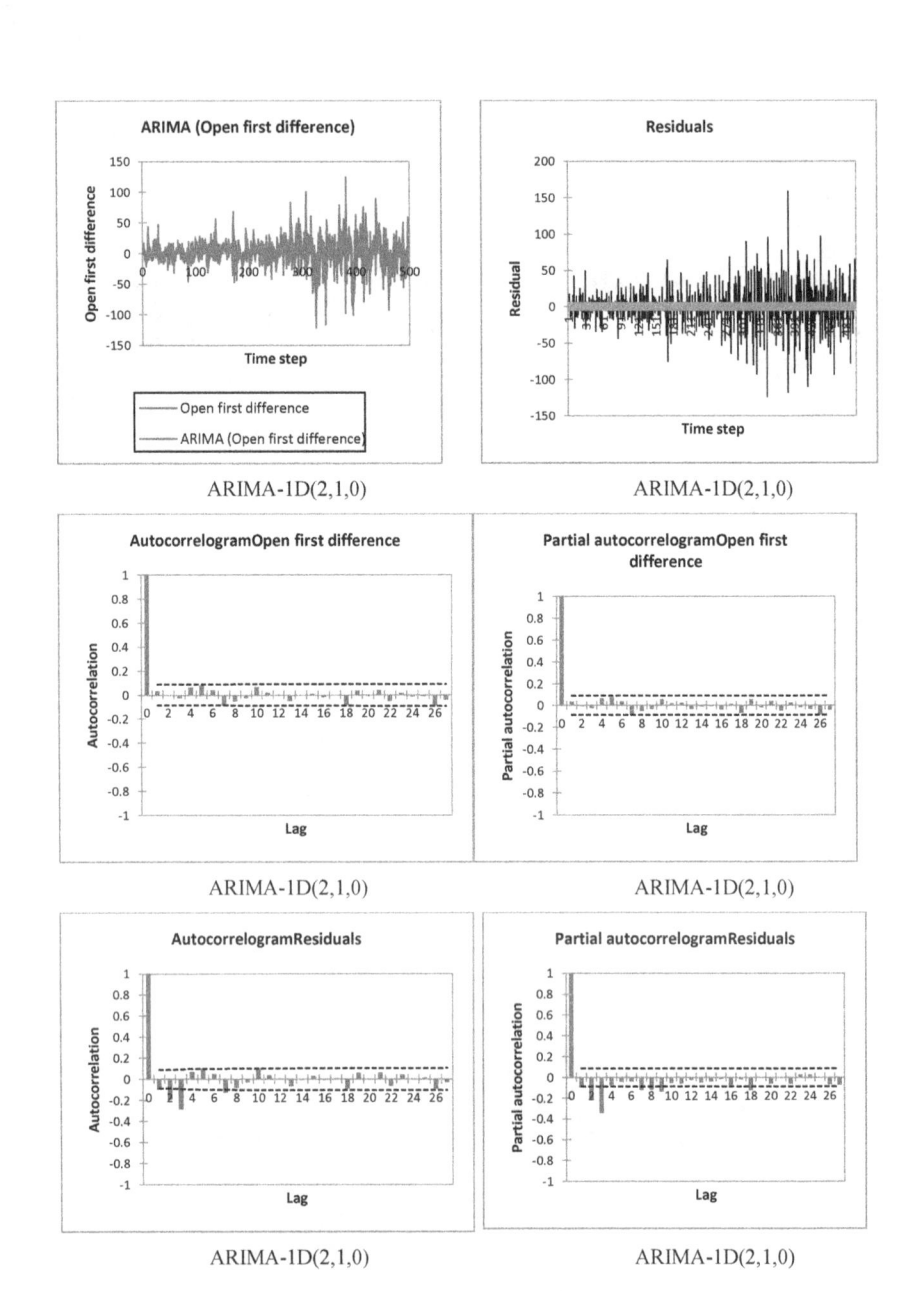

Fig 4.24: The correlogram of LUPIN Stock Price At [p=2 d=1 q=0]

ARIMA-1D(0,1,2)　　　　　　　　ARIMA-1D(0,1,2)

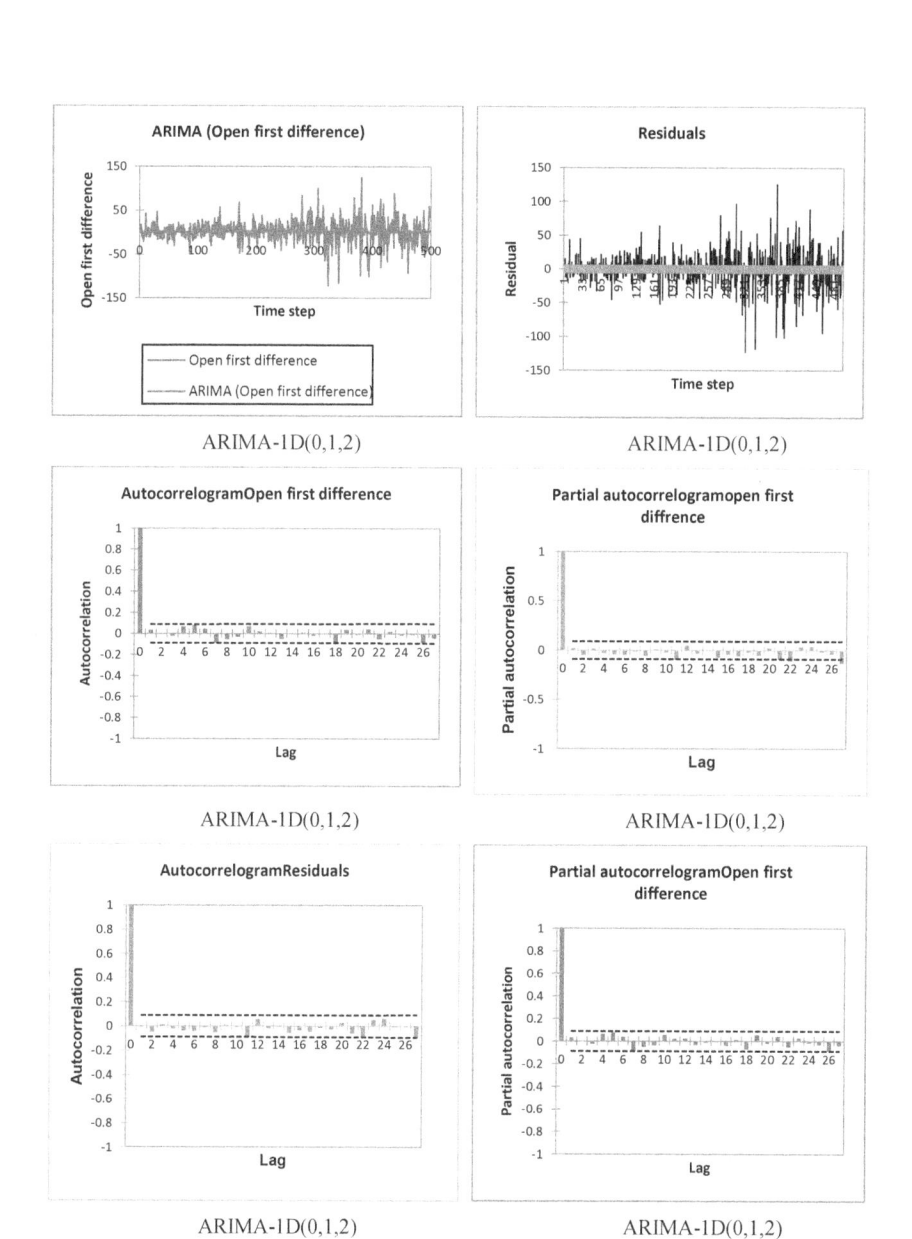

ARIMA-1D(0,1,2)　　　　　　　　ARIMA-1D(0,1,2)

ARIMA-1D(0,1,2)　　　　　　　　ARIMA-1D(0,1,2)

Fig 4.25: The correlogram of LUPIN Stock Price At [p=0 d=1 q=2]

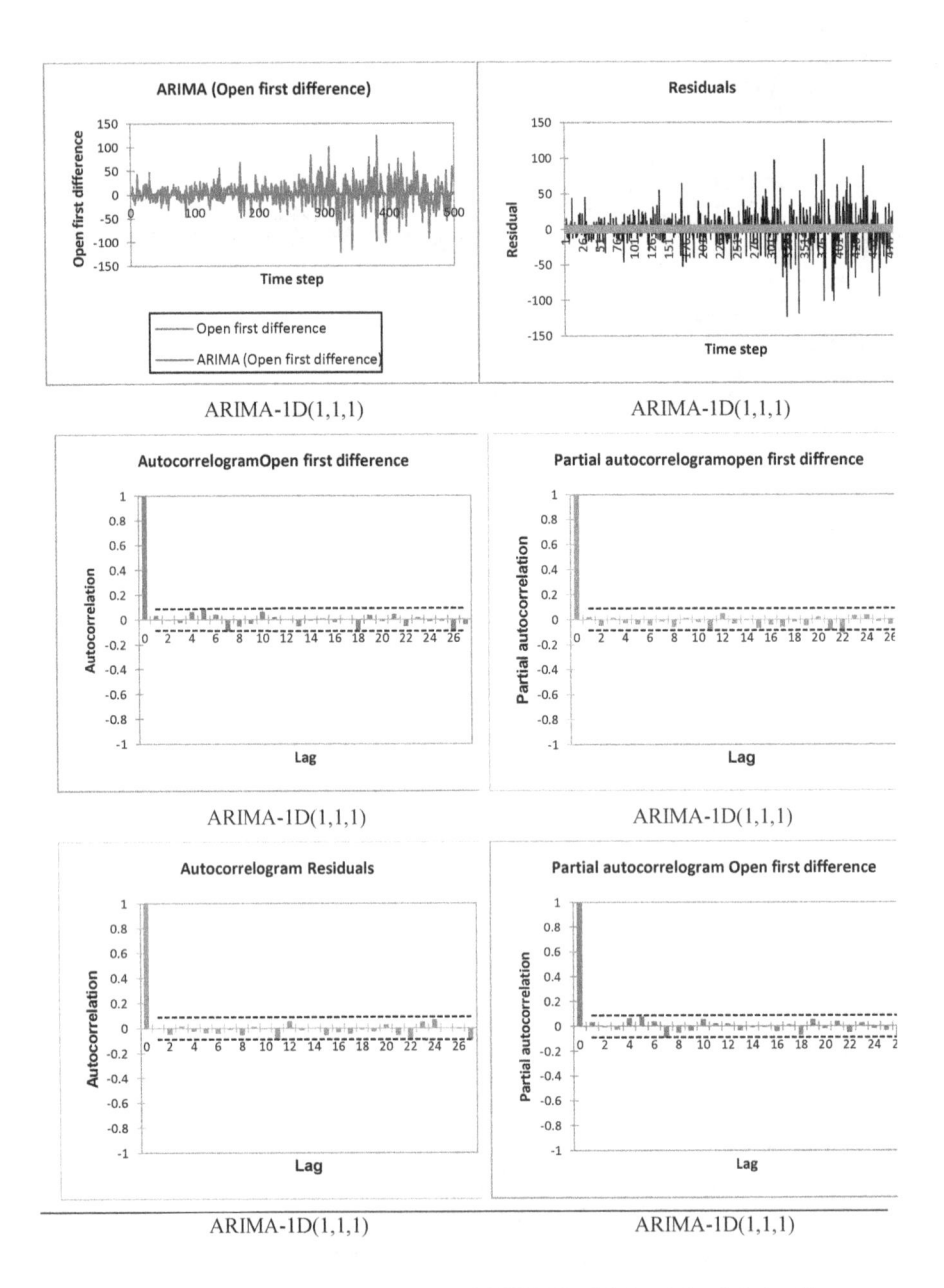

Fig 4.26: The correlogram of LUPIN Stock Price At [p=1 d=1 q=1]

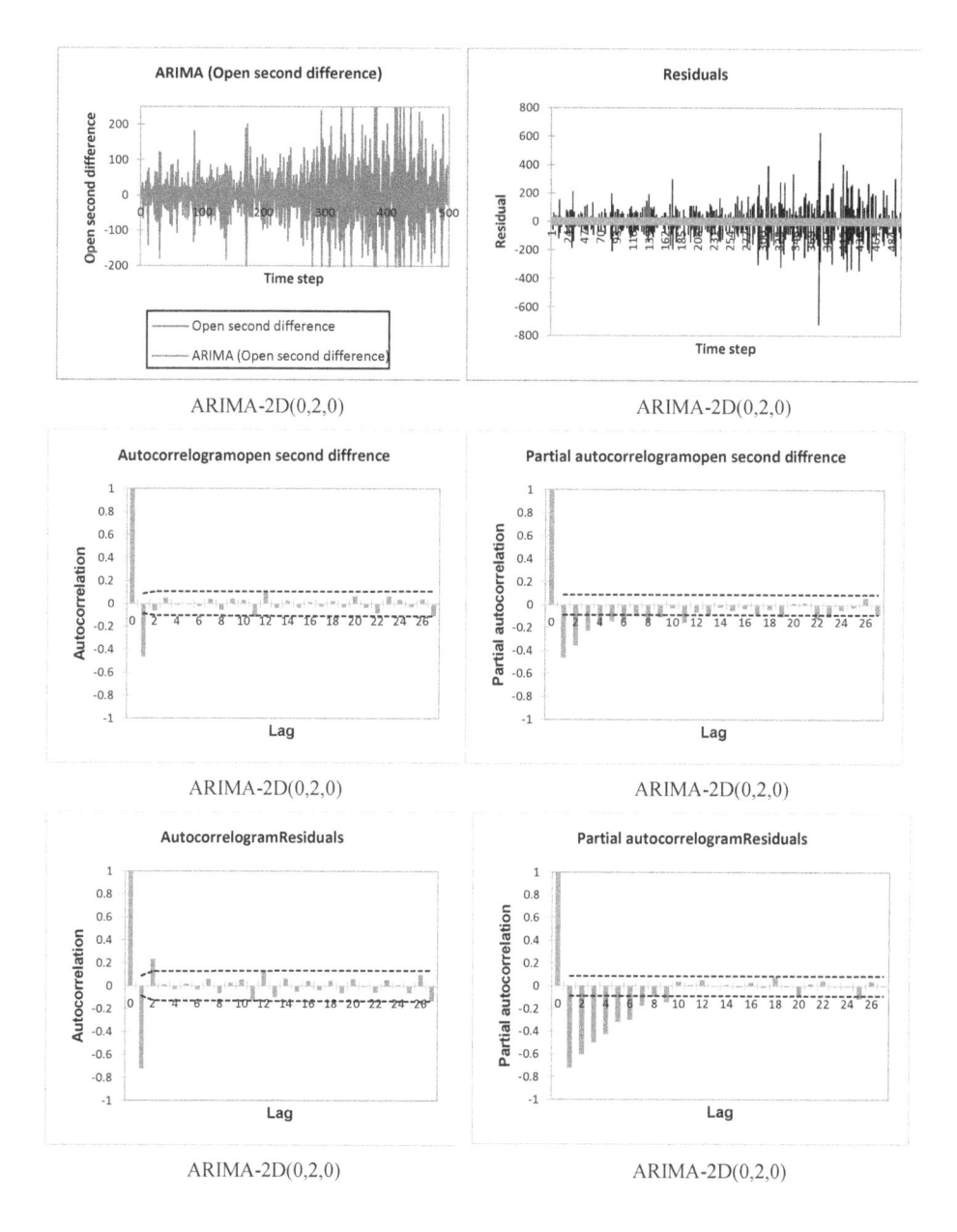

Fig 4.27: The correlogram of LUPIN Stock Price At [p=0 d=2 q=0]

ARIMA-2D(1,2,0)　　　　　　　　　　　ARIMA-2D(1,2,0)

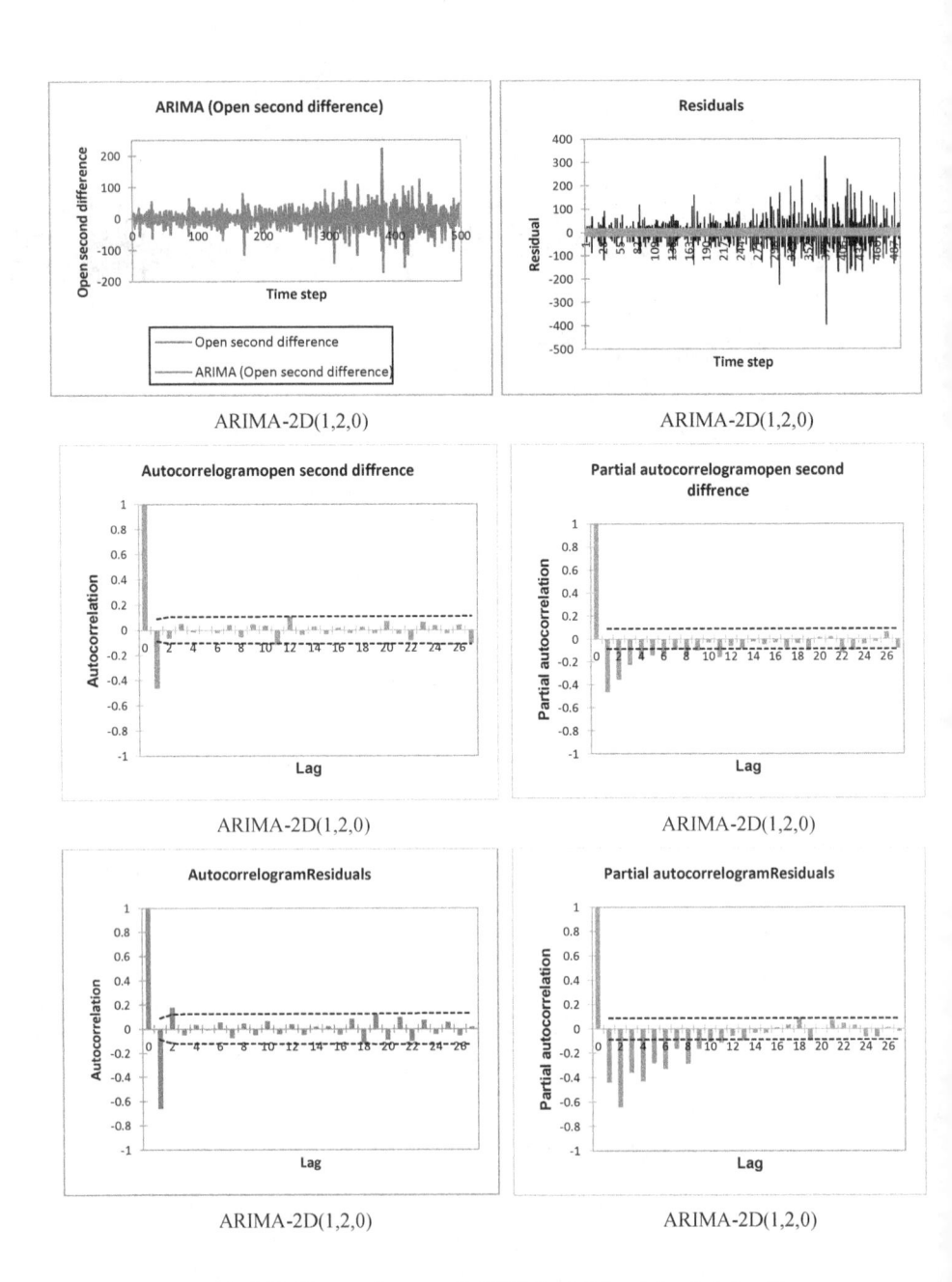

ARIMA-2D(1,2,0)　　　　　　　　　　　ARIMA-2D(1,2,0)

ARIMA-2D(1,2,0)　　　　　　　　　　　ARIMA-2D(1,2,0)

Fig 4.28: The correlogram of LUPIN Stock Price At [p=1 d=2 q=0]

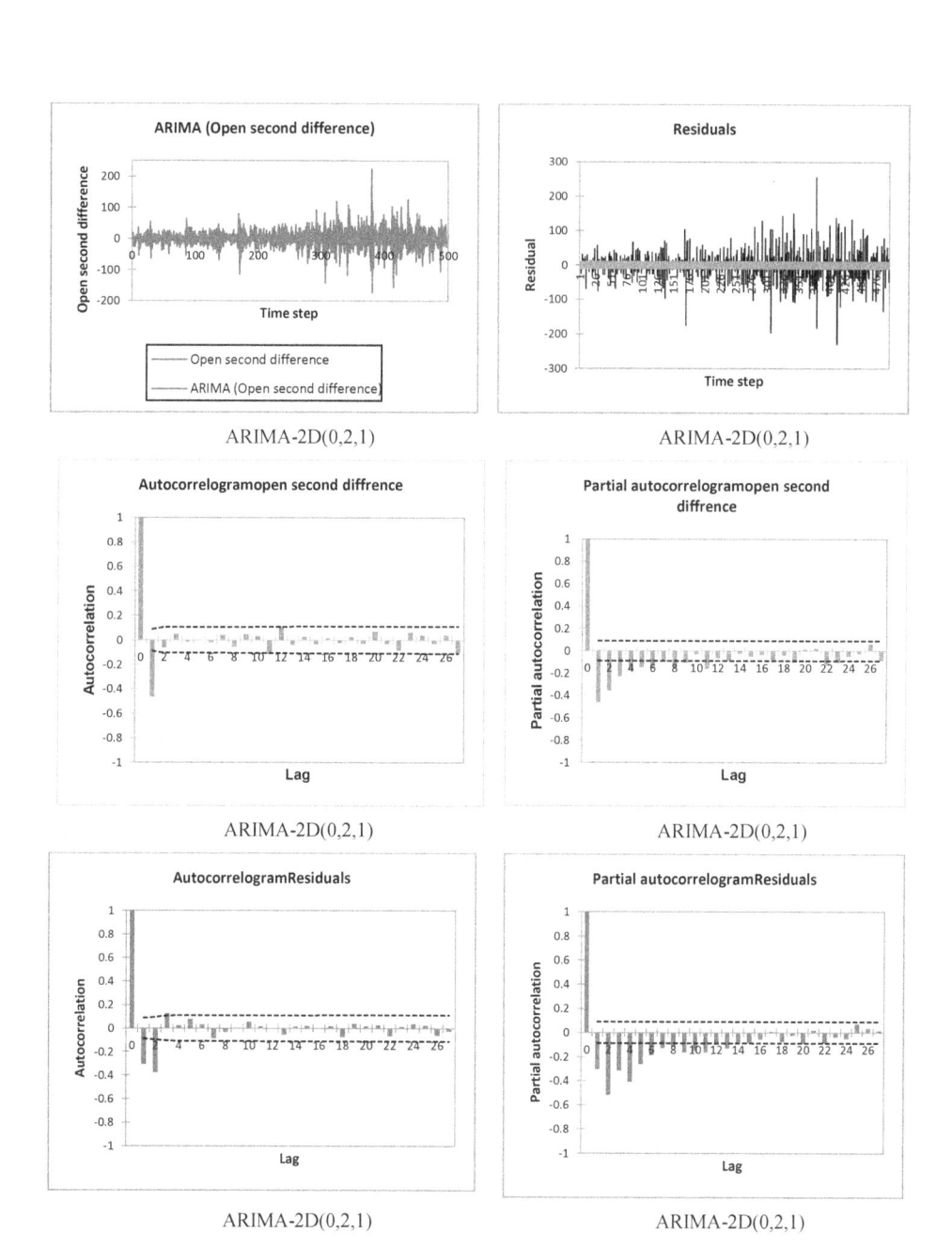

Fig 4.29: The correlogram of LUPIN Stock Price At [p=0 d=2 q=1]

ARIMA-2D(1,2,1)   ARIMA-2D(1,2,1)

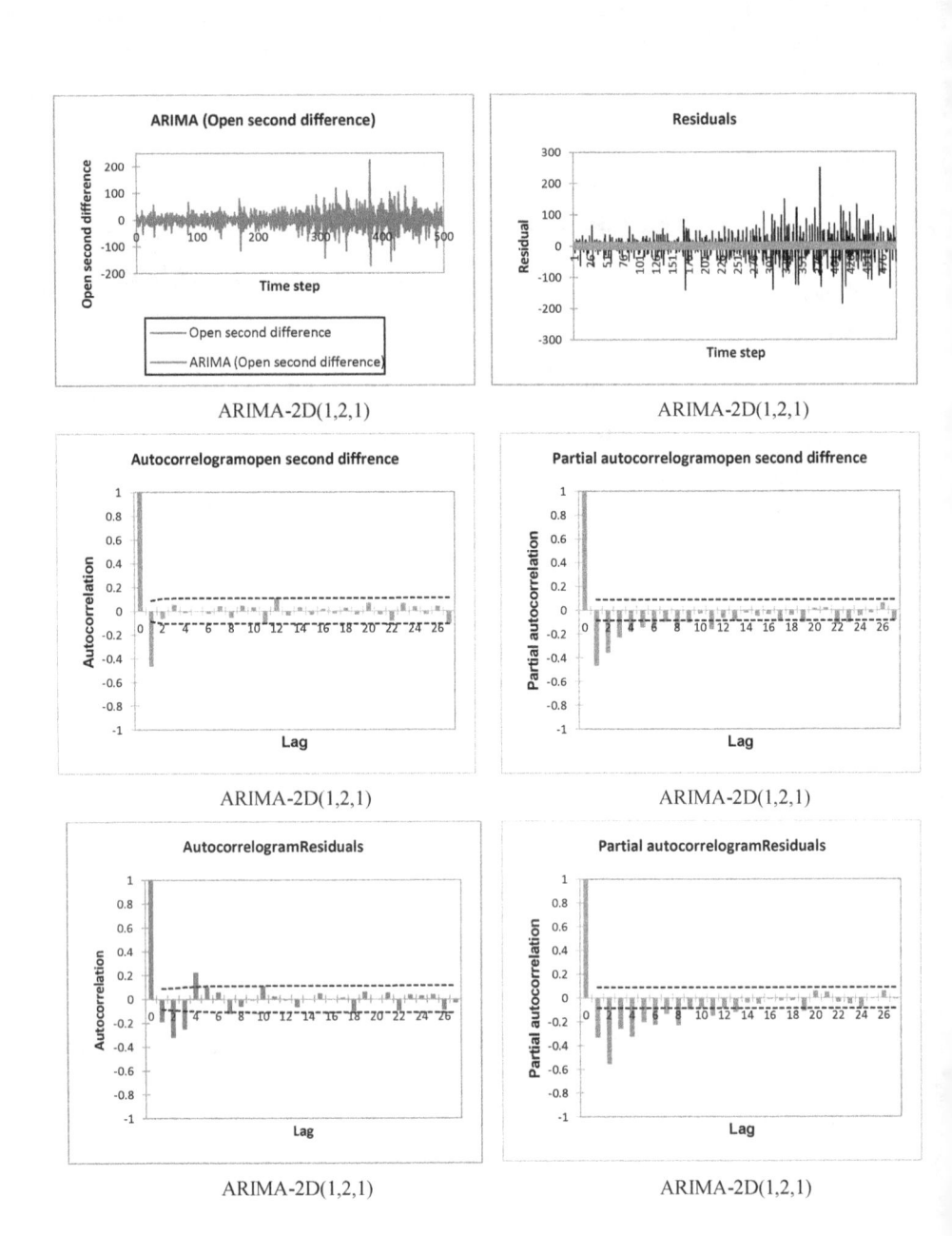

ARIMA-2D(1,2,1)   ARIMA-2D(1,2,1)

ARIMA-2D(1,2,1)   ARIMA-2D(1,2,1)

Fig 4.30: The correlogram of LUPIN Stock Price At [p=1 d=2 q=1]

ARIMA-2D(2,2,1)   ARIMA-2D(2,2,1)

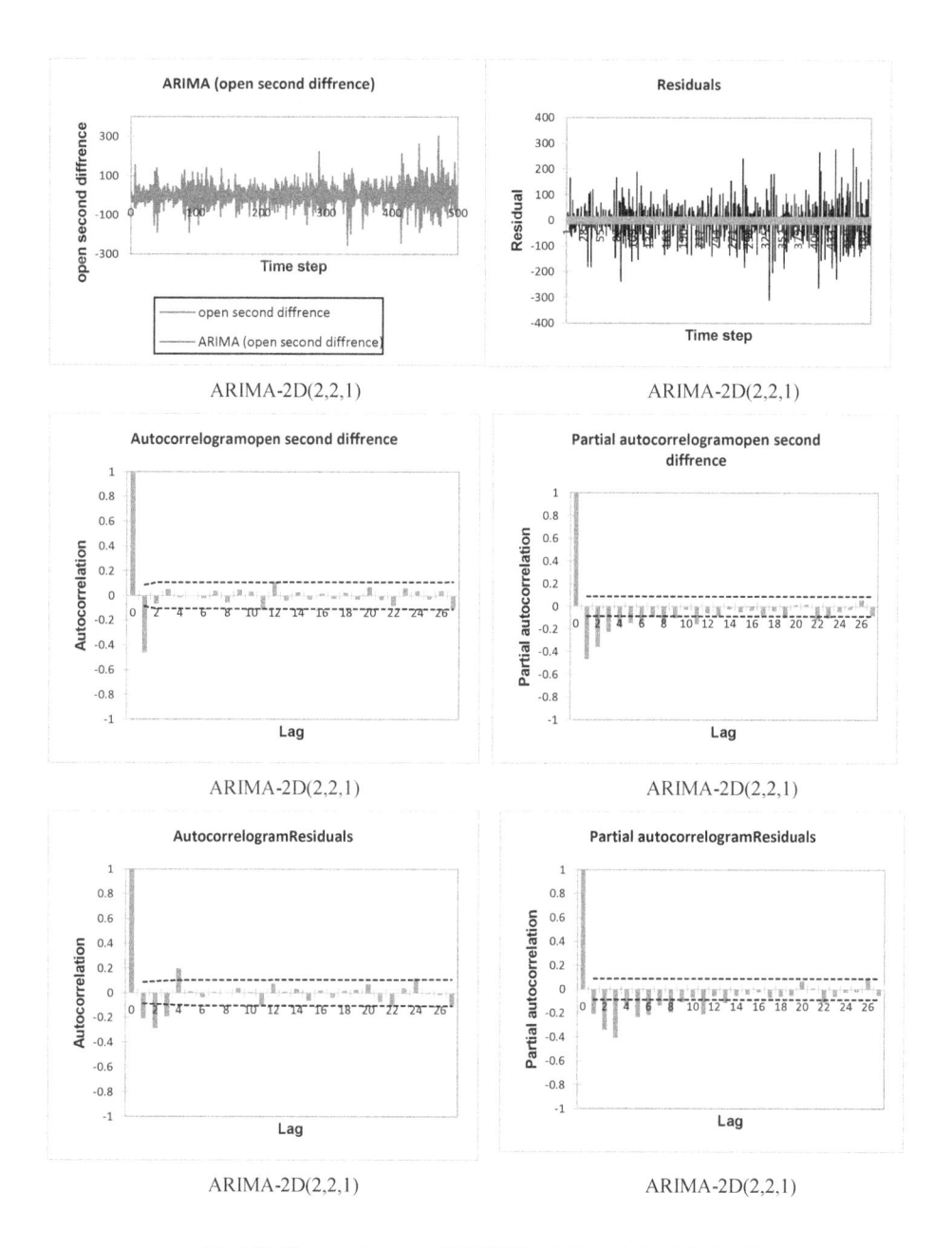

ARIMA-2D(2,2,1)   ARIMA-2D(2,2,1)

ARIMA-2D(2,2,1)   ARIMA-2D(2,2,1)

Fig 4.31: The correlogram of LUPIN Stock Price At [p=2 d=2 q=1]

ARIMA-2D(1,2,2)   ARIMA-2D(1,2,2)

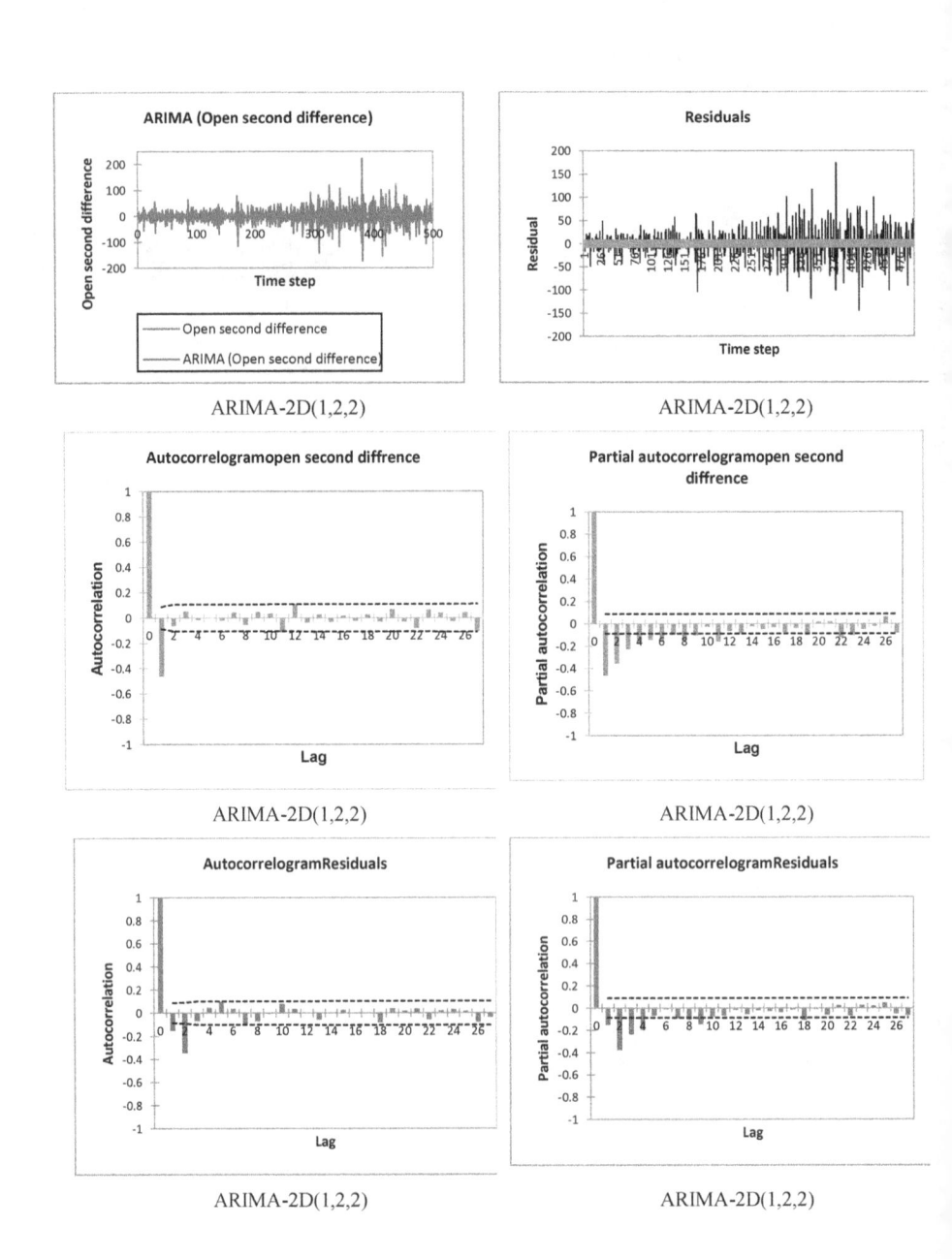

ARIMA-2D(1,2,2)   ARIMA-2D(1,2,2)

ARIMA-2D(1,2,2)   ARIMA-2D(1,2,2)

Fig 4.32: The correlogram of LUPIN Stock Price At [p=1 d=2 q=2]

4.7.2 Illustration and interpretation of the experimental results of Lupin limited

Table 4.13: ARIMA Model at first Difference for opening price of *Lupin limited* stock at BSE

Model	(0,1,0)	(1,1,0)	(0,1,1)	(2,1,0)	(0,1,2)	(1,1,1)	(2,1,1)	(2,1,2)	(1,1,2)
SE	723378	555177	374520	500995	374112	374116	**374102**	374120	556140
MSE	1455.49	1117.06	753.561	1008.04	752.74	752.748	**752.721**	752.757	1123.52
RMSE	38.1509	33.4224	27.4511	31.7496	27.4361	27.4363	**27.4358**	27.4364	33.5189
VN Variance	1455.49	1117.06	753.561	1008.04	752.74	752.748	**752.721**	752.757	1123.52
MAPE(Diff)	100.071	184.49	167.404	221.548	163.216	163.299	**163.042**	163.448	83.6218
MAPE	328.067	267.312	**107.069**	245.56	109.258	109.348	108.986	109.658	176.804
Log(Like.)		4898.86	4709.17	4848.03	4708.56	4708.56	**4708.55**	4708.55	4901.54
PE	1455.49	1121.56	753.561	1016.18	**752.74**	755.783	758.803	758.839	1128.06
IC		4902.86	**4713.17**	4854.03	4714.56	4714.56	4716.55	4718.55	4909.54
ICC		4902.88	**4713.19**	4854.08	4714.61	4714.61	4716.63	4718.67	4909.62
BC		4911.28	**4721.58**	4866.65	4727.18	4727.19	4733.39	4739.59	4926.35

Table 4.14 ARIMA Model at Second Difference for opening price of LUPIN stock at BSE

Model	(0,2,0)	(1,2,0)	(0,2,1)	(1,2,1)	(2,2,1)	(1,2,2)	(0.2.2)	(2,2,0)	(2,2,2)
SSE	7108483	3090853	2143479	1209045	952965	556140	724636	2101332	503348
MSE	14360.6	6244.15	4330.26	2442.51	1925.18	1123.52	1463.91	4245.12	1016.8
RMSE	119.836	79.0199	65.8047	49.4218	43.8769	33.5189	38.2611	65.1546	31.888
WN Variance	14360.6	6244.15	4330.26	2442.51	1925.18	1123.52	1463.91	4245.12	1016.8
MAPE(Diff)	100.131	147.35	88.3428	110.469	107.614	83.6218	**77.4709**	140.6	83.924
MAPE	843.83	566.903	377.609	287.57	235.011	176.804	**106.02**	521.352	203.92
-2Log(Like.)		5731.58	5555.78	5273.92	5157.34	4901.54	5030.27	5541.34	4853.2
FPE	14360.6	6269.43	4330.26	2452.4	1940.8	1128.06	1463.91	4279.56	1025.1
AIC		5735.58	5559.78	5279.92	5165.34	4909.54	5036.27	5547.34	4863.2
AICC		5735.61	5559.81	5279.97	5165.42	4909.62	5036.32	5547.39	4863.
SBC		5743.99	5568.19	5292.54	5182.16	4926.35	5048.88	5559.96	4884.

Analysis of results of time series data of Lupin Limited (for non- normal distribution) at first difference based on the statistics of goodness of fit / accuracy using ARIMA models:

i)   Some of Squares due to Error

Different ARIMA models are compared for SSE values and it is observed that **ARIMA (2,1,1)** has **lowest value SSE 374102.10** in comparison to ARIMA (0,1,0) having value 723377.50, ARIMA (1,1,0) having value 555176.70, ARIMA (0,1,1) having value 374520, ARIMA (2,1,0) having value 500994.50 and ARIMA (0,1,2) having value 374111.60, ARIMA (1,1,1) having value 374115.80, ARIMA (2,1,2) having value 374120 and ARIMA (1,1,2) having value 556139.70 respectively.

ii)   Mean Squared Error

MSE value are analyzed for different ARIMA models and it is observed that **ARIMA (2,1,1)** has **lowest value MSE (752.72)** in comparison to ARIMA (0,1,0) having value 1455.48, ARIMA (1,1,0) having value 1117.05, ARIMA (0,1,1) having value 753.56, ARIMA (2,1,0) having value 1008.37 and ARIMA (0,1,2) having value 752.73, ARIMA (1,1,1) having value 752.74, ARIMA (2,1,2) having value 752.75 and ARIMA (1,1,2) having value 1123.51 respectively.

iii)   Root Mean Squared Error

Different ARIMA models are compared for RMSE value and it is found that **ARIMA (2,1,1)** has **lowest value RMSE 27.43** in comparison to ARIMA (0,1,0) having value 38.15, ARIMA (1,1,0) having value 33.42, ARIMA (0,1,1) having value 27.45, ARIMA (2,1,0) having value 31.74 and ARIMA (0,1,2) having value 27.43, ARIMA (1,1,1) having value 27.43, ARIMA (2,1,2) having value 27.43 and ARIMA (1,1,2) having value 33.51 respectively.

iv)   White Noise Variance

WN Variance value are analyzed for different ARIMA models and it is observed that **ARIMA (2,1,1)** has **lowest value WN Variance (752.72)** in comparison to ARIMA (0,1,0) having value 1455.48, ARIMA (1,1,0) having value 1117.05, ARIMA (0,1,1) having value 753.56, ARIMA (2,1,0) having value 1008.37 and ARIMA (0,1,2) having value 752.73, ARIMA (1,1,1) having value 752.74, ARIMA (2,1,2) having value 752.75 and ARIMA (1,1,2) having value 1123.51 respectively.

v) Mean Absolute Percentage Error

Different ARIMA models are compared for MAPE value and it is found that **ARIMA (0,1,1)** has **lowest MAPE value 107.06** in comparison to ARIMA (0,1,0) having value 328.06, ARIMA (1,1,0) having value 267.31, ARIMA (2,1,0) having value 245.55 and ARIMA (0,1,2) having value 109.25, ARIMA (1,1,1) having value 109.34, ARIMA (2,1,2) having value 109.65, ARIMA (1,1,2) having value 176.80 and ARIMA (2,1,1) having value 108.98 respectively.

vi) Final Prediction Error (FPE)

FPE values are analyzed for different ARIMA models and it is observed that **ARIMA (0,1,2)** has **lowest FPE value 752.73** in comparison to ARIMA (0,1,0) having value 1455.48, ARIMA (1,1,0) having value 1121.56, ARIMA (0,1,1) having value 753.56, ARIMA (2,1,0) having value 1016.83, ARIMA (1,1,1) having value 755.78, ARIMA (2,1,2) having value 758.83, ARIMA (1,1,2) having value 1028.06 and ARIMA (2,1,1) having value 758.80 respectively.

vii) Akaike Information Criterion

Different ARIMA models are compared for AIC value and it is found that **ARIMA (0,1,1)** has **lowest AIC value 4713.16** in comparison to ARIMA (1,1,0) having value 4902.85, ARIMA (2,1,0) having value 4854.02, ARIMA (0,1,2) having value 4714.55 ARIMA (1,1,1) having value 4714.56, ARIMA (2,1,2) having value 4718.55, ARIMA (1,1,2) having value 4909.53 and ARIMA (2,1,1) having value 4716.55 respectively.

viii) Correction of AIC

AICC values are analyzed for different ARIMA models and it is observed that **ARIMA (0,1,1)** has **lowest AICC value 4713.19** in comparison to ARIMA (1,1,0) having value 4902.88, ARIMA (2,1,0) having value 4854.07, ARIMA (0,1,2) having value 4714.60 ARIMA (1,1,1) having value 4714.60, ARIMA (2,1,2) having value 4718.67, ARIMA (1,1,2) having value 4909.61 and ARIMA (2,1,1) having value 4716.63 respectively.

ix) Schwarz Bayesian Information Criterion

Different ARIMA are compared to SBC values and it is found that **ARIMA (0,1,1)** has **lowest SBC value 4721.58** in comparison to ARIMA (1,1,0) having value 4911.27, ARIMA (2,1,0) having value 4866.65, ARIMA (0,1,2) having value 4727.18, ARIMA (1,1,1) having value 4727.18, ARIMA (2,1,2) having value 4739.59, ARIMA (1,1,2) having value 4926.35 and ARIMA (2,1,1) having value 4733.38 respectively.

Analysis of results of time series data of Lupin Limited (for non-normal distribution) at second difference based on the statistics of goodness of fit / accuracy using ARIMA model.

i) Some of Squares due to Error

Different ARIMA models are compared for SSE value and it is found that **ARIMA (2,2,2) has lowest value SSE value 503348.20** in comparison to ARIMA (0,2,0) having value 7108483, ARIMA (1,2,0) having value 3090853, ARIMA (0,2,1) having value 2143479, ARIMA (1,2,1) having value 1209045, ARIMA (2,2,1) having value 953964.80, ARIMA (1,2,2) having value 556139.70, ARIMA (2,2,0) having value 2101332 and ARIMA (0,2,2) having value 724635 respectively.

ii) Mean Squared Error

MSE values are analyzed for different ARIMA models and it is observed that **ARIMA (2,2,2) has lowest MSE (1016.86)** in comparison to ARIMA (0,2,0) having value 14360.57, ARIMA (1,2,0) having value 6244.16, ARIMA (0,2,1) having value 4330.26, ARIMA (1,2,1)having value 2442.51, ARIMA (2,2,1) having value 1925.18, ARIMA (1,2,2) having value 1123.51, ARIMA (2,2,0) having value 4245.11 and ARIMA (0,2,2) having value 1463.91 respectively.

iii) Root Mean Squared Error

Different ARIMA models are compared for RMSE value and it is found that **ARIMA (2,2,2) has lowest RMSE value 31.88** in comparison to ARIMA (0,2,0) having value 119.83, ARIMA (1,2,0) having value 79.01, ARIMA (0,2,1) having value 65.80, ARIMA (1,2,1)having value 49.42, ARIMA (2,2,1) having value 43.87, ARIMA (1,2,2) having value 33.51, ARIMA (2,2,0) having value 65.15 and ARIMA (0,2,2) having value 38.26 respectively.

iv) White Noise Variance

WN Variance value is analyzed for different ARIMA models and it is observed that **ARIMA (2,2,2) has lowest WN Variance value 1016.86** in comparison to ARIMA (0,2,0) having value 14360.57, ARIMA (1,2,0) having value 6244.16, ARIMA (0,2,1) having value

4330.26, ARIMA (1,2,1)having value 2442.51, ARIMA (2,2,1) having value 1925.18, ARIMA (1,2,2) having value 1123.51, ARIMA (2,2,0) having value 4245.11 and ARIMA (0,2,2) having value 1463.91 respectively.

v)   Mean Absolute Percentage Error

Different ARIMA models are compared for MAPE values and it is found that **ARIMA (0,2,2)** has **lowest MAPE value 106.01** in comparison to ARIMA (0,2,0) having value 843.82, ARIMA (1,2,0) having value 566.90, ARIMA (0,2,1) having value 377.60, ARIMA (1,2,1)having value 287.56, ARIMA (2,2,1) having value 235.01, ARIMA (1,2,2) having value 176.80, ARIMA (2,2,2) having value 203.92 and ARIMA (2,2,0) having value 521.35 respectively.

vi)   Final Prediction Error

FPE values are analyzed for different ARIMA models and it is observed that **ARIMA (2,2,2)** has **lowest FPE value 1025.11** in comparison to ARIMA (0,2,0) having value 14360.57, ARIMA (1,2,0) having value 6269.42, ARIMA (0,2,1) having value 4330.26, ARIMA (1,2,1) having value 2452,40, ARIMA (2,2,1) having value 1940.80, ARIMA (1,2,2) having value 1128.06, ARIMA (2,2,0) having value 4279.55 and ARIMA (0,2,2) having value 1463.91 respectively.

vii)   Akaike Information Criterion (AIC)

Different ARIMA models are compared for AIC values and it is found that **ARIMA (2,2,2)** has lowest AIC value of 4863.27 in comparison to ARIMA (1,2,0) having value 5735.58, ARIMA (0,2,1) having value 5559.78, ARIMA (1,2,1) having value 5279.92, ARIMA (2,2,1) having value 5165.33, ARIMA (1,2,2) having value 4909531, ARIMA (2,2,0) having value 5547.34 and ARIMA (0,2,2) having value 5036.26 respectively.

viii)   Correction of AIC

AICC values are analyzed for different ARIMA models and it is observed that **ARIMA (2,2,2)** has **lowest AICC value 4863.39** in comparison to ARIMA (1,2,0) having value 5735.60, ARIMA (0,2,1) having value 5559.80, ARIMA (1,2,1) having value 5279.97, ARIMA (2,2,1) having value 5165.41, ARIMA (1,2,2) having value 4909.61, ARIMA (2,2,0) having value 5547.39 and ARIMA (0,2,2) having value 5036.31 respectively.

ix) Schwarz Bayesian Information Criterion

Different ARIMA models are compared for SBC values and it is found that **ARIMA (2,2,2)** has **lowest SBC value 4884.29** in comparison to ARIMA (1,2,0) having value 5743.99, ARIMA (0,2,1) having value 5568.18, ARIMA (1,2,1) having value 5292.53, ARIMA (2,2,1) having value 5182.15, ARIMA (1,2,2) having value 4926.35, ARIMA (2,2,0) having value 5559.95 and ARIMA (0,2,2) having value 5048.88 respectively.

Comparison between first and second difference of analyzed ARIMA models:

i) Some of Squares due to Error

SSE value is compared for both the orders and it is found that SSE value obtained from first differencing **(374102.10)** was **lowest for ARIMA model (2,1,1)** in comparison to SSE value from second differencing (503348.20) of ARIMA model (2,2,2). Thus **ARIMA model (2,1,1)** is considered best model for prediction of stock prices amongst 18 different models of ARIMA on the basis of SSE analysis.

ii) Mean Squared Error

On comparison of the orders of differencing, it is found that MSE value obtained on first differencing **(752.72)** was **lowest for ARIMA model (2,1,1)** in comparison to MSE value from second differencing (1016.85) of ARIMA model (2,2,2). Thus **ARIMA model (2,1,1)** is considered best model for prediction of stock prices amongst 18 different models of ARIMA on the basis of MSE analysis.

iii) Root Mean Squared Error

RMSE value is compared for both the orders and it is found that RMSE value obtained from first differencing **(27.43)** was **lowest** for **ARIMA model (2,1,1)** in comparison to RMSE value from second differencing (31.88) of ARIMA model (2,2,2). Thus **ARIMA model (2,1,1)** is considered best model for prediction of stock prices amongst 18 different models of ARIMA on the basis of RMSE analysis.

iv) White Noise Variance

On comparison of the orders of differencing, it is found that WN Variance value obtained on first differencing **(752.72)** was **lowest for ARIMA model (2,1,1)** in comparison to WN value from second differencing (1016.86) of ARIMA model (2,2,2). Thus **ARIMA model (2,1,1)** is considered best model for prediction of stock prices amongst 18 different models of ARIMA on the basis of WN analysis.

v)   Mean Absolute Percentage Error

MAPE value is compared for both the orders and it is found that MAPE value obtained from first differencing **(106.01)** was lowest for **ARIMA model (0,2,2)** in comparison to MAPE value from second differencing (107.06) of ARIMA model (0,1,1). Thus **ARIMA model (0,2,2)** is considered best model for prediction of stock prices amongst 18 different models of ARIMA on the basis of MAPE analysis.

vi)   Final Prediction Error

On comparison of the orders of differencing, it is found that FPE value obtained on first differencing **(752.73)** was **lowest for ARIMA model (0,1,2)** in comparison to FPE value from second differencing (1025.11) of ARIMA model (2,2,2). Thus **ARIMA model (0,1,2)** is considered best model for prediction of stock prices amongst 18 different models of ARIMA on the basis of FPE analysis.

vii)   Akaike Information Criterion

AIC value is compared for both the orders and it is found that AIC value obtained from first differencing **(4713.16)** was **lowest for ARIMA model (0,1,1)** in comparison to AIC value from second differencing (4863.27) of ARIMA model (2,2,2). Thus **ARIMA model (0,1,1)** is considered best model for prediction of stock prices amongst 18 different models of ARIMA on the basis of AIC analysis.

viii) Correction of AIC

On comparison of the orders of differencing, it is found that AICC value obtained on first differencing **(4713.19)** was **lowest for ARIMA model (0,1,1)** in comparison to AICC value from second differencing (4863.39) of ARIMA model (2,2,2). Thus **ARIMA model (0,1,1)** is considered best model for prediction of stock prices amongst 18 different models of ARIMA on the basis of AICC analysis.

ix)   Schwarz Bayesian Information Criterion

SBC value is compared for both the orders and it is found that SBC value obtained from first differencing **(4721.58)** was **lowest for ARIMA model (0,1,1)** in comparison to SBC value from second differencing (4884.29) of ARIMA model (2,2,2). Thus **ARIMA model (0,1,1)** is considered best model for prediction of stock prices amongst 18 different models of ARIMA on the basis of SBC analysis.

Appraisal of experiment:

On the considered time series stock prices data, eighteen ARIMA models are applied and the best fit model is selected on the basis of maximum number of votes for lowest value of each statistics for goodness of fit for final analysis. ARIMA model (2,1,1) at first differencing earned five votes for lowest value of each for SSE, MSE, RMSE, White Noise and -2 log like in comparison to four votes obtained by ARIMA model (0,1,1). Thus **ARIMA Model (2,1,1)** resulted best method amongst different methods of ARIMA Model.

Similarly, results of other 18 stocks in which time series data was not normally distributed were observed and it was found that ARIMA Model (1,1,1) for Adani Port, Bajaj Autos, Cipla, Tata Steel, TCS, ARIMA Model (0,1,2) for Axis Bank, Bharti Airtel, Dr. Reddy, HDFC Bank, HDFC Finance, Lupin Limited, Maruti Suzuki, ONGC, Power Grid, State Bank of India, Wipro, ARIMA Model (2,1,0) for ICIC Bank, ARIMA Model (2,2,1) for Infosys and ARIMA Model (0,2,1) for L&T is resulted as the best method amongst different methods of ARIMA models for stock prices of companies under consideration.

CHAPTER V
ANALYSIS OF STOCK PRICES DATA USING ARTIFICIAL NEURAL NETWORKS

5.1 INTRODUCTION

Forecasting time series is a crucial and constantly growing discipline which includes different areas such as investment analysis, bank loan risk evaluation, speech recognition, monitoring, marketing, character recognition, image segmentation, etc. In addition, artificial neural networks are used to detect patterns and trends which are not easily identifiable with traditional methods. Further, artificial neural networks can recognize relationship among hundreds of variables (Bylinsky, 1993). Artificial neural networks are also gifted with the capacity to dig out unknown trends and relationships from very large volumes of data (Dineley, 2001) often stored in a data warehouse and on-line transaction processing systems. A neural network approach is used in situations where traditional methods like linear and nonlinear regression, ARIMA, logistic regression, etc. do not generate desired accuracy in forecasting due to large and complex nature of data or presence of noise. One of the advantages of ANN is that it even takes up the smaller size of data set for analysis. In traditional statistical models of forecasting, stationarity of the data is pre-requisite for analysis whereas ANN takes up the data as it is without setting any parameters or conditions in advance. It does analysis on non- stationary and non-linear data sets. It works on both normal as well as non-normal data. Neural network offers a modeling and forecasting approach which saves time and energy of a researcher, provides accuracy and analyze large amount of information which is not being analyzed by other classical methods (Jones, 2004). Thus, neural network is a single tool for solving all problems faced in traditional methods and it drastically reduces the time needed to generate a model. Keeping in view of positive side of ANN, this chapter is dedicated for the analysis of time series data of stocks using artificial neural networks.

The chapter is divided into eight sub-sections. The first section 5.1 presents a brief of the chapter which is followed by various definitions of artificial neural networks in section 5.2. The section 5.3 gives the architecture of artificial neural network whereas section 5.4 describes how a neural network is trained for testing the data and section 5.5 emphasize on the features of Artificial Neural Network. The next section 5.6 details the various types of artificial neural networks used in statistics. Section 5.7 describes the methodology and data processing techniques used for analysis of the time series data and finally section 5.8 discusses the observations and concludes the chapter with results obtained.

5.2 ARTIFICIAL NEURAL NETWORK

Artificial Neural Network (ANN) theory is evolved from Artificial Intelligence. It is a program which is intended to learn like a human brain. In literature it is defined by different researchers in the different ways. Some of the definitions are described as follows:

Definition 1: "An artificial neural network is a computing architecture comprising of simple processing elements, neurons that work in parallel and connect with each other by sending signals" (Krawiec and Stefanowski, 2003).

Definition 2: "A neural network is a massively parallel distributed processor that has a natural propensity for storing experiential knowledge and making it available for use. It resembles the brain in two respects: Knowledge is acquired by the network through a learning process and interneuron connection strengths known as synaptic weights are used to store the knowledge" (Haykin, 1994).

Definition 3: "An artificial neural network is a circuit composed of a very large number of simple processing elements that are neurally based. Each element operates only on local information. Furthermore, each element operates asynchronously; thus there is no overall system clock." (Nigrin, 1993).

Definition 4: "Artificial neural systems, or neural networks, are physical cellular systems which can acquire, store, and utilize experiential knowledge." (Zurada, 1992)

Definition 5: "A neural network is a system composed of many simple processing elements operating in parallel whose function is determined by network structure, connection strengths, and the processing performed at computing elements or nodes" (Source: DARPA Neural Network Study, 1988)

5.3 ARCHITECTURE OF ARTIFICIAL NEURAL NETWORKS

This section of the chapter describes the basic architecture of artificial neurons and the way these neurons are connected to build artificial neural networks.

Artificial Neuron

Biological neuronal assembly stimulates artificial neurons. Through synapses signals are transmitted from one neuron to other neuron. It is an intricate process. The most popular neuron model is depicted in Figure 5.1.

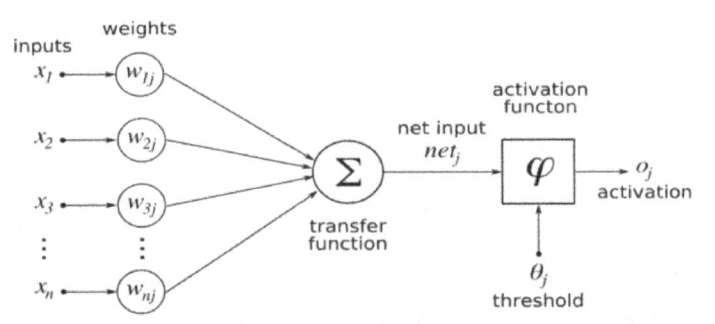

Figure 5.1: Structure of Artificial Neuron
(Source:https://en.wikibooks.org/wiki/Artificial_Neural_Networks/Print_Version)

The artificial neuron shown in the above figure has n inputs, denoted as $x_1, x_2, ..., x_n$. Some weight is allocated to each input connecting to the neuron is allocated a weight and these weights are represented as $w_{1j}, w_{2j}, ..., w_{nj}$. These weights are changed in a learning process. Synaptic connections of human neurons correspond to weights in the artificial model of a neural network. In an artificial neuron, 'θ' denotes threshold and the activation is represented as:

$$a = \sum_{j=1}^{N} w_{1j} x_j + \theta \qquad (5.1)$$

The weights and inputs represent real values. Positive value for a weight is known as excitatory connection and a negative value shows an inhibitory connection.

Summation function is very essential part of the processing in an artificial neuron. Some of the very popular functions used for analysis are Sum, Max, Min, Majority, Product etc. The summation part of threshold is combined with an imaginary input $x_0=+1$ and a connection weight $w_{0j}=\theta$.

Hence forth the activation formula turns out to be:

$$a = \sum_{j=0}^{N} w_{1j} x_j \qquad (5.2)$$

The output value of the neuron is a function of its activation and is denoted as:

$$x = (a) \qquad (5.3)$$

The activation function can be expressed in two different ways, i.e., linear or nonlinear.

The most common and widely used activation functions for various artificial neural networks are step, sigmoid, Gaussian, etc. Some of the functions are listed as under:

Function 1:

Linear function: $f(x) = ax+b$ \qquad (5.4)

Function 2:

Sigmoid: $f(x) = \frac{1}{1+e^{-\beta x}}$ (5.5)

Function 3:

Hyperbolical tangent: $f(x) = \tanh\frac{\beta x}{2} = \frac{1-e^{-\beta x}}{1+e^{-\beta x}}$ (5.6)

Function 4:

Inverted Tangent: $f(x) = \frac{2}{\pi} \tan^{-1}(\frac{\beta x}{2})$ (5.7)

Function 5:

Threshold function (step function): $f(x) = \begin{cases} 1, & x > 0 \\ -1, & x < 0 \end{cases}$ (5.8)

Function 6:

Gaussian Function: $f(x) = \exp[\frac{-(x-\mu)^2}{\sigma^2}]$ for given parameter μ and σ (5.9)

Function 7:

Sinusoidal function: $f(x) = \sin(\beta x)$ (5.10)

In neural networks construction, the input of one neuron is generally the output of the preceding neuron. This is done in a situation where one artificial neuron is unable to implement the Boolean function. In a system with several neurons, indices are assigned to the neurons. The below formula represents the activation:

$a_i = \sum_{j=1}^{N} w_{ji} x_j + \theta_i$ (5.11)

where x_j may be an external input or the output of another neuron.

In Artificial Neural Network, numerous architectures are used. The first and simplest kind of artificial neural network is feed forward neural network where neurons is structured in layers. The information flow in these network is always forward, i.e., the input of one neuron is generally the output of the preceding neuron only. There are three types of layers in ANN:

(i) Input layer,
(ii) Hidden layer, i.e., the layer between input layer and last layer and,
(iii) Last layer of neurons is called the output layer.

The input layer is comprised of special input neurons which transfers only the external input to produce output.

"A generalized feed forward network is the one wherein connections can jump over one or more layers. Such networks are said to decode the problem with much more efficiency" (Sanger, 1989). It is also observed that a standard Multilayer Perceptron (discussed below) requires substantially more training epoch than the Generalized Feed Forward network.

A network with one input layer and only one layer of output is called single layer network. Networks which have more than one hidden layer are known as multilayer networks. The third type of networks are called recurrent network where neurons are connected to the same layer or to the previous layers.

5.4 TRAINING OF ARTIFICIAL NEURAL NETWORK

The Training of the network happens in the said manner: "The output values set for the neurons of one layer are placed on the inputs of neurons in the next layer. An exception is the first layer (called the input layer) consisting of neurons, at whose inputs are values brought from the outside of the network (concerning the values of input variables that appear in the solved problem as a prerequisite for inferences) and the last layer (output layer consisting of neurons designating values) later sent outside as whole network output values (treated in the solved problem as conclusions of reasoning)" (Lula et al, 2007).

There are three ways of training the networks , i.e., supervised and unsupervised and data set.

Supervised Learning:

The first method of training , i.e., supervised method involves input and output signals (also known as reference signals). For example, the data of credit card issued by the banks can be trained in two different ways as good risk and bad risk.

Unsupervised Learning:

Unsupervised method is contrary to that of supervised learning which comprises only of input signals and not reference (output) signal (Hopfield, 1982). For example, banks while issuing credit card consider 4 to 5 parameters like income, age, employment status, repayment default status, past repayment history, etc.

Data Set:

For fitting and validation of a model the time series data is always divided into two parts as: (i) Training set data (ii) Test set data.

5.5 CHARACTERISTICS OF ARTIFICIAL NEURAL NETWORKS

ANN is widely used because of their capability to "learn". These networks easily adapt to all the parameters and learn suitable responses to a specific set of stimulation. A network operates appropriately in situations where there is some damage to few elements, connections are broken, or there is loss of information.

Other features of artificial neural networks include "the ability to process information that is fuzzy, chaotic, incomplete or even contradictory; fast and efficient processing of large amounts of data; parallel, distributed processing; associative access to the information contained in the network the so-called associative memory" (Witkowska, 2000).

5.6 ANTIQUITY OF ARTIFICIAL NEURAL NETWORKS

There are various architectures of Artificial Neural Networks that are commonly used. Another popular method of classifying Artificial Neural Networks as stated above is with the help of training algorithms used, some use supervised training while others use unsupervised or self-organizing (Kosko, 1992). Some networks are categorized as Feed Forward while others are known as Recurrent (those which implement feedback) depending on the training method used and data processing done throughout the network. The most popular network architecture is the Multilayer Perceptron (Minsky, 1969), (Rosenblatt, 1958) which is trained with the back propagation algorithm, radial basis function, Hopfield, and Kohonen algorithms (Kohonen, 1997).

A few widely used algorithms are detailed as under:

5.6.1 Multilayer Perceptrons and Back Propagation Algorithm

Multilayer Perceptrons (MLP) are usually layered Feed Forward networks. Static back propagation algorithm is always used in conjunction with MLP as the training of MLP is done with the help of back propagation algorithm. These networks are widely used in various applications requiring static pattern classification. Easy to use and approximation of input/output map is their distinct feature whereas the only disadvantages is that they are trained slowly and need a large training data set (Almeida, 1987).

The concept of a single perceptron was introduced by Rosenblatt in 1958. The Perceptron from a set of input factors computes a single output and then uses nonlinear activation function to the output. A pictorial representation is as follows:

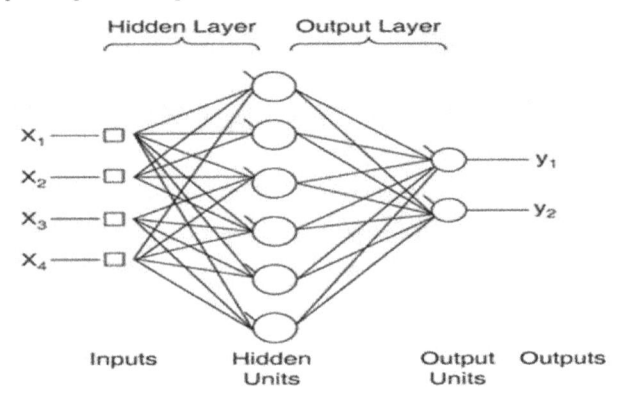

Figure 5.2: Structure of layered network

(Source: https://www.researchgate.net/figure/287280850_fig5_Structure-of-the-three-layers-of-a-neural-network)

Mathematically this can be written as:

$$y = \varphi \sum_{i=1}^{n} w_i \, x_i + b) = \varphi \, (w^T x + b) \qquad (5.12)$$

where,

'y' depicts the output, 'w' represents the weights of the vector, 'x' is the vector of inputs, 'b' is the bias and 'φ' is the activation function.

The training of a multilayer perceptron is achieved with the help of back propagation (BP) algorithm (Amrender, 2012). The BP has two phases, namely, forward phase and backward phase.

Forward phase: In this phase, error signal is computed by propagating the input signal and keeping all the free parameters of the network fixed. The mathematical representation of the error signal is:

$$e_i = d_i - y_i \qquad (5.13)$$

where d_i is the desired response, y_i is the output produces in response to input x_i.

Backward phase: In this phase, the error signal e_i is propagated in a reverse direction which denotes the name of the algorithm, i.e., back propagation algorithm. The free parameters which were fixed in the first phase are adjusted in this phase to minimize the error e_i.

5.6.2 Radial Basis Function

Radial basis function is a type of nonlinear hybrid networks which contains only one hidden layer of perceptron. The hidden layer in multilayer perceptron uses a standard Sigmoidal functions whereas a radial basis function network uses Gaussian transfer functions.

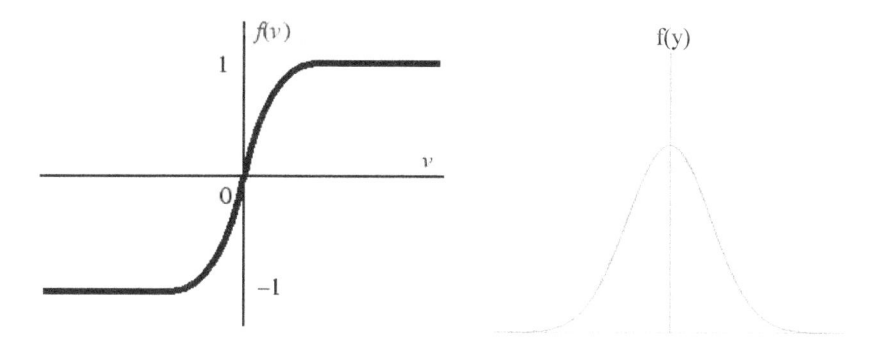

Figure 5.3: Sigmoid Function   Figure 5.4: Gaussian Function

A RBF Neuron is made up of input vector, RBF neurons and an output layer. Each RBF neuron has a "prototype" vector which is one of the vectors from the training set. Each RBF neuron tries to compare every input vector to its model (prototype), and outputs a value between *zero* and *one* which is a measure of similarity. The output of that RBF neuron is *one* when the input is equal to the prototype. As the distance between the input and prototype grows, the response, i.e., output falls off exponentially and tends to *zero*. The shape of the RBF neuron's response is a bell curve. The neuron's response value is also called its "activation" value.

RBF Neuron Activation Function

Each RBF neuron calculates the degree of similarity between the input vector and its prototype which is taken from the training sets. Input vectors which are more similar to the prototype give a result closer to *one*. The most popular similarity function is the Gaussian function. The equation for a Gaussian with a one-dimensional input.

$$f(x) = \frac{1}{\sigma \sqrt{2\pi}} e^{\frac{-(x-\mu)^2}{2\sigma^2}} \qquad (5.14)$$

where, x is the input, μ is the mean, and σ is the standard deviation. This is also graphically represented as bell curve shown below, which is centered at the mean, μ (here, the mean is 5 and σ is 1).

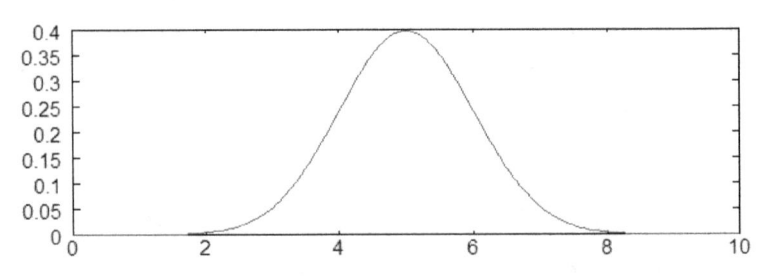

Figure 5.5: Gaussian Function Bell Curve
(Source: http://mccormickml.com/2013/08/15/the-gaussian-kernel/)

The RBF neuron activation function written as:

$$\varphi(x) = e^{-\beta(x-\mu)^2} \quad (5.15)$$

The properties of the Gaussian transfer functions, the center and width are determined by unsupervised learning rule and the output layer involves supervised learning. These networks have a very high learning rate in comparison to Multilayer Perceptrons (Source: http://mccormickml.com/2013/08/15/radial-basis-function-network-rbfn-tutorial).

5.6.3 Hopfield Network:

Artificial neurons are the basic building block of Hopfield. The total number of inputs is represented by N where i is the input and a weight w_i is associated with it. The output remains the same until the values of neuron is updated. The updation process of a neuron takes place in the following manner:

- In the first step, input value, x_i is calculated and then P_i w_i x_i (weighted sum) is calculated.
- In the second step, output state is set according to the weighted input sum. It is set to +1 if the weighted sum ≥ 0. It is set to -1 if the weighted sum ≤ 0.

The above process is mathematically represented as:

$$o = \begin{cases} 1 : \sum_i w_i x_i \geq 0 \\ -1 : \sum_i w_i x_i < 0 \end{cases} \quad (5.16)$$

A Hopfield network is a network of N such artificial neurons, which are fully connected.

5.6.4 Self Organizing Maps: Kohonen Algorithm

Self-organizing maps (SOM) were first introduced by Kohonen (1990). It is a typical feed forward network which contains a single computational layer of neurons arranged in rows and columns.

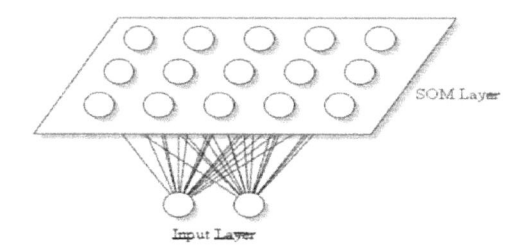

Figure 5.6: Kohonen Self Organizing Map
[Source: Kohonen, Self Organizing maps, springer 1997]

The step by step working of SOM algorithms is summarized as follows:
1. **Initialization**: For initial weight vector 'wj' random values are considered.
2. **Sampling**: From the input space a sample training input vector 'x' is drawn.
3. **Matching**: A winning neuron I(x) having weight vector closest to the input vector is figured out, i.e., the minimum value of dj (x) = $\sum_{i=1}^{D}(x_i - w_{ji})^2$.
4. **Updating:** Thereafter, the following weight updating equation is applied.
$\Delta w_{ji} = \eta(t) T_{j, I(x)}(t)(x_i - w_{ji})$, where $T_{j,I(x)}(t)$ is a Gaussian neighborhood and $\eta(t)$ is the learning rate.
5. **Continuation**–Finally keep on repeating the above said steps until the feature map stops changing.

5.7 METHODOLOGY FOR STOCK PRICE DATA FORECASTING

The neural networks are mostly used to project what will happen most likely. Nowadays, it is used in almost all branches of business, science, communication, economics, etc. for forecasting purpose. Prediction of stock prices has always been a challenging task for researchers and investors. Neural networks are the algorithms which have the capability to make the profoundly complex systems very easy to handle.

Most of the applications of neural networks fall into the following five categories:
- Prediction

- Classification
- Data association
- Data conceptualization
- Data filtering

In this study, the stock price data under consideration fall into the first category, , i.e.,, prediction. For prediction of time series analysis, various neural networks are applied. Some of the most popular networks are listed below:

- Back-propagation
- Delta Bar Delta
- Extended delta bar delta
- Directed random search
- Higher order neural networks
- Self-Organizing Map into Back-propagation

In this research, we have used Back-propagation algorithm using three layers of different activation functions. These are namely, threshold, hyperbolic tangent, zero-based log sigmoid, log-sigmoid and bipolar sigmoid.

The time series stock prices data under consideration is comprised of listed 25 BSE Sensex companies. The variables observed are date, opening price, closing price, high price, low price and volume in number of shares traded on a particular day are taken into consideration. Out of these, only four variables are taken into account , i.e., the opening price, closing price, high price and the low price. The output consists of a single variable , i.e., the opening value. The data is further divided into the ratio of 95:5 for training and testing respectively. The stock prices data is analyzed with software Neuro XL predictor.

Input and output ranges for training set and prediction of the results along with the parameters for neural networks are specified for processing the data

Then, the graphical learning process is recorded. Neural network allows its parameters to specify the initial weights, learning rate, momentum, selection of activation function and the number of neurons in the hidden layer , i.e., layer 1, layer 2, layer 3,etc.

In this research, following parameters are used to train the input data set.

Index/parameter	Value	Range

Initial weight	0.3	0 to initial weight
Learning Rate	0.3	0 to 1
Momentum Rate	0.6	0 to 1
Number of epochs	1000	Maximum : 3000
Neurons in hidden layer	1,2,3	-

Initial weights:

The synapses of every neuron are initialized with random values varying from 0 to the initial weights. In this research value of initial weight is 0.3.

Learning rate:

It is the rate of learning for the networks and its value ranges between 0-1. If the rate of learning is increased then there are chances of oscillation and non-convergence. However, in this research the considered learning rate is 0.3.

Momentum:

Non- convergence may occur if the learning rate is too high due to weight change oscillations during the training process. To provide a smoothing effect, momentum changes the next weight, a function of the previous weight change. The value for momentum is in the range 0 to 1 which also determines the proportion of the weight change. Rate of momentum used in this study is 0.6.

Neurons in hidden layer:

It is mandatory to set the number of neurons in the hidden layers. Number of neuron used in this research varies from 1-3. Generally the default values of these parameters are used for analysis. It is assumed that each change made in layers may produce better results than the previous ones.

Epochs:

A complete cycle of neural network training on the entire training data set is known as an epoch. It is a parameter which decided the maximum number of epoch cycles to reach a defined minimum weight delta. In this study the number of epochs fixed for the analysis is 1000. The maximum number of epochs goes up to 3000.

Minimum weight delta:

Synapses weights are corrected during training process. When the network is trained enough then the desired lowermost weight correction value is defined by minimum weight delta.

Activation Functions:

The activation functions used in the study are threshold, hyperbolic tangent, zero-based log sigmoid, log-sigmoid and bipolar sigmoid. The mathematical representation of the functions used is as follows:

1. **Threshold function (step function):**

$$f(x) = \begin{cases} 1, & x > 0 \\ -1, & x < 0 \end{cases} \quad (5.17)$$

2. **Hyperbolical tangent:**

$$f(x) = \tanh \frac{\beta x}{2} = \frac{1 - e^{-\beta x}}{1 + e^{-\beta x}} \quad (5.18)$$

3. **Sigmoid:**

$$f(x) = \frac{1}{1 + e^{-\beta x}} \quad (5.19)$$

4. **Log Sigmoid:**

$$f(x) = \frac{1}{1 + e^{-x}} \quad (5.20)$$

5. **Bipolar sigmoid:**

$$f(x) = -1 + \frac{2}{(1 + e^{-x})} \quad (5.21)$$

The select companies are analyzed on the basis of the results obtained from the methodology mentioned above. The companies under consideration are Sun Pharmaceutical and Lupin Limited taken from pharmaceutical sector. Out of 25, only 2 companies are discussed in detail in this research due to space constraint. The companies are selected on the basis of normality test, i.e., Jarque-Bera test. (Refer Table 2.4)

- Normal distribution: Sun Pharmaceutical Industries Limited.
- Non-Normal Distribution: Lupin Limited.

Graphical Representation of Training Data Set:

Graphical analysis is done to analyze the basic nature of time series data, i.e., to check if it is stationary or non – stationary. It can be easily inferred from the graphs given below that the nature of data is non-stationary. Neural network has the ability to predict outputs directly from non-stationary data set whereas traditional methods first convert the entire data set to stationary and then analyze the data set. Neural networks is advantageous as it requires less formal statistical training, it makes use of multiple training algorithm and has the ability to detect complex nonlinear relationships between dependent and independent variables.

Training the data under consideration graphically determines the effectiveness of the training process. The experiment needs to be done with different parameters if the predicted values do not closely match the actual values. During training process, various models of artificial neural network are fitted to the data set. The graphical representations below illustrate the training process.

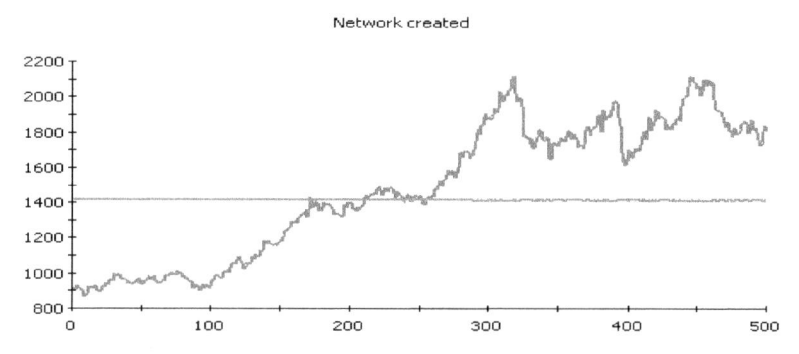

Figure 5.7: Graph showing network creation of the input data of Lupin Limited.

In the above graph, input data, i.e., open price, closing price, high price and low price of Lupin limited are fed to the neural network and a network is created for training the data set. In a training process, data set is fitted to a model which is most suitable for predicting the opening price of Lupin Limited.

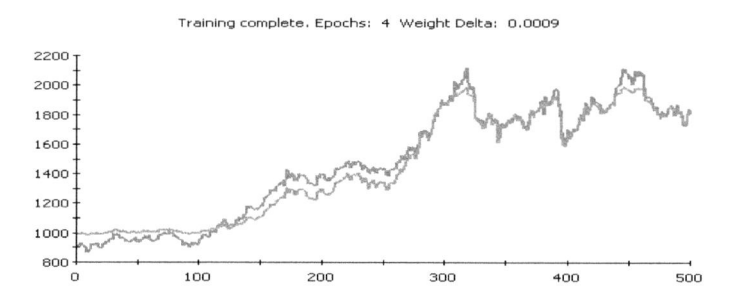

Figure 5.8: Graph showing training of input data of Lupin Limited

Network created

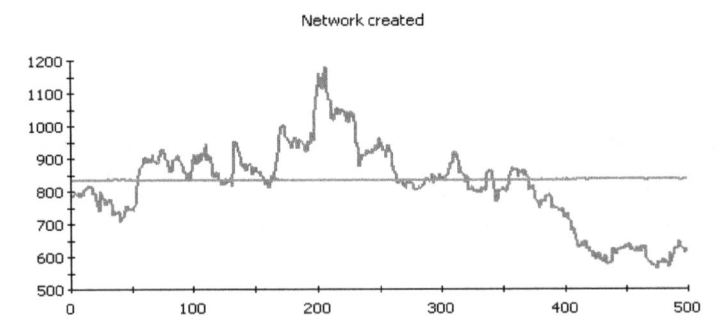

[Figure 5.9 chart]

Figure 5.9: Graph showing network creation of the input data of Sun Pharmaceutical

Training complete. Epochs: 10 Weight Delta: 0.0009

[Figure 5.10 chart]

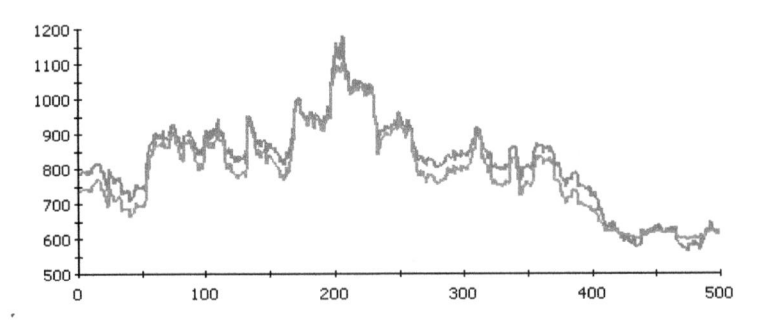

Figure 5.10: Graph showing training of input data of Sun Pharmaceutical

Observations:

a) The x-axis in the above graph represents the total number of observations, i.e., 500.

b) The y-axis represents the actual value of all the stock prices.

In the graph, actual values of stock price are represented by green lines and the predictions are represented by red lines. As the neural network converges, predicted value of a given stock tends towards the actual value of that same stock.

5.8 ANALYSIS OF RESULTS AND ITS INTERPRETATION

When the training is complete, input and output ranges are specified for the prediction of stock prices of Lupin Limited and Sun Pharmaceutical under layer 1, layer 2 and layer 3 of different activation functions.

The different ANN models, i.e., threshold, hyperbolic tangent, zero-based log sigmoid, log-sigmoid and bipolar sigmoid are applied on the historical stock prices of 2 years under consideration. Results obtained under hidden layer 1 are using different ANN models and test statistics, i.e., Mean Absolute Error (MAE), Mean Absolute Percentage Error (MAPE), Mean Squared Error (MSE), Root Mean Squared Error (RMSE), Root Absolute Error (RAE) and Relative Root Absolute Error (RRSE) are calculated.

Similarly, results are obtained for hidden layer 2 and 3 to find out the best and accurate prediction model out of all other ANN models. The model is said to be "best fit model" if it has minimum values of MAE, MAPE, MSE, RMSE, RAE and RRSE.

5.8.1 Analysis of results obtained of Lupin Limited (Normal Distribution)

Table 1: Analysis of results of Lupin Limited

	MAE	MAPE	MSE	RMSE	RAE	RRSE
Zero-based Log-Sigmoid						
Layer 1	88.433	5.123	626.892	20.629	0.051	0.209
Layer 2	82.597	4.791	675.329	20.850	0.048	0.200
Layer 3	53.309	3.062	1566.233	24.101	0.031	0.157
Threshold						
Layer 1	1052.803	59.490	59809.709	244.119	0.595	0.771
Layer 2	502.072	28.543	13831.947	116.584	0.285	0.533
Layer 3	502.072	28.543	48977.407	187.509	0.285	0.533
Hyperbolic tangent						
Layer 1	54.293	3.148	266.914	12.754	0.031	0.159
Layer 2	46.201	2.668	196.644	10.854	0.027	0.147
Layer 3	55.700	3.229	1570.799	25.868	0.032	0.160
Bipolar-Sigmoid						
Layer 1	56.090	3.245	269.320	13.144	0.032	0.166
Layer 2	56.307	3.256	269.734	13.194	0.033	0.166
Layer 3	55.490	3.209	1667.455	25.777	0.032	0.165
Log-Sigmoid						
Layer 1	54.129	3.132	258.604	12.725	0.031	0.158
Layer 2	62.180	3.614	355.957	14.571	0.036	0.170
Layer 3	71.079	4.132	2509.851	32.824	0.041	0.180

It can be observed from the result obtained above, that the technique of hidden layer 2 under hyperbolic tangent function of neural network is the best method of ANN models for predicting stock market prices in normal distribution of time series.

5.8.2: Analysis of results obtained of Sun Pharmaceutical (Non-normal Distribution)

Table 2: Analysis of results of Sun Pharmaceutical

	MAE	MAPE	MSE	RMSE	RAE	RRSE
Zero-based Log-Sigmoid						
Layer 1	44.632	7.475	115.626	10.398	0.075	0.271
Layer 2	27.776	4.675	66.381	7.079	0.047	0.203
Layer 3	28.899	4.862	222.249	11.616	0.049	0.209
Threshold						
Layer 1	110.720	18.427	662.603	25.641	0.184	0.429
Layer 2	656.780	109.540	23273.266	152.405	1.095	1.046
Layer 3	110.720	18.427	1858.038	38.856	0.184	0.429
Hyperbolic tangent						
Layer 1	1206.336	201.167	78459.893	279.893	2.012	1.418
Layer 2	1205.873	201.074	78474.924	279.794	2.011	1.418
Layer 3	1206.562	201.206	237973.953	432.796	2.012	1.418
Bipolar-Sigmoid						
Layer 1	25.205	4.241	44.193	5.901	0.042	0.195
Layer 2	21.155	3.564	33.308	4.962	0.036	0.176
Layer 3	21.058	3.547	126.949	8.573	0.035	0.175
Log-Sigmoid						
Layer 1	44.068	7.399	125.328	10.303	0.074	0.264
Layer 2	43.378	7.285	123.694	10.147	0.073	0.261
Layer 3	45.619	7.655	490.234	17.881	0.077	0.270

It can be observed from the result obtained above, that the technique of hidden layer 3 under Bipolar-sigmoid function of neural network is the best method of ANN models for predicting stock market prices in non- normal distribution of time series.

The predicted values of stocks of Sun Pharmaceutical are analyzed by fitting 15 models to find out the best ANN model for prediction of stock prices on the basis of goodness of fit statistics. The analysis of goodness of fit statistics such as Mean Absolute Error (MAE), Mean Absolute Percentage Error (MAPE), Mean Squared Error (MSE), Root Mean Squared Error (RMSE), Relative Absolute Error (RAE) and Root Relative Squared Error (RRSE) are detailed as follows:

(i)   Mean Absolute Error (MAE)

a) MAE is analyzed for hidden layer 1 for different activation functions and it is observed that Bipolar-sigmoid results in **lowest MAE of 25.21** in comparison to Zero based Log-sigmoid (44.63), Threshold (110.72), Hyperbolic Tangent (1206.34) and Log-sigmoid (44.07).
b) MAE is analyzed for hidden layer 2 for different activation functions and it is observed that Bipolar-sigmoid results in **lowest MAE of 25.21** in comparison to Zero based Log-sigmoid (27.78), Threshold (656.78), Hyperbolic Tangent (1205.87) and Log-sigmoid (43.38).
c) MAE is analyzed for hidden layer 3 for different activation functions and it is observed that Bipolar-sigmoid results **lowest MAE of 21.06** in comparison to Zero based Log-sigmoid (28.90), Threshold (110.72), Hyperbolic Tangent (1206.56) and Log-sigmoid (45.62).

In the next step, all three values chosen above for all the 3 different hidden layers are analyzed, compared and it is observed that MAE for 3rd layer is **lowest (21.06)** using Bipolar-Sigmoid activation function in comparison to MAE (21.15) of Bipolar-Sigmoid layer 2 and MAE (25.21) of layer 1 of Bipolar-Sigmoid. Therefore, we conclude on the analysis of all 15 models that layer 3 of Bipolar-sigmoid model is considered best for prediction of stock prices using Artificial Neural Networks.

(ii)   Mean Absolute Percentage Error (MAPE)

a) MAPE is analyzed in hidden layer 1 for different activation functions and it is observed that Bipolar-sigmoid results in **lowest MAPE of 4.24** in comparison to Zero based Log-sigmoid (7.48), Threshold (18.43), hyperbolic tangent (201.17) and Log-sigmoid (7.40).
b) MAPE is analyzed in hidden layer 2 for different activation functions and it is observed that Bipolar-sigmoid results in **lowest MAPE of 3.56** in comparison to Zero based Log-sigmoid (4.68), Threshold (109.54), hyperbolic tangent (201.07) and Log-sigmoid (7.29).
c) MAPE is analyzed in hidden layer 3 for different activation functions and it is observed that Bipolar-sigmoid results in **lowest MAPE of 3.55** in comparison to Zero based Log-sigmoid (4.86), Threshold (18.43), hyperbolic tangent (201.21) and Log-sigmoid (7.65).

In the next step, all three lowest MAPE values are analyzed for 3 hidden layers, they are compared and it is found that **MAPE (3.55) is lowest** for layer 3 for Bipolar-Sigmoid function in comparison to MAPE (3.56) of Bipolar-Sigmoid layer 2 and MAPE (4.24) of layer 1 of Bipolar-Sigmoid. Therefore, we conclude that on the basis of MAPE analysis of all 15 models, layer 3 of Bipolar-sigmoid model is considered best fit for prediction of stock prices using Artificial Neural Networks.

(iii) Mean Squared Error (MSE)

a) MSE is analyzed for hidden layer 1 for different activation functions and it is observed that Bipolar-sigmoid results in **lowest MSE of 44.19** in comparison to Zero based Log-sigmoid (115.63), Threshold (662.60), hyperbolic tangent (78459.89) and Log-sigmoid (125.33).

b) MSE is analyzed for hidden layer 2 for different activation functions and it is observed that Bipolar-sigmoid results in **lowest MSE of 33.31** in comparison to Zero based Log-sigmoid (66.38), Threshold (23273.27), hyperbolic tangent (78474.92) and Log-sigmoid (123.69).

c) MSE is analyzed for hidden layer 3 for different activation functions and it is observed that Bipolar-sigmoid results in **lowest MSE of 126.95** in comparison of Zero based Log-sigmoid (222.25), Threshold (1858.04), hyperbolic tangent (237973.95) and Log-sigmoid (490.23).

In the next step, all three lowest values of MSE for 3 hidden layers are analyzed; it is compared and observed that **MSE (33.31) is lowest** for layer 2 using Bipolar-Sigmoid function in comparison to MSE (44.91) of layer 1 which uses Bipolar-Sigmoid and MSE (126.95) of layer 3 using Bipolar-Sigmoid. Therefore, on the basis of MSE analysis for all 15 models, result show that layer 3 of Bipolar-sigmoid model is considered the best fir for prediction of stock prices using Artificial Neural Networks.

(iv) Root Mean Squared Error (RMSE)

a) RMSE is analyzed for hidden layer 1 for different activation functions and it is observed that Bipolar-sigmoid results in **lowest RMSE of 5.90** in comparison to Zero based Log-sigmoid (10.40), Threshold (25.64), Hyperbolic Tangent (279.89) and Log-sigmoid (10.30).

b) RMSE is analyzed for hidden layer 2 for different activation functions and it is observed that Bipolar-sigmoid results in **lowest RMSE of 4.96** in comparison to Zero based Log-sigmoid (7.08), Threshold (152.41), Hyperbolic Tangent (279.79) and Log-sigmoid (10.15).

c) RMSE is analyzed for hidden layer 3 for different activation functions and it is observed that Bipolar-sigmoid results in **lowest RMSE of 8.57** in comparison to Zero based Log-sigmoid (11.62), Threshold (38.86), Hyperbolic Tangent (432.80) and Log-sigmoid (17.88).

In the next step, all three lowest RMSE resulted for 3 hidden layers are analyzed; it is compared and found out that **RMSE (4.96) is lowest** for layer 2 of Bipolar-Sigmoid in comparison to RMSE (5.90) of Bipolar-Sigmoid layer 1 and RMSE (8.57) of layer 3 of Bipolar-Sigmoid. Therefore, on the basis of RMSE analysis for all 15 models, layer 3 of Bipolar-sigmoid model is considered best fit for prediction of stock prices using Artificial Neural Networks.

(v) **Relative Absolute Error (RAE)**
  a) RAE is analyzed for hidden layer 1 for different activation functions and it is observed that Bipolar-sigmoid results in **lowest RAE of 0.04** in comparison to Zero based Log-sigmoid (0.07), Threshold (0.18), Hyperbolic Tangent (12.01) and Log-sigmoid (0.07).
  b) RAE is analyzed for hidden layer 3 for different activation functions and it is observed that Bipolar-sigmoid results in **lowest RAE of 0.04** in comparison to Zero based Log-sigmoid (0.05), Threshold (1.10), Hyperbolic Tangent (2.01) and Log-sigmoid (0.07).
  c) RAE is analyzed for hidden layer 3 for different activation functions and it is observed that Bipolar-sigmoid results in **lowest RAE of 0.04** in comparison to Zero based Log-sigmoid (0.05), Threshold (0.18), Hyperbolic Tangent (2.01) and Log-sigmoid (0.08).

In the next step, all three lowest RAE resulted for 3 hidden layers are analyzed, it is compared and observed that **RAE (0.04) are equal** for layer 1, Layer 2 and layer 3 for Bipolar-Sigmoid function. Therefore, on the basis of RMSE analysis of all 15 model, Bipolar-sigmoid model is considered the best fit for prediction of stock prices using Artificial Neural Networks.

(vi) **Root Relative Squared Error (RRSE)**
  a) RRSE is analyzed for hidden layer 1 for different activation functions and it is observed that Bipolar-sigmoid is resulted **lowest RRSE of 0.20** in comparison to Zero

based Log-sigmoid (0.27), Threshold (0.43), Hyperbolic Tangent (1.42) and Log-sigmoid (0.26).

b) RRSE is analyzed for hidden layer 2 for different activation functions and it is observed that Bipolar-sigmoid results in the **lowest RRSE value of 0.18** in comparison to Zero based Log-sigmoid (0.20), Threshold (1.05), Hyperbolic Tangent (1.42) and Log-sigmoid (0.26).

c) RRSE is analyzed for 3rd hidden layer for different activation functions and it is observed that Bipolar-sigmoid results in the **lowest RRSE value of 0.18** in comparison to Zero based Log-sigmoid (0.21), Threshold (0.43), Hyperbolic Tangent (1.42) and Log-sigmoid (0.27).

In the next step, all the three lowest RRSE resulted for 3 hidden layers are analyzed, it is compared and observed that **RRSE (0.18) is lowest** for layer 3 using Bipolar-Sigmoid function in comparison to Bipolar-Sigmoid value for layer 2 and layer 1. Therefore, on the basis of RRSE analysis of all 15 models, results of layer 3 of Bipolar-sigmoid model is considered best fit for prediction of stock prices using Artificial Neural Networks.

On comparison of results for hidden layer 1 using different activation functions, the results of Bipolar-sigmoid are found better in comparison to other functions as layer 1 of Bipolar-sigmoid has got six number of votes for lowest values of MAE, MAPE, MSE, RMSE, RAE and RRSE. Similarly on comparison of the results for layer 2 using different activation functions, the results of Bipolar-sigmoid are found better in comparison to the results of other functions as layer 2 of Bipolar-sigmoid has received the six votes for lowest value of MAE, MAPE, MSE, RMSE, RAE and RRSE. Also for layer 3 is it observed that the results of Bipolar-sigmoid are better in comparison to the results of other functions as layer 3 of Bipolar-sigmoid has got six votes for lowest values of MAE, MAPE, MSE, RMSE, RAE and RRSE.

Finally, best fit of Artificial Neural Network is selected on the basis of maximum number of votes for lowest value of each statistics for goodness of fit under Layer 1, Layer 2 and Layer 3. Results of layer 2 improved in comparison of layer 1 as value of different statistics of goodness of fit have been decreased. Layer 2 and Layer 3 are considered best of Bipolar-sigmoid got maximum number of votes for each therefore on the basis of minimum value of MSE (33.31) of Layer 2 of Bipolar-sigmoid model in comparison of MSE (126.95) of Layer 3 Bipolar-sigmoid, prediction of stock prices using hidden layer 2 of Bipolar-sigmoid is considered best model of Artificial Neural Networks

5.9 CONCLUSION

In this research, company's stock exchange prices are predicted using neural networks. Daily stock price data is taken from Yahoo Finance for a period of 2 years from 20.01.2014 to 20.01.2016. Various neural network models with different parameters are applied for prediction of stock prices of historical data. On the basis of goodness of fit statistics and machine learning processes, it is observed from the analysis that Hyperbolic Tangent function of neural network is the best method for predicting stock prices in case of normal distribution of time series data while Bipolar-Sigmoid function of neural network is the best method of ANN models for predicting stock market prices in non- normal distribution of time series.

CHAPTER VI
TIME SERIES ANALYSIS USING GENETIC ALGORITHMS

6.1 INTRODUCTION

Computer scientists came up with the idea that evolution could be used as an optimization tool for solving engineering problems during 1960s. The ideology in all these systems was to create a number of solutions to a given problem using genetic variation and natural selection.

A search technique called genetic algorithm was introduced by John Holland to be used in computing to find exact or approximate solutions to search and optimisation solutions. Inspired by Darwin's theory of evolution, his idea was to study the natural phenomenon of adaptation and then develop mechanism to import the natural adaptation into computer systems (Holland, 1975).

The chapter is divided into seven sub-sections. The first section 6.1 gives a brief introduction of the chapter, section 6.2 includes a brief review of literature in relation to the application of time series analysis using Genetic Algorithms, followed by section 6.3 introducing all the terms used in genetic algorithm. The next section 6.4 specifies basic elements of the simplest framework of genetic algorithm whereas Section 6.5 describes the working of a genetic algorithm and why it is used. The various applications of GA are presented in section 6.6, followed by processing for the experiments conducted in section 6.7. Further, experimental results obtained are presented and discussed in section.

6.2 Brief Overview of Some Related Literature

Mahfoud and Mani (1996) presented that combining genetic algorithm system with neural network system significantly produced better result in comparison to both systems individually. In this study genetic algorithm system is compared to an established neural network system in the domain of financial forecasting, using the results from over 1600 stocks and roughly 5000 experiments. Genetic algorithm system was benchmarked a better methodology in comparison to artificial neural network system.

Neely et al (1997) explored the technical trading rules related to evidence of significant returns using genetic programming techniques. They found significant improvement in the performance of models when dollar/deutschemark rules got permission to decide trades in the other markets as except to deutschemark/yen. They observed that patterns which were not apprehended by prevailing statistical models were detected by trading rules and genetic algorithm techniques.

Thomas and Sycara (1999) tried to discover trading rule based on genetic programming. The performance of the model was verified over real world exchange rate data in the doller /dm and dollar /yen market and better results were obtained from the dollar / yen market. The study analysed the aspects of system that helped to fight over-fitting specially validation methodologies and rule complexity.

Allen and Karjalainen (1999) used genetic algorithm to learn technical trading rules for S&P stock and used every day prices for a period of 1928-1995. They tested their model on low transaction cost of liquid markets, including financial features, commodity and foreign exchange markets. The result showed a relationship between volatility and trading rule. Returns were lower when volatility was higher and vice versa.

Kim and Han (2000) tried to reduce the complexity in feature space and improved the learning algorithm by employing genetic algorithm. Genetic Algorithm optimized related weight between layers and threshold for feature discretization. With the help of feature discretization, they tried to minimize the complexity of the feature space and eliminate the factors which are not relevant. The result showed that genetic algorithm approach for feature discretization models increased performance for prediction of stock price in comparison to gradient descent algorithm.

Lin et al (2000) presented genetic algorithm as the best technique for forecasting the prices of stock market and financial fields in real time analysis The stock data is selected from Australian Stock Exchange (ASX) beginning from 1992-2002. GA makes the possible of real time analysis in comparison to greedy algorithm which takes a lot of time to get the most profit combination. It helped the investors to solve the problematic areas for selecting the values of trading rules and get the best possible combination for investment. The objective of the study was to provide the combination of parameters which could produce the maximum profit and give reasonable trading options.

Abraham et al (2005) introduced a genetic program technique for the prediction of two stock indices. In this study, comparison was carried out between five different intelligent paradigms which were combined using an ensemble and two well-known optimization algorithms namely PAES and NSGA II algorithms in order to obtain the most favourable combination which can optimize the presentation of four different measures. It was found that resulting ensemble gave the best result.

Canillas et al (2009) presented an advanced technique which was used in the field of genetic programming such as Linear Genetic Programming (LGP). The forecast was done on consumer price index (CPI) and price of soybean per ton for a certain period. They used LGP to forecast time series with two objectives , i.e., (i) to explain the variations of time series in the past while and (ii) to predict the future behaviour of the time series.

Nair et al (2010) proposed a new system to optimize the decision tree-support vector machine (SVM) hybrid system used with genetic algorithm which helped in forecasting the stock market trends one day ahead. The prediction model applied on BSE stock market data for listed companies for the period from January2, 2007 to July 30, 2010. The accuracy was higher for GA optimized decision tree-SVM hybrid system. Both the system under consideration gave more trading profits for the investors. The study showed that the hybrid system was best fit for forecasting of stock market trends.

Mandziuk and Jaruszewicz (2011) focused on short term index prediction using neuron genetic system. The study discussed a mechanism by adding a new type of crossover to control the range of chromosomes' sizes to enhance the procedure of genetic algorithm. The qualitative observations and numerical results concluded that the choice of network's architecture and the evolutionary-based input variables selection are reasonable. They proposed neuro-genetic hybrid system to enhance the results.

Mousavishiri and Saeidi (2013) designed a hybrid model to predict stock prices. The model was a combination of genetic algorithms and neural networks. The prediction based on this model was better during uncertain market conditions. The problems which were difficult to identify with traditional methods were identified and solved by artificial intelligence techniques such as fuzzy logic, genetic algorithm and artificial neural networks. The performance of the model was found best when neural network was combined with genetic algorithm.

Zareimoravej et al (2013) presented the prediction model based on genetic theory of rhythm patterns and a hybrid model using a measure of error (MSE). The nonlinear nature of price behaviour of stocks was analysed in the study by taking sample stocks from Tehran stock exchange from year 2002 to 2012. A combined forecasting model based on set theory and genetic algorithms reduced the errors in forecasting stock prices. The results proved that genetic algorithm model gave better results of prediction than the traditional models.

Bonde and Khaled (2015) used genetic algorithm for optimization of weights of neural network and trained neural network for prediction of stock prices proposing a hybrid genetic approach combined with neural network for better accuracy. The data used for the study was google (GOOG), TCS (TCS.BE), Infosys (INFY.BO), HCLTECH.NS and Wipro (WIPRO.BO) beginning from 1st January 2004 to 31st December 2014. Six attributes of each company , i.e., opening price, closing price, highest price, lowest price, volume and adjusted closing price were used for prediction. They found that results of prediction were accurate upto 70%.

Patil et al (2016) developed a system for predictions of the stock market movements in the Indonesia stock exchange market which followed two main phases, one is for fragment based association mining and other focus on optimization for predictions provided by genetic algorithms. They analysed stock price movements of the companies by implementing the association rule-mining algorithm to mine rules of relationship amid movements of the stock prices from time to time. The study also examined and evaluated various factors that affect number of rules generated.

6.3 TERMINOLOGY USED IN GA

The structure of genetic algorithm is based on biological factors like mutation, crossover of genetic information, selection and reproduction (Melanie, 1999).Like in natural world, the evolution of the fittest offspring depends on mix match between various genetic features of species, similarly, in genetic algorithms; the most optimal solution is produced from fittest a potential solution which is produced by matching fitness of various potential solutions.

A major innovation was done by Holland's population based algorithm with inversion, crossover and mutation. Genetic algorithms are derived from genomic terminology. A human body is made up of various cells, each cell in our body constitutes of the same set of chromosomes. Each chromosome is divided into genes containing DNA, this DNA acts as a blueprint for making every individual different. The mix matching of DNA ensures that each individual has different set of features known as traits such as hair colour, eye colour, etc. The different traits are known as "alleles" and each gene is located at a particular "locus" of the chromosome. A new human is formed by the recombination or crossover during reproduction. Mutation done in DNA ensures random and rare features of every individual and finally offspring's fitness is evaluated in terms of viability or fertility.

In genetic algorithms, in a given problem, chromosome represents one of the candidate solutions. Each chromosome is represented in the form of bit strings and each locus is represented in the form of allele: 0 and 1. In a search space, chromosomes represent a point. While processing a GA population, a set of chromosomes is replaced by another set. Further, to find out the fitness (score) of each chromosome in the population, a "fitness function" is used. The score depends on how well the chromosome solves a particular problem.

The fitness function is denoted by $f(x)$, which is a real valued function used on the chromosomes (candidate solutions). During fitness evaluation, the 'x' in $f(x)$ denotes numeric value of chromosomes.

An important application of GA is function optimization. A simple example can be to optimize the real valued function

$$f(x) = x + |\sin(32x)|$$

Overall values of x between 0 and π (Riolo,1992). Here the candidate solutions are values of x which are encoded as bit strings. A given bit string is translated to a real number x with the help of fitness calculation and then value is evaluated. The fitness of that particular string is the function value at that point.

For the selection of most optimal solution from various solutions available is done from "search space" a terminology used in GA which refers to collection of candidate solutions for a given problem whereas the term " fitness landscape" is used to represent a space of all possible genotypes and their fitness.

6.4 ELEMENTS OF GENETIC ALGORITHM

It is observed that no particular definition exists from genetic algorithm but most of the algorithms used genetics have below mentioned common features which differentiate it from other evolutionary computation methods.

1. Selection: In GA processing, this operator is used to select a chromosome from the population. Each chromosome is evaluated by the fitness function. The fitter the chromosome, more likely it is selected to reproduce.
2. Crossover: This operator is used to choose a locus , i.e., a particular point in candidate chromosome to reproduce. The recombination is used to produce two offspring's by combing the genes of parent's in different ways. For example, in binary representation, two stings 00000000 and 11111111 could be crossed over at the sixth locus in each to generate the two new offspring 10111000 and 00101011.
3. Mutation: This operator randomly changes some of the bits in a string to protect them against premature convergence.The crossover can happen at every bit but with a very less probability of occurring.

The same cycle happens and evaluates fitness. In each cycle, the old population is replaced by the new population by selecting the fittest candidate with the help of above operators.

6.5: FUNCTIONING OF GENETIC ALGORITHM

To solve a given problem with a bit string representing candidate solutions, GA follows below mentioned steps to find optimal solution or the fittest solution:

1. A randomly generate population is selected with n bit chromosomes. Each chromosome here represents a candidate solution to a given problem.
2. The, the fitness f(x) of each chromosome 'x' is calculated in the population.
3. Repeat the above 2 steps until offspring n is created:
   a. A pair of parent chromosome is selected from the population (selection depend on fitness of chromosome). A single chromosome can be selected multiple times if it continues to be the fittest.
   b. The crossover happens at probability p_c (crossover probability)at a randomly chosen point to produce offspring. An exact copy of parents is produced as offspring's if no crossover takes place.
   c. Then, mutation of offspring's takes place with probability p_m (mutation probability) and they are placed in new population.
4. The old population , i.e., the current population is replaced by the new population generated with the help of offspring's
5. Go back to Step 2.

A GA is iterated from 50 to 500 times and each iteration is known as "generation". "Run" is the term used for each set of "generation".

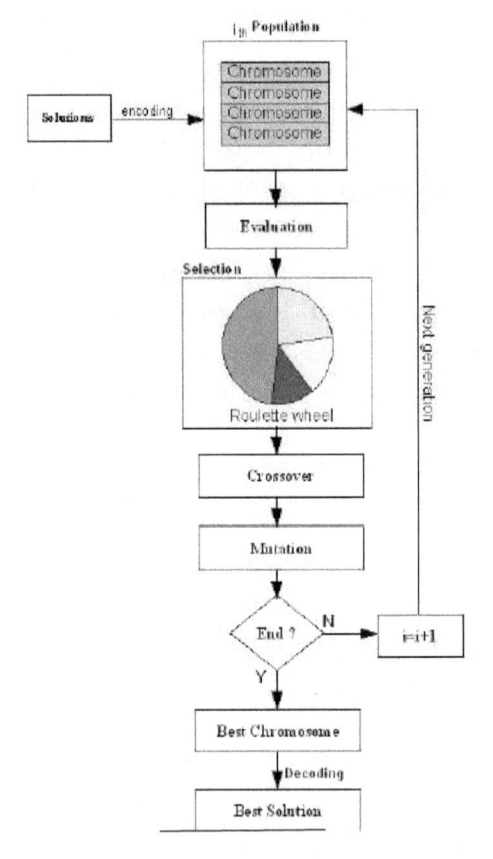

Figure 6.3: Flow chart of genetic algorithm

This is the simplest form of GA which is the basis of a number of complex models and engineering problems.

6.6 APPLICATION OF GENETIC ALGORITHM
1. Optimization
Optimization is the most important feature of GA. They have been used in a number of optimization tasks such as numerical optimization and also combinatorial optimization problems like job scheduling.

2. Machine Learning

Machine learning applications use GA for classification and prediction tasks like prediction of weather. GAs is also being widely used in machine-learning systems such as weights for neural networks and also in sensors for robots.

3. Automatic Programming

GAs is also used in evolving computer programs for specific tasks and computational structures such as sorting networks and cellular automata.

4. Economic Models

GAs is widely being used in processes of innovation, emergence of economic markets and development strategies.

5. Forecasting Models

These days for forecasting stock price data, researchers are frequently using genetic algorithms along with other time series models with the perceptions of optimizing the results. Some of the applications of genetic algorithms, used for forecasting the stock price data are listed here. Genetic Programming technique-Multi Expression programming (Abraham et al, 2005), GP-based stock price models-MLP and Neuro Fuzzy Model-Trading Rules (Rajabioun and Rahimi-Kian, 2008), Neuro Genetic (Mandziuk and Jaruszewicz, 2011), genetic algorithm with ANN, MLP, GFF, ANFIS-Trading Rules (Mousavishiri and Saeidi, 2013), genetic algorithm-hybrid clustering, i.e., Fuzzy C Means and K-Medoids (Chandrika et al, 2014), LM algorithms and quasi newton algorithm, Sigmoid function, linear function (Sabri and Mogadam, 2014), genetic algorithm with support vectorn mechanism (SVM) (Jena and Padhy, 2014), genetic algorithm to optimize artificial neural network (Amin et al, 2014), hybrid neuro genetic data mining technique (Bonde and Khaled, 2015), training an ANN using genetic algorithms (Olsson and Magnusson, 2016).

6.7: EXPERIMENTAL PROCESS

In this research, software Weka is used to analyze the time series stock prices data under consideration. Software Weka has a dedicated time series analysis environment that allows forecasting to be developed, evaluated and visualized. The data is comprised of 25 BSE Sensex companies. It consists of date, opening price, closing price, high, low and volume in number of shares traded on the day. Out of these, only four variables were taken into account, the opening price, closing price, high price and the low price. The output consists of a single variable, i.e., the opening value. The data is further divided into 95:5 ratios for training and testing respectively.

In data processing procedure, input and output ranges for training set are specified. The attribute function selection is done by three methods known as M5 method, Greedy and no attribute selection. The default method selected, i.e., 0 = M5 method, 1= none (no attribute selection) and 2= greedy method.

In each iteration, the **M5 prime** feature selection selects the attribute with the smallest standardized coefficient, removes it and performs another regression. If the result improves AIC, the attribute is dropped. This is repeated until no attribute is dropped anymore.

The **greedy** feature selection however selects a random attribute (that's why it is called greedy) and checks if removing it, improves the AIC. This is also repeated until no attribute is dropped anymore.

Descriptive attributes statistics, i.e., Mean absolute error (MAE), Mean squared error (MSE), Root Mean squared error (RMSE), Relative absolute error (RAE) and Root relative squared error (RRSE) are calculated for further analysis. Maximum least values of the above test statistics are calculated to identify the best fit method for prediction of stock prices.

6.7.1: GRAPHICAL REPRESENTATION OF SUN PHARMACEUTICAL:
Training Prediction at Differents Stages/Steps:

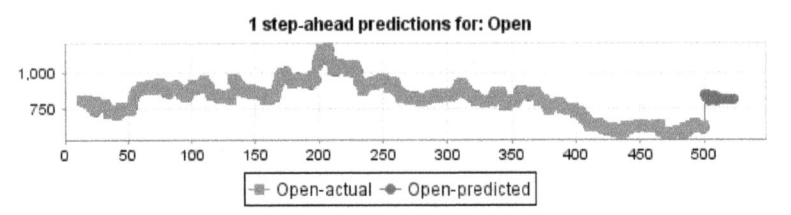

Figure 6.4: Graph of Training Prediction at First Step

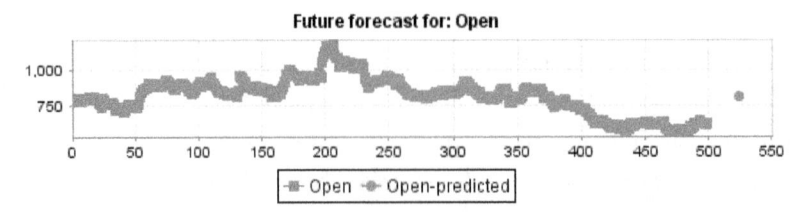

Figure 6.5: Graph of Future Forecast for open

6.7.2 EXPERIMENTAL RESULTS OF SUN PHARMACEUTICAL

Evaluation of results obtained, using three different attribute selection methods of genetic algorithms are as under:

Table 6.1: Descriptive Statistics for goodness of Fit

Minimum	566.00
Maximum	1180.00
Mean	817.65
Standard Deviation	127.17

Table 6.2: Results of Sun Pharmaceutical Stock index with different Genetic Algorithms

Method Used	M5	Greedy	No Attribute Selection
Observations	500	500	500
Mean absolute error	12.19	12.19	12.18
Root relative squared error	97.35	97.35	96.69
Direction accuracy	48.55	48.55	48.76
Relative absolute error	98.93	98.93	98.80
Mean absolute percentage error	1.47	1.47	1.48
Root mean squared error	17.06	17.06	16.94
Mean squared error	291.07	291.07	287.26

INTERPRETATION

On the basis of the results obtained above it is deduced that mean absolute error, root relative squared error, relative absolute error, root mean square error, mean squared error are having the least value for no attribute selection method. Therefore, no attribute selection method is chosen as the best fit method amongst different models of genetic algorithm for prediction of time series stock prices data following a normal distribution.

Evaluation of the results of Sun Pharmaceutical (normal distribution) based on statistics of goodness of fit/accuracy.

i) MAE

Different values of mean absolute error are analysed and compared for different genetic algorithm models. It is observed that **No Attribute Selection method** has the least **MAE**

(12.18) value when compared with MAE (12.19) for M5 Method and MAE (12.19) for Greedy Method respectively.

ii) RRSE

Values of root relative squared error are analysed for different genetic algorithm models. It is found that No **Attribute Selection method** has the least **RRSE (96.69)** value when compared with RRSE (97.35) for M5 Method and RRSE (97.35) for Greedy Method respectively.

iii) Direction Accuracy

Different values of root relative squared error are analysed and compared for different genetic algorithm models. It is observed that **No Attribute Selection method has the least DA value (48.55)** when compared with DA (48.57) for M5 Method and DA (48.57) for Greedy Method respectively.

iv) RAE

Values of relative absolute error are analysed for different genetic algorithm models and it is observed that **No Attribute Selection method has the least RAE (98.80)** when compared with RAE (98.93) for M5 Method and RAE (98.93) for Greedy Method respectively.

v) MAPE

Different values of mean absolute percentage error are analysed and compared for different genetic algorithm models. It is found that **Greedy method has the least MAPE (1.47)** when compared with MAPE (1.47) for M5 Method and MAPE (1.48) for No Attribute Selection method respectively.

vi) RMSE

Values of root mean squared error are analysed and compared for different genetic algorithm models. It is observed that **No Attribute Selection method resulted into the least RMSE (16.94)** when compared with RMSE (17.06) for M5 Method and RMSE (17.06) for Greedy Method respectively.

vii) MSE

Different values of mean squared error are analysed and compared for different genetic algorithm models. It is found that **No Attribute Selection method has the least MSE**

(287.26) when compared with MSE (291.07) for M5 Method and MSE (291.07) Greedy Method respectively.

The best fit method for genetic algorithm is selected on the basis of maximum number of votes earned for the least value of each statistics for goodness of fit/accuracy. No attribute selection method earned 5 votes on the basis of least value of each statistics , i.e., MAE, RRSE, RAE, RMSE and MSE respectively. On the other hand only two votes are allocated to greedy method for least value of DA and MAPE whereas none of the vote is earned by M5 method. Thus, no selection attribute method is concluded as the best fit method amongst different methods of genetic algorithms.

Appraisal of the experiment:

Similarly, results of other five stocks in which time series data is normally distributed are analysed. It is found that no attribute selection method earned maximum numbers of votes for the least value of statistics for goodness of fit for Coal India, Gail, Hero Motor Corp., NTPC and Reliance Industries respectively. It is deduced from the above analysis that no selection attribute method is declared as the best fit method amongst different methods of genetic algorithms for forecasting stock prices time series data. The result analysis of all the companies stated above is listed in the following table.

Table No 6.3: Result analysis of stocks (normal distribution) using GA models

Model	No of companies	Name of the companies
M5	-	Nil
Greedy	-	Nil
No attribute selection	6	Coal India, Gail, Hero Motor Corp., NTPC and Reliance Industries, Sun Pharmaceutical

6.7.3: GRAPHICAL REPRESENTATION OF LUPIN LIMTED:

Training Prediction At Differenents Stages/Steps:

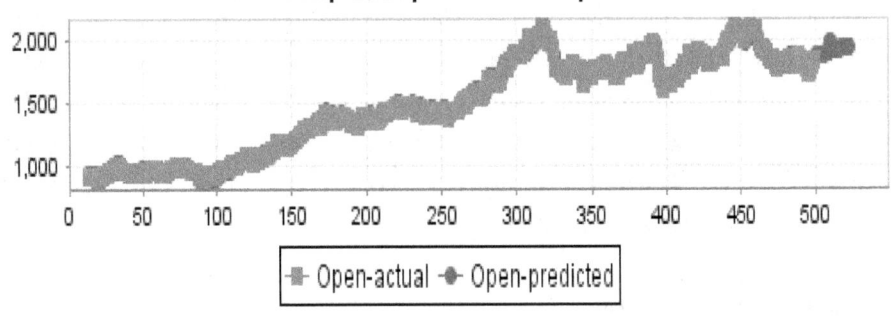

Figure 6.6: Graph of Training Prediction at First Step

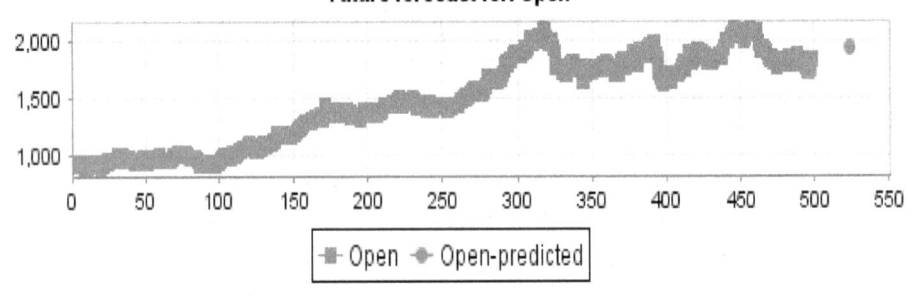

Figure 6.7: Graph of Future Forecast for open

6.7.4 EXPERIMENTAL RESULTS OF LUPIN LIMITED

Analysis of genetic algorithm results obtained by using three different attributes selection methods are as under:

Table6.4: Goodness of fit statistics for Lupin Limited (non-normal distribution)

Mean	1475.15
Minimum	871.00
Maximum	2114.90
Standard Deviation	377.56

Table6.5: Statistical Results of different Genetic Algorithms for Lupin Stock index

Method Used	M5	Greedy	No Attribute Selection
Observations	500	500	500
Mean absolute error	21.86	21.86	**21.71**
Root relative squared error	105.58	105.58	**105.10**
Direction accuracy	51.23	**51.23**	52.05
Relative absolute error	112.27	**112.27**	111.56
Mean absolute percentage error	1.46	1.46	**1.44**
Root mean squared error	29.25	29.25	**29.10**
Mean squared error	855.76	855.76	**847.12**

INTERPRETATION:

On the basis of the results obtained above it is deduced that mean absolute error, root relative squared error, relative absolute error, root mean square error, mean squared error are having the least value for no attribute selection method. Therefore, no attribute selection method is chosen as the best fit method amongst different models of genetic algorithm for prediction of time series stock prices data following a normal distribution.

Evaluation of the results of Lupin Limited (non-normal distribution) based on statistics of goodness of fit/accuracy.

i) MAE

Different values of mean absolute error are analysed and compared for different genetic algorithm models. It is observed that **No Attribute Selection method has value the least**

MAE (21.71) when compared with MAE (21.86) for M5 Method and MAE (21.86) for Greedy Method respectively.

ii) RRSE

Values of root relative squared error are analysed for different genetic algorithm models and observed that **No Attribute Selection method has the least RRSE (105.10)** when compared with RRSE (105.58) for M5 Method and RRSE (105.58) for Greedy Method respectively.

iii) Direction Accuracy

Different values of root relative squared error are analysed and compared for different genetic algorithm models. It is found that **M5 method and Greedy method has the least DA (51.23)** when compared with DA (52.05) for No attribute selection Method respectively.

iv) RAE

Values of relative absolute error values are analysed for different genetic algorithm models and it is found that **No Attribute Selection method has the least RAE (111.56)** when compared with RAE (112.27) for M5 Method and RAE (112.27) for Greedy Method respectively.

v) MAPE

Different values of mean absolute percentage error are analysed and compared for different genetic algorithm models. It is observed that **Greedy method has the least MAPE (1.44)** when compared with MAPE (1.46) for M5 Method and MAPE (1.46) for No Attribute Selection method respectively.

vi) RMSE

Values of root mean squared errors are analysed and it is observed that **No Attribute Selection method has the least RMSE (29.10)** when compared with RMSE (29.25) for M5 Method and RMSE (29.25) for Greedy Method respectively.

vii) MSE

Different values of mean squared error values are analysed and compared for different genetic algorithm models. It is found that **No Attribute Selection method has the least**

MSE (847.12) when compared with MSE (855.76) for M5 Method and MSE (855.76) Greedy Method respectively.

As stated in the previous experiment for Sun Pharmaceutical here also the best fit method of genetic algorithm is selected on the basis of maximum number of votes for the least value of each statistics of goodness of fit/accuracy. No attribute selection method scored 6 votes on the basis of the least value of each statistics, i.e., MAE, RRSE, RAE, MAPE, RMSE and MSE respectively. On the other hand only one vote is allocated to greedy method for least value of DA whereas none of the vote is earned by M5 method. Thus, no selection attribute method is concluded as the best fit method amongst different methods of genetic algorithms.

Appraisal of the experiment

Similarly, results of other 18 stocks (non-normal distribution) are analysed. It is found that no attribute selection method earned maximum numbers of votes for the least values of statistic for goodness of fit/accuracy for Adani Port, Axis Bank, Bharti Airtel, Bajaj Autos, Cipla, Dr. Reddy, HDFC Bank, HDFC Finance ICICI Bank, Infosys, L&T, Lupin, Maruti Suzuki, ONGC, Power Grid, State Bank of India, Tata Steel, TCS and Wipro respectively. It is deduced from the above analysis that no selection attribute method is declared as the best fit method amongst different methods of genetic algorithms for forecasting stock prices time series data of all companies. The result analysis of all the companies stated above is listed in the following table.

Table No 6.6: Analysis of stocks (non-normal distribution) using GA models

Model	No of companies	Name of the companies
M5	-	Nil
Greedy	-	Nil
No attribute selection	19	Adani Port, Axis Bank, Bharti Airtel, Bajaj Autos, Cipla, Dr. Reddy, HDFC Bank, HDFC Finance ICICI Bank, Infosys, L&T, Lupin, Maruti Suzuki, ONGC, Power Grid, State Bank of India, Tata Steel, TCS and Wipro

CHAPTER VII
RESULTS AND DISCUSSIONS

7.1 INTRODUCTION

The stock market is comprised of various participants with different risk capacity and return characteristics, different perceptions and expectations about stocks and the economy. Investors interpret and react on the information/news in different ways. They focus on diverse pieces of information and reach different conclusions. The level of impact of such information on the stock prices Investment decisions are made by the investors mainly on fundamental and technical analysis of the stocks. Fundamentals of the stocks include study of financial statements of the company involving balance sheet analysis, profit and loss account analysis, etc. for the particular company under consideration. Promoters and management details are taken from annual report and their reputation is also considered for the investment in any stock.

Another important parameter for the investment is technical analysis of the stocks. In this study, only technical analysis has been carried out on the historical data of the stocks. The stock prices, i.e., open price, high price, low price, close price, volume and adjusted close have been analyzed under different models of Time Series Analysis namely ARIMA model, artificial neural networks and genetic algorithm. Investors/participants of the stock market are mainly interested in knowing the opening price of the next day in relation to today's close price. In this study, open price of 25 stocks are analyzed on a database of 2 years. In total, 500 observations are analyzed for forecasting stock price for 23 days under different models and finally, the best method of prediction has been selected on the basis of minimum value of test statistics.

This chapter is divided into five sections. Section 7.1 gives a brief introduction of the chapter; Section 7.2 presents the results of prediction of stock prices using ARIMA models. Further, section 7.3 presents result of stock prices predicted using Artificial Neural Network followed by section 7.4 which briefs about the results generated with the help of genetic algorithm for forecasting of stock prices. Section 7.5 presents the comparison of results obtained from different model, i.e., ARIMA, artificial neural network and genetic algorithm. Finally, section 7.6 highlights the conclusion of research work carried out.

7.2 EVALUATION OF RESULTS FORECASTED USING ARIMA MODELS:

ARIMA model is applied on historical data of stock prices. This data has been obtained over a duration of 2 years starting from 20.01.2015 to 19.01.2016 for 25 select companies belonging to different sectors, i.e., banking & finance, automobiles, coal, gas, power, energy, steel ports infrastructure and IT & telecommunication. In the first step, 9 ARIMA models, i.e., (0,1,0), (1,1,0), (0,1,1), (2,1,0), (0,1,2), (1,1,1), (2,1,2), (1,1,2) and (2,1,1) are applied at first difference for opening prices. Further, based on second differencing of time series data, 9 ARIMA models, i.e., (0,2,0), (1,2,0), (0,2,1), (1,2,1), (2,2,1), (1,2,2), (2,2,2), (2,2,0) and (0,2,2) are applied. The results so obtained for 18 different models of ARIMA are analyzed on the basis of goodness of fit statistics as follows:

7.2.1 Results of time series data of Sun Pharmaceuticals (for normal distribution) at first difference based on the statistics of goodness of fit / accuracy using ARIMA models:

i) Sum of Squares due to Error

Different ARIMA models are compared for SSE values and it is found that **ARIMA (1,1,2) has the least SSE value 149529.50** when compared with ARIMA (0,1,0) having value SSE value 282477.80, ARIMA (1,1,0) having value 1187400, ARIMA (0,1,1) having value 150181.90, ARIMA (2,1,0) having value 188472.80 and ARIMA (0,1,2) having value 149673.40, ARIMA (1,1,1) having value 149656, ARIMA (2,1,2) having value 149573.80 and ARIMA (2,1,1) having value 149596.10 respectively.

ii) Mean Squared Error

MSE value of different ARIMA models are compared and it is observed that **ARIMA (1,1,2) has the least MSE value 300.86** when compared with ARIMA (0,1,0) having value 569.36, ARIMA (1,1,0) having value 2389.13, ARIMA (0,1,1) having value 302.17, ARIMA (2,1,0) having value 379.22, ARIMA (0,1,2) having value 301.15, ARIMA (1,1,1) having value 301.11, ARIMA (2,1,2) having value 300.95 and ARIMA (2,1,1) having value 300.99 respectively.

iii) Root Mean Squared Error

Different ARIMA models are compared for RMSE values and it is found that **ARIMA (1,1,2) has the least RMSE value 17.34** when compared with ARIMA (0,1,0) having value 23.84, ARIMA (1,1,0) having value 48.87, ARIMA (0,1,1) having value 17.38, ARIMA (2,1,0) having value 19.47, ARIMA (0,1,2) having value 17.35, ARIMA (1,1,1) having value

17.35, ARIMA (2,1,2) having value 17.34 and ARIMA (2,1,1) having value 17.34 respectively.

iv) White Noise Variance

WN variance value are analyzed for different ARIMA models and it is observed that **ARIMA (1,1,2)** has **the least WN variance value 300.86** when compared with ARIMA (0,1,0) having value 569.36, ARIMA (1,1,0) having value 2389.13, ARIMA (0,1,1) having value 302.17, ARIMA (2,1,0) having value 379.22 and ARIMA (0,1,2) having value 301.15, ARIMA (1,1,1) having value 301.11, ARIMA (2,1,2) having value 300.95 and ARIMA (2,1,1) having value 300.99 respectively.

v) Mean Absolute Percentage Error

Different ARIMA models are compared for MAPE values and it is found that **ARIMA (0,1,1)** has **the least MAPE value 104.47** when compared with ARIMA (0,1,0) having value 472.24, ARIMA (1,1,0) having value 424.92, ARIMA (2,1,0) having value 266.64, ARIMA (0,1,2) having value 115.11, ARIMA (1,1,1) having value 115.37, ARIMA (2,1,2) having value 113.62, ARIMA (1,1,2) having value 124.23 and ARIMA (2,1,1) having value 114.18 respectively.

vi) Final Prediction Error

FPE values are analyzed for different ARIMA models and it is observed that **ARIMA (0,1,2)** has **the least FPE value 301.15** when compared with ARIMA (0,1,0) having value 568.36, ARIMA (1,1,0) having value 2398.76, ARIMA (0,1,1) having value 302.17, ARIMA (2,1,0) having value 382.28, ARIMA (1,1,1) having value 302.33, ARIMA (2,1,2) having value 303.38, ARIMA (1,1,2) having value 302.07 and ARIMA (2,1,1) having value 303.43 respectively.

vii) Akaike Information Criterion

Different ARIMA models are compared for AIC value and it is found that **ARIMA (0,1,1)** has **the least AIC value 4259.09** when compared with ARIMA (1,1,0) having value 5280.76, ARIMA (2,1,0) having value 4368.21, ARIMA (0,1,2) having value 4259.21 ARIMA (1,1,1) having value 4259.14, ARIMA (2,1,2) having value 4262.78, ARIMA (1,1,2) having value 4260.76 and ARIMA (2,1,1) having value 4260.90 respectively.

viii) Correction of AIC

AICC value are analyzed for different ARIMA models and it is observed that **ARIMA (0,1,1)** has **the least AICC value 4259.03** when compared with ARIMA (1,1,0) having value 5280.78, ARIMA (2,1,0) having value 4368.26, ARIMA (0,1,2) having value 4259.26

ARIMA (1,1,1) having value 4259.19, ARIMA (2,1,2) having value 4262.91, ARIMA (1,1,2) having value 4260.84 and ARIMA (2,1,1) having value 4260.98 respectively.

ix)   **Schwarz Bayesian Information Criterion**

Different ARIMA models are compared for SBC value and it is found that **ARIMA (0,1,1)** has **the least SBC value 4267.42** when compared with ARIMA (1,1,0) having value 5289.17, ARIMA (2,1,0) having value 4380.84, ARIMA (0,1,2) having value 4271.83, ARIMA (1,1,1) having value 4271.76, ARIMA (2,1,2) having value 4283.83, ARIMA (1,1,2) having value 4277.59 and ARIMA (2,1,1) having value 4277.73 respectively.

7.2.2 Results of time series data of Sun Pharmaceuticals (for normal distribution) at second difference based on the statistics of goodness of fit / accuracy using ARIMA model:

i)   **Sum of Squares due to Error**

Different ARIMA models are compared for SSE values and it is found that **ARIMA (2,2,2)** has **the least SSE value 189161.8** when compared with ARIMA (0,2,0) having value 2750243, ARIMA(1,2,0) having value 1300588, ARIMA (0,2,1) having value 835999.60, ARIMA (1,2,1) having value 487188.90, ARIMA (2,2,1) having value 341204.30, ARIMA (1,2,2) having value 217577.50, ARIMA (2,2,0) having value 762418.20 and ARIMA (0,2,2) having value 282999 respectively.

ii)   **Mean Squared Error**

MSE value is analyzed for different ARIMA models and it is observed that **ARIMA (2,2,2)** has **the least MSE value 382.145** when compared with ARIMA (0,2,0) having value 5556.04, ARIMA (1,2,0) having value 2627.45, ARIMA (0,2,1) having value 1688.88, ARIMA (1,2,1) having value 984.22, ARIMA (2,2,1) having value 689.30, ARIMA (1,2,2) having value 439.55, ARIMA (2,2,0) having value 1540.23 and ARIMA (0,2,2) having value 571.71 respectively.

iii)   **Root Mean Squared Error**

Different ARIMA models are compared for RMSE value and it is found that **ARIMA (2,2,2)** has **the least RMSE value 19.54** when compared with ARIMA (0,2,0) having value 74.53, ARIMA (1,2,0) having value 51.25, ARIMA (0,2,1) having value 41.09, ARIMA (1,2,1) having value 31.37, ARIMA (2,2,1) having value 26.25, ARIMA (1,2,2) having value 20.96, ARIMA (2,2,0) having value 39.24 and ARIMA (0,2,2) having value 23.91 respectively.

iv) White Noise Variance

WN variance value is compared for different ARIMA models and it is observed that **ARIMA (2,2,2)** has **the least WN variance value 382.145** when compared with ARIMA (0,2,0) having value 5556.04, ARIMA (1,2,0) having value 2627.45, ARIMA (0,2,1) having value 1688.88, ARIMA (1,2,1) having value 984.22, ARIMA (2,2,1) having value 689.30, ARIMA (1,2,2) having value 439.55, ARIMA (2,2,0) having value 1540.23 and ARIMA (0,2,2) having value 571.71 respectively.

v) Mean Absolute Percentage Error

Different ARIMA models are compared for MAPE value and it is found that **ARIMA (0,2,2)** has **the least MAPE value 101.88** when compared with ARIMA (0,2,0) having value 1122.04, ARIMA (1,2,0) having value 531.63, ARIMA (0,2,1) having value 424.03, ARIMA (1,2,1) having value 325.03, ARIMA (2,2,1) having value 306.45, ARIMA (1,2,2) having value 210.12, ARIMA (2,2,2) having value 208.33 and ARIMA (2,2,0) having value 506.27 respectively.

vi) Final Prediction Error

FPE value is analyzed for different ARIMA models and it is observed that **ARIMA (2,2,2)** has **the least FPE value 385.24** when compared with ARIMA (0,2,0) having value 5556.04, ARIMA (1,2,0) having value 2638.08, ARIMA (0,2,1) having value 1688.88, ARIMA (1,2,1) having value 988.20, ARIMA (2,2,1) having value 694.89, ARIMA (1,2,2) having value 441.33, ARIMA (2,2,0) having value 1552.73 and ARIMA (0,2,2) having value 571.71 respectively.

vii) Akaike Information Criterion

Different ARIMA models are compared for AIC value and it is found that **ARIMA (2,2,2)** has **the least AIC value 4379.274** when compared with ARIMA (1,2,0) having value 5307.01, ARIMA (0,2,1) having value 5093.70, ARIMA (1,2,1) having value 4829.95, ARIMA (2,2,1) having value 4657.22, ARIMA (1,2,2) having value 4444.93, ARIMA (2,2,0) having value 5045.70 and ARIMA (0,2,2) having value 4570.77 respectively.

viii) Correction of AIC

AICC value is analyzed for different ARIMA models and it is observed that **ARIMA (2,2,2)** has **the least AICC value 4379.39** when compared with ARIMA (1,2,0) having value 5307.03, ARIMA (0,2,1) having value 5093.70, ARIMA (1,2,1) having value 4830.00, ARIMA (2,2,1) having value 4657.30, ARIMA (1,2,2) having value 4445.01, ARIMA (2,2,0) having value 5045.75 and ARIMA (0,2,2) having value 4570.80 respectively.

ix) Schwarz Bayesian Information Criterion

Different ARIMA models are compared for SBC value and it is found that **ARIMA (2,2,2)** has **the least SBC value 4400.29** when compared with ARIMA (1,2,0) having value 5315.42, ARIMA (0,2,1) having value 5102.11, ARIMA (1,2,1) having value 4842.56, ARIMA (2,2,1) having value 4674.04, ARIMA (1,2,2) having value 4461.75, ARIMA (2,2,0) having value 5058.31 and ARIMA (0,2,2) having value 4583.38 respectively.

7.2.3 Comparison between first and second difference results analyzed of ARIMA:

All statistics of goodness of fitness are compared for first and second difference of time series data.

i) Sum of Squares due to Error

SSE value is compared for both the orders and it is found that SSE value obtained from first differencing **(149529.50)** is the least for **ARIMA model (1,1,2)** when compared with SSE value for second differencing (189161.80) of ARIMA model (2,2,2). Thus, **ARIMA model (1,1,2)** is considered best model for prediction of stock prices amongst 18 models of ARIMA on the basis of SSE analysis.

ii) Mean Squared Error

On comparison of the orders of differencing, it is found that MSE value obtained on first differencing **(300.86)** is the least for **ARIMA model (1,1,2)** when compared with MSE value obtained on second differencing (382.14) of ARIMA model (2,2,2). Thus, **ARIMA model (1,1,2)** is considered best model for prediction of stock prices amongst 18 ARIMA models on the basis of MSE analysis.

iii) Root Mean Squared Error

RMSE value is compared for both the orders and it is found that RMSE value obtained from first differencing (17.34) is the least for ARIMA model (1,1,2) when compared with RMSE value for second differencing (19.54) of ARIMA model (2,2,2). Thus, **ARIMA model (1,1,2)** is considered best model for prediction of stock prices amongst 18 different models of ARIMA on the basis of RMSE analysis.

iv) White Noise Variance

On comparison of the orders of differencing, it is found that WN variance value obtained on first differencing **(300.86)** is the least for **ARIMA model (1,1,2)** when compared with WN variance value for second differencing (382.14) of ARIMA model (2,2,2). Thus, **ARIMA model (1,1,2)** is considered best model for prediction of stock prices amongst 18 different models of ARIMA on the basis of WN analysis.

v)   **Mean Absolute Percentage Error**

MAPE value is compared for both the orders and it is found that MAPE value obtained from first differencing **(99.80)** is the least for **ARIMA model (0,1,0)** when compared with MAPE value for second differencing (190.68) of ARIMA model (0,2,0). Thus, **ARIMA model (0,1,0)** is considered best model for prediction of stock prices amongst 18 different models of ARIMA on the basis of MAPE analysis.

vi)   **Final Prediction Error**

On comparison of the orders of differencing, it is found that FPE value obtained on first differencing **(301.15)** is the least for **ARIMA model (0,1,2)** when compared with FPE value for second differencing (385.24) of ARIMA model (2,2,2). Thus, **ARIMA model (0,1,2)** is considered best model for prediction of stock prices amongst 18 different models of ARIMA on the basis of FPE analysis.

vii)   **Akaike Information Criterion**

AIC value is compared for both the orders and it is found that AIC value obtained from first differencing **(4259.00)** is the least for **ARIMA model (0,1,1)** when compared with AIC value for second differencing (4379.27) of ARIMA model (2,2,2). Thus, **ARIMA model (0,1,1)** is considered best model for prediction of stock prices amongst 18 different models of ARIMA on the basis of AIC analysis.

viii)   **Correction of AIC**

On comparison of the orders of differencing, it is found that AICC value obtained on first differencing **(4259.03)** is the least for **ARIMA model (0,1,1)** when compared with AICC value for second differencing (4379.39) of ARIMA model (2,2,2). Thus, **ARIMA model (0,1,1)** is considered best model for prediction of stock prices amongst 18 different models of ARIMA on the basis of AICC analysis.

ix)   **Schwarz Bayesian Information Criterion**

SBC value is compared for both the orders and it is found that SBC value obtained from first differencing **(4267.42)** is the least for **ARIMA model (0,1,1)** when compared with SBC value for second differencing (4400.29) of ARIMA model (2,2,2). Thus, **ARIMA model (0,1,1)** is considered best model for prediction of stock prices amongst 18 different models of ARIMA on the basis of SBC analysis.

For final analysis, the best fit method of ARIMA model is selected on the basis of maximum number of votes for the least value of each statistic for goodness of fit. ARIMA model (1,1,2) at first difference got five number of votes for the least value of each for SSE, MSE, RMSE,

White Noise and -2 log like when compared with four votes of ARIMA model (0,0,1). Thus, **ARIMA Model (1,1,2)** resulted best method amongst different methods of ARIMA Model.

Appraisal of experiment:
Similarly, results of other five stocks where time series data is normally distributed are observed. It is concluded that ARIMA Model (1,1,1) turned out to be the best model for 3 companies namely Coal India, Hero Motor Corporation, Reliance Industries. ARIMA Model (0,1,1) for Gail and ARIMA Model (0,1,2) for NTPC respectively. The results are presented in the following table

Table No 7.1: Analysis of stocks (normal distribution) using ARIMA models

Model	No of companies	Name of the companies
(1,1,1)	4	Coal India, Hero Motor Corp, Reliance Industries, Sun Pharmaceuticals
(0,1,1)	1	GAIL
(0,1,2)	1	NTPC

7.2.4 Results of time series data of Lupin Limited (for non-normal distribution) at first difference based on the statistics of goodness of fit / accuracy using ARIMA model:

i) **Sum of Squares due to Error**

Different ARIMA models are compared for SSE values and it is observed that **ARIMA (2,1,1)** has **the least value SSE374102.10** when compared with ARIMA (0,1,0) having value 723377.50, ARIMA (1,1,0) having value 555176.70, ARIMA (0,1,1) having value 374520, ARIMA (2,1,0) having value 500994.50 and ARIMA (0,1,2) having value 374111.60, ARIMA (1,1,1) having value 374115.80, ARIMA (2,1,2) having value 374120 and ARIMA (1,1,2) having value 556139.70 respectively.

ii) **Mean Squared Error**

MSE value are analyzed for different ARIMA models and it is observed that **ARIMA (2,1,1)** has **the least value MSE (752.72)** when compared with ARIMA (0,1,0) having value 1455.48, ARIMA (1,1,0) having value 1117.05, ARIMA (0,1,1) having value 753,56, ARIMA (2,1,0) having value 1008.37 and ARIMA (0,1,2) having value 752.73, ARIMA (1,1,1) having value 752.74, ARIMA (2,1,2) having value 752.75 and ARIMA (1,1,2) having value 1123.51 respectively.

iii) Root Mean Squared Error

Different ARIMA models are compared for RMSE value and it is found that **ARIMA (2,1,1)** has **the least value RMSE 27.43** when compared with ARIMA (0,1,0) having value 38.15, ARIMA (1,1,0) having value 33.42, ARIMA (0,1,1) having value 27.45, ARIMA (2,1,0) having value 31.74 and ARIMA (0,1,2) having value 27.43, ARIMA (1,1,1) having value 27.43, ARIMA (2,1,2) having value 27.43 and ARIMA (1,1,2) having value 33.51 respectively.

iv) White Noise Variance

WN Variance value are analyzed for different ARIMA models and it is observed that **ARIMA (2,1,1)** has **the least value WN Variance (752.72)** when compared with ARIMA (0,1,0) having value 1455.48, ARIMA (1,1,0) having value 1117.05, ARIMA (0,1,1) having value 753,56, ARIMA (2,1,0) having value 1008.37 and ARIMA (0,1,2) having value 752.73, ARIMA (1,1,1) having value 752.74, ARIMA (2,1,2) having value 752.75 and ARIMA (1,1,2) having value 1123.51 respectively.

v) Mean Absolute Percentage Error

Different ARIMA models are compared for MAPE value and it is found that **ARIMA (0,1,1)** has **the least MAPE value 107.06** when compared with ARIMA (0,1,0) having value 328.06, ARIMA (1,1,0) having value 267.31, ARIMA (2,1,0) having value 245.55 and ARIMA (0,1,2) having value 109.25, ARIMA (1,1,1) having value 109.34, ARIMA (2,1,2) having value 109.65, ARIMA (1,1,2) having value 176.80 and ARIMA (2,1,1) having value 108.98 respectively.

vi) Final Prediction Error (FPE)

FPE values are analyzed for different ARIMA models and it is observed that **ARIMA (0,1,2)** has the least FPE value 752.73 when compared with ARIMA (0,1,0) having value 1455.48, ARIMA (1,1,0) having value 1121.56, ARIMA (0,1,1) having value 753.56, ARIMA (2,1,0) having value 1016.83, ARIMA (1,1,1) having value 755.78, ARIMA (2,1,2) having value 758.83, ARIMA (1,1,2) having value 1028.06 and ARIMA (2,1,1) having value 758.80 respectively.

vii) Akaike Information Criterion

Different ARIMA models are compared for AIC value and it is found that **ARIMA (0,1,1)** has **the least AIC value 4713.16** when compared with ARIMA (1,1,0) having value 4902.85, ARIMA (2,1,0) having value 4854.02, ARIMA (0,1,2) having value 4714.55 ARIMA (1,1,1) having value 4714.56, ARIMA (2,1,2) having value 4718.55, ARIMA (1,1,2) having value 4909.53 and ARIMA (2,1,1) having value 4716.55 respectively.

viii) **Correction of AIC**

AICC values are analyzed for different ARIMA models and it is observed that **ARIMA (0,1,1)** has **the least AICC value 4713.19** when compared with ARIMA (1,1,0) having value 4902.88, ARIMA (2,1,0) having value 4854.07, ARIMA (0,1,2) having value 4714.60 ARIMA (1,1,1) having value 4714.60, ARIMA (2,1,2) having value 4718.67, ARIMA (1,1,2) having value 4909.61 and ARIMA (2,1,1) having value 4716.63 respectively.

ix) **Schwarz Bayesian Information Criterion**

Different ARIMA are compared to SBC values and it is found that **ARIMA (0,1,1)** has **the least SBC value 4721.58** when compared with ARIMA (1,1,0) having value 4911.27, ARIMA (2,1,0) having value 4866.65, ARIMA (0,1,2) having value 4727.18, ARIMA (1,1,1) having value 4727.18, ARIMA (2,1,2) having value 4739.59, ARIMA (1,1,2) having value 4926.35 and ARIMA (2,1,1) having value 4733.38 respectively.

7.2.5 Results of time series data of Lupin Limited (for non-normal distribution) at second difference based on the statistics of goodness of fit / accuracy using ARIMA model.

i) **Sum of Squares due to Error**

Different ARIMA models are compared for SSE value and it is found that **ARIMA (2,2,2)** has **the least value SSE value 503348.20** when compared with ARIMA (0,2,0) having value 7108483, ARIMA (1,2,0) having value 3090853, ARIMA (0,2,1) having value 2143479, ARIMA (1,2,1) having value 1209045, ARIMA (2,2,1) having value 953964.80, ARIMA (1,2,2) having value 556139.70, ARIMA (2,2,0) having value 2101332 and ARIMA (0,2,2) having value 724635 respectively.

ii) **Mean Squared Error**

MSE values are analyzed for different ARIMA models and it is observed that **ARIMA (2,2,2)** has **the least MSE (1016.86)** when compared with ARIMA (0,2,0) having value 14360.57, ARIMA (1,2,0) having value 6244.16, ARIMA (0,2,1) having value 4330.26, ARIMA (1,2,1) having value 2442.51, ARIMA (2,2,1) having value 1925.18, ARIMA (1,2,2) having value 1123.51, ARIMA (2,2,0) having value 4245.11 and ARIMA (0,2,2) having value 1463.91 respectively.

iii) **Root Mean Squared Error**

Different ARIMA models are compared for RMSE value and it is found that **ARIMA (2,2,2)** has **the least RMSE value 31.88** when compared with ARIMA (0,2,0) having value 119.83, ARIMA (1,2,0) having value 79.01, ARIMA (0,2,1) having value 65.80, ARIMA (1,2,1) having value 49.42, ARIMA (2,2,1) having value 43.87, ARIMA (1,2,2) having value 33.51, ARIMA (2,2,0) having value 65.15 and ARIMA (0,2,2) having value 38.26 respectively.

iv)   White Noise Variance

WN Variance value is analyzed for different ARIMA models and it is observed that **ARIMA (2,2,2)** has **the least WN Variance value 1016.86** when compared with ARIMA (0,2,0) having value 14360.57, ARIMA (1,2,0) having value 6244.16, ARIMA (0,2,1) having value 4330.26, ARIMA (1,2,1) having value 2442.51, ARIMA (2,2,1) having value 1925.18, ARIMA (1,2,2) having value 1123.51, ARIMA (2,2,0) having value 4245.11 and ARIMA (0,2,2) having value 1463.91 respectively.

v)   Mean Absolute Percentage Error

Different ARIMA models are compared for MAPE values and it is found that **ARIMA (0,2,2)** has **the least MAPE value 106.01** when compared with ARIMA (0,2,0) having value 843.82, ARIMA (1,2,0) having value 566.90, ARIMA (0,2,1) having value 377.60, ARIMA (1,2,1) having value 287.56, ARIMA (2,2,1) having value 235.01, ARIMA (1,2,2) having value 176.80, ARIMA (2,2,2) having value 203.92 and ARIMA (2,2,0) having value 521.35 respectively.

vi)   Final Prediction Error

FPE values are analyzed for different ARIMA models and it is observed that **ARIMA (2,2,2)** has **the least FPE value 1025.11** when compared with ARIMA (0,2,0) having value 14360.57, ARIMA (1,2,0) having value 6269.42, ARIMA (0,2,1) having value 4330.26, ARIMA (1,2,1) having value 2452,40, ARIMA (2,2,1) having value 1940.80, ARIMA (1,2,2) having value 1128.06, ARIMA (2,2,0) having value 4279.55 and ARIMA (0,2,2) having value 1463.91 respectively.

vii) Akaike Information Criterion (AIC)

Different ARIMA models are compared for AIC values and it is found that **ARIMA (2,2,2)** has the least AIC value of 4863.27 when compared with ARIMA (1,2,0) having value 5735.58, ARIMA (0,2,1) having value 5559.78, ARIMA (1,2,1) having value 5279.92, ARIMA (2,2,1) having value 5165.33, ARIMA (1,2,2) having value 4909531, ARIMA (2,2,0) having value 5547.34 and ARIMA (0,2,2) having value 5036.26 respectively.

viii) Correction of AIC

AICC values are analyzed for different ARIMA models and it is observed that **ARIMA (2,2,2)** has **the least AICC value 4863.39** when compared with ARIMA (1,2,0) having value 5735.60, ARIMA (0,2,1) having value 5559.80, ARIMA (1,2,1) having value 5279.97,

ARIMA (2,2,1) having value 5165.41, ARIMA (1,2,2) having value 4909.61, ARIMA (2,2,0) having value 5547.39 and ARIMA (0,2,2) having value 5036.31 respectively.

ix)   Schwarz Bayesian Information Criterion

Different ARIMA models are compared for SBC values and it is found that **ARIMA (2,2,2)** has **the least SBC value 4884.29** when compared with ARIMA (1,2,0) having value 5743.99, ARIMA (0,2,1) having value 5568.18, ARIMA (1,2,1) having value 5292.53, ARIMA (2,2,1) having value 5182.15, ARIMA (1,2,2) having value 4926.35, ARIMA (2,2,0) having value 5559.95 and ARIMA (0,2,2) having value 5048.88 respectively.

7.2.6 Comparison between first and second difference of analyzed ARIMA model:

i)   Sum of Squares due to Error

SSE value is compared for both the orders and it is found that SSE value obtained from first differencing **(374102.10)** is **the least for ARIMA model (2,1,1)** when compared with SSE value from second differencing (503348.20) of ARIMA model (2,2,2). Thus **ARIMA model (2,1,1)** is considered best model for prediction of stock prices amongst 18 different models of ARIMA on the basis of SSE analysis.

ii)   Mean Squared Error

On comparison of the orders of differencing, it is found that MSE value obtained on first differencing **(752.72)** is **the least for ARIMA model (2,1,1)** when compared with MSE value from second differencing (1016.85) of ARIMA model (2,2,2). Thus **ARIMA model (2,1,1)** is considered best model for prediction of stock prices amongst 18 different models of ARIMA on the basis of MSE analysis.

iii)   Root Mean Squared Error

RMSE value is compared for both the orders and it is found that RMSE value obtained from first differencing **(27.43)** is **the least** for **ARIMA model (2,1,1)** when compared with RMSE value from second differencing (31.88) of ARIMA model (2,2,2). Thus **ARIMA model (2,1,1)** is considered best model for prediction of stock prices amongst 18 different models of ARIMA on the basis of RMSE analysis.

iv)   White Noise Variance

On comparison of the orders of differencing, it is found that WN Variance value obtained on first differencing **(752.72)** is **the least for ARIMA model (2,1,1)** when compared with WN value from second differencing (1016.86) of ARIMA model (2,2,2). Thus **ARIMA model (2,1,1)** is considered best model for prediction of stock prices amongst 18 different models of ARIMA on the basis of WN analysis.

v) Mean Absolute Percentage Error

MAPE value is compared for both the orders and it is found that MAPE value obtained from first differencing (**106.01**) is the least for **ARIMA model (0,2,2)** when compared with MAPE value from second differencing (107.06) of ARIMA model (0,1,1). Thus **ARIMA model (0,2,2)** is considered best model for prediction of stock prices amongst 18 different models of ARIMA on the basis of MAPE analysis.

vi) Final Prediction Error

On comparison of the orders of differencing, it is found that FPE value obtained on first differencing (**752.73**) is **the least for ARIMA model (0,1,2)** when compared with FPE value from second differencing (1025.11) of ARIMA model (2,2,2). Thus **ARIMA model (0,1,2)** is considered best model for prediction of stock prices amongst 18 different models of ARIMA on the basis of FPE analysis.

vii) Akaike Information Criterion

AIC value is compared for both the orders and it is found that AIC value obtained from first differencing (**4713.16**) is **the least for ARIMA model (0,1,1)** when compared with AIC value from second differencing (4863.27) of ARIMA model (2,2,2). Thus **ARIMA model (0,1,1)** is considered best model for prediction of stock prices amongst 18 different models of ARIMA on the basis of AIC analysis.

viii) Correction of AIC

On comparison of the orders of differencing, it is found that AICC value obtained on first differencing (**4713.19**) is **the least for ARIMA model (0,1,1)** when compared with AICC value from second differencing (4863.39) of ARIMA model (2,2,2). Thus **ARIMA model (0,1,1)** is considered best model for prediction of stock prices amongst 18 different models of ARIMA on the basis of AICC analysis.

ix) Schwarz Bayesian Information Criterion

SBC value is compared for both the orders and it is found that SBC value obtained from first differencing (**4721.58**) is **the least for ARIMA model (0,1,1)** when compared with SBC value from second differencing (4884.29) of ARIMA model (2,2,2). Thus **ARIMA model (0,1,1)** is considered best model for prediction of stock prices amongst 18 different models of ARIMA on the basis of SBC analysis.

INTERPRETATION:

Finally, the best fit method of ARIMA model is selected on the basis of maximum number of votes for the least value of each statistics for goodness of fit. ARIMA model (2,1,1) at first differencing got five number of votes for the least value of each for SSE, MSE, RMSE, White Noise and -2 log like when compared with four votes obtained by ARIMA model (0,1,1). Thus **ARIMA Model (2,1,1)** resulted best method amongst different methods of ARIMA Model.

Appraisal of experiment:

Similarly, results of other 18 stocks in which time series stock prices data is distributed non-normally are analyzed. It is found that ARIMA (0,1,2) model turns out to be the best model for Axis Bank, Bharti Airtel, Dr. Reddy, HDFC Bank, HDFC Finance, Maruti Suzuki, ONGC, Power Grid, State Bank of India, Wipro. ARIMA (1,1,1) model for Adani Port, Bajaj Autos, Cipla, Tata Steel, TCS. ARIMA (2,1,0) model for ICICI Bank, ARIMA (2,2,1) model for Infosys and ARIMA (0,2,1) model for L&T company. The result analysis of all the companies stated above is listed in the following table.

Table No 7.2: **Analysis of stocks (non-normal) using ARIMA models**

Model	No of companies	Name of the companies
(1,1,1)	5	Adani Port, Bajaj Autos, Cipla, Tata Steel, TCS
(0,1,2)	11	Axis Bank, Bharti Airtel, Dr. Reddy, HDFC Bank, HDFC Finance, Maruti Suzuki, ONGC, Power Grid, State Bank of India, Wipro, Lupin Limited
(2,1,0)	1	ICICI Bank
(2,2,1)	1	Infosys
(0,2,1)	1	L&T

7.3 EVALUATION OF RESULTS FORECASTED USING ARTIFICIAL NEURAL NETWORKS:

This study is comprised of the time series data of listed 25 BSE companies. The variables considered for analysis are (i) opening price (ii) closing price (iii) high price (iv) low price (v) volume of trades and (vi) Adjacent closing price for a particular stock on that day. The time series stock prices data is analyzed with the software Neuro excel predictor. The data is divided into two parts: Training set-95% (500 observations) and testing set-5% (23 observations).

To proceed further with the study four attributes are selected. These are: opening price, closing price, high price and low price for each stock. The output consists of a single attribute which is the opening price.

Parameters are then set for training the input and output ranges. On completion of training, input and output values are specified for prediction of stock prices based on the historical prices. Neural network parameters allow specifying initial weights, learning rate, momentum rate, number of epochs and number of neurons in hidden layers.

Activation functions used for the analysis are: Threshold, Hyperbolic tangent, Zero-based Log-sigmoid, Log-sigmoid and Bipolar-sigmoid. These functions are applied for simulation and stock prices are predicted using the number of neurons in the hidden layers for different layers, i.e., layer 1, layer 2 and layer 3 respectively.

The results obtained for 25 companies are then analyzed with the help of 15 models applied for prediction of stock prices. The best ANN model for prediction is decided on the basis of goodness of fit statistics. The measures applied for the accuracy of the results are Mean Absolute Error (MAE), Mean Absolute Percentage Error (MAPE), Mean Squared Error (MSE), Root Mean Squared Error (RMSE), Relative Absolute Error (RAE) and Root Relative Squared Error (RRSE).

7.3.1 Results of time series data of Sun Pharmaceuticals (for normal distribution) based on the statistics of goodness of fit / accuracy using ANN models:

i) Mean Absolute Error

Different ANN models are compared for MAE values. These values are compared for all the three layers of hidden network for all the five activation functions. On analyzing hidden **layer 1** for different activation functions it is observed that Bipolar-sigmoid has the least MAE value 25.21 when compared with Zero based Log-sigmoid (44.63), Threshold (110.72), Hyperbolic tangent (1206.34) and Log-sigmoid (44.07).

Similarly, MAE values are compared for different activation functions in **hidden layer 2** and it is found that Bipolar-sigmoid has the least MAE value 25.21 when compared with Zero based Log-sigmoid (27.78), Threshold (656.78), Hyperbolic tangent (1205.87) and Log-sigmoid (43.38).

Likewise, MAE values for **hidden layer 3** are also compared for all activation functions. It is found that Bipolar-sigmoid has the least MAE value 21.06 when compared with Zero based

Log-sigmoid (28.90), Threshold (110.72), Hyperbolic tangent (1206.56) and Log-sigmoid (45.62).

Finally, MAE values obtained for all the three hidden layers are compared and it is concluded that MAE value 21.06 is the least value of hidden layer 3 of Bipolar-Sigmoid when compared with MAE (21.15) of Bipolar-Sigmoid hidden layer 2 and MAE (25.21) of hidden layer 1 of Bipolar-Sigmoid. On the basis of the analysis of MAE values of all 15 models, Bipolar-sigmoid: layer 3 is considered as the best model for prediction of stock prices using artificial neural networks.

ii) Mean Absolute Percentage Error

MAPE values are analyzed for different activation functions for all the three layers of hidden network. It is found on reviewing that **hidden layer 1** of Bipolar-sigmoid has the least MAPE value 4.24 in comparison to Zero based Log-sigmoid (7.48), Threshold (18.43), Hyperbolic tangent (201.17) and Log-sigmoid (7.40).

Likewise, MAPE values are compared for different activation functions in **hidden layer 2** and it is observed that Bipolar sigmoid has the least MAPE value 3.56 when compared with Zero based Log-sigmoid (4.68), Threshold (109.54), Hyperbolic tangent (201.07) and Log-sigmoid (7.29).

In the same manner MAPE values for **hidden layer 3** are compared for all used activation functions. It is observed that Bipolar-sigmoid has the least MAPE 3.55 in comparison to Zero based Log-sigmoid (4.86), Threshold (18.43), Hyperbolic tangent (201.21) and Log-sigmoid (7.65).

At last, MAPE values obtained from all the three hidden layers are compared. It is obtained that the value of MAPE (3.55) for hidden layer 3 of Bipolar-Sigmoid is least when compared with MAPE (3.56) of Bipolar-Sigmoid layer 2 and MAPE (4.24) of layer 1 of Bipolar-Sigmoid. On the basis of analysis of MAPE values of all 15 models, Bipolar-sigmoid: layer 3 is considered as the best model for forecasting the stock prices using artificial neural networks.

iii) Mean Squared Error

Different ANN models are compared for MSE values. These values are compared for all the three layers of hidden network for all the five activation functions. On analyzing of **hidden layer 1** for different activation functions it is observed that Bipolar-sigmoid has the least MSE value 44.19 when compared with Zero based Log-sigmoid (115.63), Threshold (662.60), Hyperbolic tangent (78459.89) and Log-sigmoid (125.33).

Similarly, MSE values are compared for different activation functions in **hidden layer 2** and it is found that Bipolar-sigmoid had the least MSE 33.31 when compared with Zero based Log-sigmoid (66.38), Threshold (23273.27), Hyperbolic tangent (78474.92) and Log-sigmoid (123.69).

Likewise, MSE values for **hidden layer 3** are also compared for all activation functions. It is found that Bipolar-sigmoid had the least MSE value 126.95 when compared with Zero based Log-sigmoid (222.25), Threshold (1858.04), Hyperbolic tangent (237973.95) and Log-sigmoid (490.23).

Finally, MSE values obtained for all three hidden layers are compared and it is concluded that MSE value 33.31 is the least value of hidden layer 2 of Bipolar-Sigmoid when compared with MSE (44.91) of Bipolar-Sigmoid layer 1 and MSE (126.95) of layer 3 of Bipolar-Sigmoid. On the basis of the analysis of MSE values of all 15 models, Bipolar-sigmoid: layer 3 is considered as the best model for prediction of stock prices using artificial neural networks.

iv)   Root Mean Squared Error

RMSE values are analyzed for different activation functions for all the three layers of hidden network. It is found on reviewing that **hidden layer 1** of Bipolar-sigmoid has the least RMSE value 5.90 when compared with Zero based Log-sigmoid (10.40), Threshold (25.64), Hyperbolic tangent (279.89) and Log-sigmoid (10.30).

Likewise, RMSE values are compared for different activation functions in **hidden layer 2** and it is observed that Bipolar-sigmoid has the least RMSE 4.96 when compared with Zero based Log-sigmoid (7.08), Threshold (152.41), Hyperbolic tangent (279.79) and Log-sigmoid (10.15).

In the same manner RMSE values for **hidden layer 3** are compared for all used activation functions. It is observed that Bipolar-sigmoid has the least RMSE 8.57 when compared with Zero based Log-sigmoid (11.62), Threshold (38.86), Hyperbolic tangent (432.80) and Log-sigmoid (17.88).

At last, RMSE values obtained from all the three hidden layers are compared. It is obtained that the value of RMSE (4.96) is the least for layer 2 of Bipolar-Sigmoid when compared with RMSE (5.90) of Bipolar-Sigmoid layer 1 and RMSE (8.57) of layer 3 of Bipolar-Sigmoid. On the basis of analysis of RMSE values of all 15 models, layer 3 of Bipolar-sigmoid model is considered as the best model for prediction of stock prices using artificial neural networks.

v) Relative Absolute Error

Different ANN models are compared for RAE values. These values are compared for all the three layers of hidden network for all the five activation functions. On analyzing of **hidden layer 1** for different activation functions it is observed that Bipolar-sigmoid has the least RAE value 0.04 when compared with Zero based Log-sigmoid (0.07), Threshold (0.18), Hyperbolic tangent (12.01) and Log-sigmoid (0.07).

Similarly, RAE values are compared for different activation functions in **hidden layer 2** and it is found that Bipolar-sigmoid has the least RAE 0.04 when compared with Zero based Log-sigmoid (0.05), Threshold (1.10), Hyperbolic tangent (2.01) and Log-sigmoid (0.07).

Likewise, RAE values for **hidden layer 3** are also compared for all activation functions. It is found that Bipolar-sigmoid has the least RAE 0.04 when compared with Zero based Log-sigmoid (0.05), Threshold (0.18), Hyperbolic tangent (2.01) and Log-sigmoid (0.08).

Finally, RAE values obtained for all three hidden layers are compared and it is concluded that RAE value of 0.04 is equal for layer 1, Layer 2 and layer 3 of Bipolar-Sigmoid. On the basis of RAE analysis, Bipolar-sigmoid model is considered the best model for prediction of stock prices using artificial neural networks.

vi) Root Relative Squared Error

RRSE values are analyzed for different activation functions for all the three layers of hidden network. It is found on reviewing that **hidden layer 1** of Bipolar-sigmoid has the least RRSE value 0.20 when compared with Zero based Log-sigmoid (0.27), Threshold (0.43), Hyperbolic tangent (1.42) and Log-sigmoid (0.26).

Likewise, RRSE values are compared for different activation functions in **hidden layer 2** and it is observed that Bipolar-sigmoid has the least RRSE value 0.18 when compared with Zero based Log-sigmoid (0.20), Threshold (1.05), Hyperbolic tangent (1.42) and Log-sigmoid (0.26).

In the same manner RRSE values for **hidden layer 3** are compared for all used activation functions. It is observed that Bipolar-sigmoid has the least RRSE 0.18 when compared with Zero based Log-sigmoid (0.21), Threshold (0.43), Hyperbolic tangent (1.42) and Log-sigmoid (0.27).

Finally, RRSE values obtained from all the three hidden layers are compared. It is obtained that RRSE (0.18) is the least for layer 3 of Bipolar-Sigmoid when compared with RRSE (0.18) of Bipolar-Sigmoid layer 2 and RRSE (0.20) of layer 1 of Bipolar-Sigmoid. On the basis of analysis of RRSE values of all 15 models, layer 3 of Bipolar-sigmoid model is considered as the best model for prediction of stock prices using artificial neural networks.

Further, different sigmoid functions are compared for hidden layer 1 and it is found that Bipolar-sigmoid layer 1 is better when compared with the results obtained from other functions. The hidden layer 1 of Bioplar-sigmoid got six numbers of votes for the least values of MAE, MAPE, MSE, RMSE, RAE and RRSE. Similarly, on comparison for hidden layer 2, the results of Bipolar-sigmoid layer 2 are better when compared with the results obtained from other functions. Layer 2 of Bioplar-sigmoid got six numbers of votes for the least values of MAE, MAPE, MSE, RMSE, RAE and RRSE. Similarly, Bipolar-sigmoid layer 3 is found better when compared with the results of other functions as layer 3 of Bioplar-sigmoid got six number of votes for each vote of the least MAE, MAPE, MSE, RMSE, RAE and RRSE.

Finally, the best fit method of artificial neural network is selected on the basis of maximum number of votes for the least value of each statistics for goodness of fit under Layer 1, Layer 2 and Layer 3. Results of layer 2 improved when compared with layer 1 as value of different statistics of goodness of fit seemed to decrease. Layer 2 and Layer 3 are considered best of Bipolar-sigmoid as it got maximum number of votes for each. Therefore, on the basis of minimum value of MSE (33.31) Layer 2 of Bipolar-sigmoid model when compared with MSE (126.95) of Layer 3 Bipolar-sigmoid, prediction of stock prices using hidden layer 2 of Bipolar-sigmoid is considered best model of Artificial Neural Networks

Appraisal of experiment:

Similarly, results of other five stocks in which time series data is normally distributed are observed and it is found that ANN Hyperbolic tangent Layer 2 turns out to be best model for Coal India, GAIL and NTPC. Zero based Log-sigmoid Layer 1 for Hero Motor Corp. and Reliance Industries. The result analysis of all the companies stated above is listed in the following table.

Table No 7.3: Analysis of stocks (normal distribution) using ANN models

Activation function	Model	No of companies	Name of the companies
Hyperbolic tangent	Layer 2	3	Coal India, GAIL and NTPC
Zero based Log-sigmoid	Layer 1	2	Hero Motor Corp. and Reliance Industries
Bipolar-sigmoid	Layer 2	1	Sun Pharmaceuticals

7.3.2 Results of time series data of Lupin Limited (for non-normal distribution) based on the statistics of goodness of fit / accuracy using ANN models:

i) Mean Absolute Error

Different ANN models are compared for MAE values. These values are compared for all the three layers of hidden network for all the five activation functions. On analyzing hidden **layer 1** for different activation functions it is observed that Log-sigmoid has the least MAE value 54.13 when compared with Zero based Log-sigmoid (88.43), Threshold (1052.80), Hyperbolic tangent (54.29) and Bipolar-sigmoid (56.09).

Similarly, MAE values are compared for different activation functions in **hidden layer 2** and it is found that Hyperbolic tangent has the least MAE value 46.20 when compared with Zero based Log-sigmoid (82.80), Threshold (502.07), Log-sigmoid (62.18) and Bipolar-sigmoid (56.31).

Likewise, MAE values for **hidden layer 3** are also compared for all activation functions. It is found that Zero based Log-sigmoid has the least MAE 53.31 when compared with Threshold (502.07), Hyperbolic tangent (55.70) and Log-sigmoid (71.08), Bipolar-sigmoid (55.49).

Finally, MAE values obtained for all the three hidden layers are compared and it is concluded that MAE (46.20) is the least for layer 2 of Hyperbolic tangent when compared with MAE (53.31) of Zero Base Log-Sigmoid layer 3 and MAE (25.21) of layer 1 of Log-Sigmoid and on the basis of MAE analysis of all 15 models results of layer 2 of Hyperbolic tangent model is considered best model for prediction of stock prices using Artificial Neural Networks.

ii) Mean Absolute Percentage Error

MAPE values are analyzed for different activation functions for all the three layers of hidden network. On analysis of **hidden layer 1**, it is found that Log-sigmoid has the least MAPE value 3.13 when compared with Zero based Log-sigmoid (5.12), Threshold (59.49), Hyperbolic Tangent (3.15) and Bipolar-sigmoid (3.24).

Likewise, MAPE values are compared for different activation functions in **hidden layer 2** and it is observed that Hyperbolic Tangent has the least MAPE value 2.67 when compared with Zero based Log-sigmoid (4.79), Threshold (28.54), Log-sigmoid (3.61) and Bipolar-sigmoid (3.26).

In the same manner MAPE values for **hidden layer 3** are compared for all used activation functions. It is observed that Zero based Log-sigmoid has the least MAPE value 3.06 in comparison to with Threshold (28.54), Hyperbolic tangent (3.23) and Log-sigmoid (4.13), Bipolar-sigmoid (3.21).

Finally, MAPE values obtained from all the three hidden layers are compared. It is obtained that the value of MAPE (2.67) for hidden layer 3 of Hyperbolic tangent is least when compared with MAPE (3.06) of Zero Base Log-Sigmoid layer 3 and MAPE (3.13) of layer 1 of Log-Sigmoid. On the basis of analysis of MAPE values of all 15 models, Hyperbolic tangent: layer 3 is considered as the best model for prediction of stock prices using Artificial Neural Networks.

iii) Mean Squared Error

Different ANN models are compared for MSE values. These values are compared for all the three layers of hidden network for all the five activation functions. On analysis of **hidden layer 1** for different activation functions it is observed that Log-sigmoid has the least MSE value 258.60 when compared with Zero based Log-sigmoid (626.89), Threshold (59809.71), Hyperbolic tangent (266.91) and Bipolar-sigmoid (269.32).

Similarly, MSE values are compared for different activation functions in **hidden layer 2** and it is found that Hyperbolic tangent has the least MSE value 196.64 when compared with Zero based Log-sigmoid (675.33), Threshold (13831.95), Log-sigmoid (355.96) and Bipolar-sigmoid (269.73).

Likewise, MSE values for **hidden layer 3** are also compared for all activation functions. It is found that Zero based Log-sigmoid has the least MSE 1566.23 when compared with Threshold (13831.95), Hyperbolic tangent (1570.80) and Log-sigmoid value (2509.85), Bipolar-sigmoid (1667.46).

Finally, MSE values obtained for all three hidden layers are compared and it is concluded that MSE value 196.64 is the least for layer 2 of Hyperbolic tangent when compared with MSE (258.80) of Log-Sigmoid layer 3 and MSE (1566.23) of layer 1 of Zero Base Log-Sigmoid. On the basis of the analysis of MSE values of all 15 models, Hyperbolic tangent: layer 2 is considered the best model for prediction of stock prices using artificial neural networks.

iv) Root Mean Squared Error

RMSE values are analyzed for different activation functions for all the three layers of hidden network. It is found on reviewing that **hidden layer 1** of Log-sigmoid has the least RMSE value 12.73 when compared with Zero based Log-sigmoid (20.63), Threshold (244.12), Hyperbolic tangent (12.75) and Bipolar-sigmoid (13.14).

Likewise, RMSE values are compared for different activation functions in **hidden layer 2** and it is observed that Hyperbolic tangent has the least RMSE 10.85 in comparison to Zero based Log-sigmoid (20.85), Threshold (116.58), Log-sigmoid (14.57) and Bipolar-sigmoid (13.19).

In the same manner RMSE values for **hidden layer 3** are compared for all used activation functions. It is observed that Zero based Log-sigmoid has the least RMSE value 24.10 when compared with Threshold (116.58), Hyperbolic tangent (25.87) and Log-sigmoid (32.82), Bipolar-sigmoid (25.78).

At last, RMSE values obtained from all the three hidden layers are compared. It is obtained that the value of RMSE (10.85) is the least for layer 2 of Hyperbolic tangent in comparison to RMSE (12.73) of Log-Sigmoid layer 3 and RMSE (24.10) of layer 1 of Zero Base Log-Sigmoid. On the basis of RMSE analysis, layer 2 of Hyperbolic tangent model is considered best model for prediction of stock prices using Artificial Neural Networks.

v)   **Relative Absolute Error**

Different ANN models are compared for RAE values. These values are compared for all the three layers of hidden network for all the five activation functions. On analysis of **hidden layer 1** for different activation function it is observed that Log-sigmoid has the least RAE value of 0.03 when compared with Zero based Log-sigmoid (0.05), Threshold (0.59), Hyperbolic tangent (0.03) and Bipolar-sigmoid (0.03).

Similarly, RAE values are compared for different activation functions in **hidden layer 2** and it is found that Hyperbolic tangent has the least RAE value of 0.03 in comparison to Zero based Log-sigmoid (0.05), Threshold (0.29), Log-sigmoid (0.04) and Bipolar-sigmoid (0.03).

Likewise, RAE values for **hidden layer 3** are also compared for all activation functions. It is found Zero based Log-sigmoid has the least RAE value of 0.03 when compared with Threshold (0.29), Hyperbolic tangent (0.03) and Log-sigmoid (0.04), Bipolar-sigmoid (0.03).

Finally, RAE values obtained for all three hidden layers are compared and it is concluded that RAE (10.85) is the least for layer 2 of Hyperbolic tangent when compared with RAE (12.73) of Log-Sigmoid layer 3 and RAE (24.10) of layer 1 of Zero Base Log-Sigmoid and on the basis of RAE analysis of all 15 models results of layer 2 of Hyperbolic tangent model is considered best model for prediction of stock prices using Artificial Neural Networks.

vi)   **Root Relative Squared Error**

RMSE values are analyzed for different activation functions for all the three layers of hidden network. It is found on reviewing that **hidden layer 1** of Log-sigmoid has the least RRSE value 0.16 when compared with Zero based Log-sigmoid (0.21), Threshold (0.77), Hyperbolic tangent (0.16) and Bipolar-sigmoid (0.17).

Likewise, RRSE values are compared for different activation functions in **hidden layer 2** and it is observed that Hyperbolic tangent has the least RRSE value 0.15 when compared with

Zero based Log-sigmoid (0.20), Threshold (0.53), Log-sigmoid (0.17) and Bipolar-sigmoid (0.17).

In the same manner RRSE values for **hidden layer 3** are compared for all used activation functions. It is observed that Zero based Log-sigmoid has the least RRSE value 0.16 when compared with Threshold (0.53), Hyperbolic tangent (0.16) and Log-sigmoid (0.18), Bipolar-sigmoid (0.16).

Finally, RRSE values obtained from all the three hidden layers are compared. It is obtained that RRSE (0.15) is the least for layer 2 of Hyperbolic tangent when compared with RRSE (0.16) of Log-Sigmoid layer 3 and RRSE (0.16) of layer 1 of Zero Base Log-Sigmoid. On the basis of RRSE analysis, layer 2 of Hyperbolic tangent model is considered best model for prediction of stock prices using Artificial Neural Networks.

On comparison of the results of hidden layer 1 for different methods of activation functions, the results of Log-sigmoid layer 1 is found better when compared with the results of other functions as layer 1 of Log-sigmoid. It got all the six number of votes for the least values of MAE, MAPE, MSE, RMSE, RAE and RRSE. Similarly, on comparison to the results of layer 2, the results of Hyperbolic-tangent layer 2 are found better when compared with the results of other functions as layer 2 of Hyperbolic-tangent got six number of votes for the least value of MAE, MAPE, MSE, RMSE, RAE and RRSE. Similarly, for hidden layer 3, the results of Zero based Log-sigmoid layer 3 found better when compared with the results of other functions as layer 3 of Log-sigmoid got all the six number of votes for each vote of the least MAE, MAPE, MSE, RMSE, RAE and RRSE.

Finally, best fit artificial neural network model is selected on the basis of maximum number of votes for the least value of each statistics for goodness of fit under Layer 1, Layer 2 and Layer 3 respectively. Results of layer 2 improved when compared with layer 1 as value of different statistics of goodness of fit started decreasing and results of layer 3 deteriorated, therefore results of Layer 2 are considered best of Hyperbolic-tangent on the basis of minimum value of MSE (196.64) of Layer 2 of Hyperbolic-tangent model when compared with MSE (258.60) of Layer 3 Log-sigmoid and MSE (1566.23) of Layer 3 of Zero Base Log-sigmoid. Thus, prediction of stock prices using hidden layer 2 of Hyperbolic-tangent is considered as the best model of artificial neural networks.

Appraisal of experiment:

Similarly, results of rest 18 stocks distributed non-normally are analyzed. It is concluded that ANN Zero Based Log-sigmoid Layer 1 turns out to be best model for Adani Port, Axis Bank, Bharti Airtel, Cipla, ICICI Bank, Wipro, ANN Zero Based Log-sigmoid Layer 2 for HDFC Finance, State Bank Of India, ANN Zero Based Log-sigmoid Layer 3 L&T, ONGC, ANN Threshold Layer 1 for Bajaj Autos, ANN Log-Sigmoid Layer 1 for Dr. Reddy, ANN Hyperbolic-tangent Layer 1 for HDFC Bank, Power Grid, Tata Steel, TCS, and ANN Hyperbolic-tangent Layer 2 for Infosys, Lupin, Maruti Suzuki were best method amongst different methods of ANN Models for stock prices of companies under consideration.

Table No 7.4: Analysis of stocks (non-normal) using ANN models

Activation function	Model	No of companies	Name of the companies
Zero Based Log-sigmoid	Layer 1	6	Adani Port, Axis Bank, Bharti Airtel, Cipla, ICICI Bank, Wipro
Zero Based Log-sigmoid	Layer 2	2	HDFC Finance, State Bank Of India
Zero Based Log-sigmoid	Layer 3	2	L&T, ONGC
Threshold	Layer 1	1	Bajaj Autos
Log-Sigmoid	Layer 1	1	DR. Reddy
Hyperbolic-tangent	Layer 1	4	HDFC Bank, Power Grid, Tata Steel, TCS
Hyperbolic-tangent	Layer 2	3	Infosys, Maruti Suzuki, Lupin Limited

7.4 EVALUATION OF RESULTS FORECASTED USING GENETIC ALGORITHMS

Genetic Algorithms are used to optimize the performance of an artificial neural network. In this research, historical data of the stock prices of 25 BSE listed companies taken from yahoo India finance for a period of 2 years (20.01.2014 to 20.01.2016) is analyzed using software Weka 3.8.0. Time series framework uses a machine learning approach to model time series data by transforming the data in a form that learning algorithm can be processed. It uses the method of time encoding with the help of additional input field known as "lagged" variables which are used to remove time-based ordering of individual input. If the data has a time stamp, and the time stamp is a date, then the system can automatically detect the periodicity of the data. Software allows user to opt to have the system compute confidence intervals for its predictions and perform an evaluation of performance on the training data. Once data has been transformed, Weka Genetic Algorithm model is applied with multiple linear regression method including non-linear methods as well. This approach to time series analysis is more flexible and powerful than classical statistical techniques such as ARMA and ANN.

Three different methods are used for forecasting the stock prices time series data. These are (i) M5 method, (ii) Greedy method and (iii) No Attribute Selection method.

All three methods are assessed to select the best genetic algorithm based on statistics of goodness of fit/ accuracy for different models. These statistics includes Mean Absolute Error (MAE), Mean Absolute Percentage Error (MAPE), Mean Squared Error (MSE), Root Mean Squared Error (RMSE), Relative Absolute Error (RAE) and Root Relative Squared Error (RRSE) respectively.

7.4.1 Evaluation of the results of Sun Pharmaceuticals (normal distribution) based on statistics of goodness of fit/accuracy.

i) MAE

Different values of mean absolute error are analyzed and compared for different genetic algorithm models. It is observed that **No Attribute Selection method** has the least **MAE (12.18)** value when compared with MAE (12.19) for M5 Method and MAE (12.19) for Greedy Method respectively.

ii) RRSE

Values of root relative squared error are analyzed for different genetic algorithm models. It is found that No **Attribute Selection method** has the least **RRSE (96.69)** value when compared with RRSE (97.35) for M5 Method and RRSE (97.35) for Greedy Method respectively.

iii) Direction Accuracy

Different values of root relative squared error are analyzed and compared for different genetic algorithm models. It is observed that **No Attribute Selection method has the least DA value (48.55)** when compared with DA (48.57) for M5 Method and DA (48.57) for Greedy Method respectively.

iv) RAE

Values of relative absolute error are analyzed for different genetic algorithm models and it is observed that **No Attribute Selection method has the least RAE (98.80)** when compared with RAE (98.93) for M5 Method and RAE (98.93) for Greedy Method respectively.

v) MAPE

Different values of mean absolute percentage error are analyzed and compared for different genetic algorithm models. It is found that **Greedy method has the least MAPE (1.47)** when compared with MAPE (1.47) for M5 Method and MAPE (1.48) for No Attribute Selection method respectively.

vi) RMSE

Values of root mean squared error are analyzed and compared for different genetic algorithm models. It is observed that **No Attribute Selection method resulted into the least RMSE (16.94)** when compared with RMSE (17.06) for M5 Method and RMSE (17.06) for Greedy Method respectively.

vii) MSE

Different values of mean squared error values are analyzed and compared for different genetic algorithm models. It is found that **No Attribute Selection method has the least MSE (287.26)** when compared with MSE (291.07) for M5 Method and MSE (291.07) Greedy Method respectively.

The best fit method for genetic algorithm is selected on the basis of maximum number of votes earned for the least value of each statistics for goodness of fit/accuracy. No attribute selection method earned 5 votes on the basis of least value of each statistics, i.e., MAE, RRSE, RAE, RMSE and MSE respectively. On the other hand only two votes are allocated to greedy method for least value of DA and MAPE whereas none of the vote is earned by M5 method. Thus, no selection attribute method is concluded as the best fit method amongst different methods of genetic algorithms.

Appraisal of the experiment:

Similarly, results of other five stocks in which time series data is normally distributed are analyzed. It is found that no attribute selection method earned maximum numbers of votes for the least value of statistics for goodness of fit for Coal India, Gail, Hero Motor Corp., NTPC and Reliance Industries respectively. It is deduced from the above analysis that no selection attribute method is declared as the best fit method amongst different methods of genetic algorithms for forecasting stock prices time series data. The result analysis of all the companies stated above is listed in the following table.

Table No 7.5: Analysis of stocks (normal distribution) using GA models

Model	No of companies	Name of the companies
M5	-	Nil
Greedy	-	Nil
No attribute selection	6	Coal India, Gail, Hero Motor Corp., NTPC and Reliance Industries, Sun Pharmaceuticals

7.4.2 Evaluation of the results of Lupin Limited (non-normal distribution) based on statistics of goodness of fit/accuracy is illustrated as under:

i) MAE

Different values of mean absolute error are analyzed and compared for different genetic algorithm models. It is observed that **No Attribute Selection method has value the least MAE (21.71)** when compared with MAE (21.86) for M5 Method and MAE (21.86) for Greedy Method respectively.

ii) RRSE

Values of root relative squared error are analyzed for different genetic algorithm models and observed that **No Attribute Selection method has the least RRSE (105.10)** when compared with RRSE (105.58) for M5 Method and RRSE (105.58) for Greedy Method respectively.

iii) Direction Accuracy

Different values of root relative squared error are analyzed and compared for different genetic algorithm models. It is found that **M5 method and Greedy method has the least DA (51.23)** when compared with DA (52.05) for No attribute selection Method respectively.

iv) RAE

Values of relative absolute error values are analyzed for different genetic algorithm models and it is found that **No Attribute Selection method has the least RAE (111.56)** when compared with RAE (112.27) for M5 Method and RAE (112.27) for Greedy Method respectively.

v) MAPE

Different values of mean absolute percentage error are analyzed and compared for different genetic algorithm models. It is observed that **Greedy method has the least MAPE (1.44)** when compared with MAPE (1.46) for M5 Method and MAPE (1.46) for No Attribute Selection method respectively.

vi) **RMSE**

Values of root mean squared errors are analyzed and it is observed that **No Attribute Selection method has the least RMSE (29.10)** when compared with RMSE (29.25) for M5 Method and RMSE (29.25) for Greedy Method respectively.

vii) **MSE**

Different values of mean squared error values are analyzed and compared for different genetic algorithm models. It is found that **No Attribute Selection method has the least MSE (847.12)** when compared with MSE (855.76) for M5 Method and MSE (855.76) Greedy Method respectively.

As stated in the previous experiment for Sun Pharmaceuticals here also the best fit method of genetic algorithm is selected on the basis of maximum number of votes for the least value of each statistics of goodness of fit/accuracy. No attribute selection method scored 6 votes on the basis of the least value of each statistics, i.e., MAE, RRSE, RAE, MAPE, RMSE and MSE respectively. On the other hand only one vote is allocated to greedy method for least value of DA whereas none of the vote is earned by M5 method. Thus, no selection attribute method is concluded as the best fit method amongst different methods of genetic algorithms.

Appraisal of the experiment

Similarly, results of other 18 stocks (non-normal distribution) are analyzed. It is found that no attribute selection method earned maximum numbers of votes for the least values of statistic for goodness of fit/accuracy for Adani Port, Axis Bank, Bharti Airtel, Bajaj Autos, Cipla, Dr. Reddy, Hdfc Bank, Hdfc Finance ICICI Bank, Infosys, L&T, Lupin, Maruti Suzuki, ONGC, Power Grid, State Bank of India, Tata Steel, TCS and Wipro respectively. It is deduced from the above analysis that no selection attribute method is declared as the best fit method amongst different methods of genetic algorithms for forecasting stock prices time series data of all companies. The result analysis of all the companies stated above is listed in the following table.

Table No 7.6: Analysis of stocks (non-normal) using GA models

Model	No of companies	Name of the companies
M5	-	Nil
Greedy	-	Nil
No attribute selection	19	Adani Port, Axis Bank, Bharti Airtel, Bajaj Autos, Cipla, Dr. Reddy, Hdfc Bank, Hdfc Finance ICICI Bank, Infosys, L&T, Lupin, Maruti Suzuki, ONGC, Power Grid, State Bank of India, Tata Steel, TCS and Wipro

7.5: COMPARISON OF RESULTS OBTAINED FROM ARIMA, ANN, GA

In this section, we present the comparison of the results obtained from all the three different models applied on the stock prices data of 25 BSE Sensex companies. These models are namely ARIMA models, ANN models, and Genetic Algorithm models. The final results are presented on the basis of comparison of 6 statistics of goodness of fit/accuracy, i.e., MAE, MAPE, RMSE, RRMSE, RAE and RRSE.

Table 7.7: Result analysis of stocks (normal distribution) using different forecasting models

TESTS STATISTICS	MAE	MAPE	RMSE	RRMSE	RAE	RRSE
COAL INDIA						
ARIMA (1,1,1)	2.93	0.92	0.85	0.70	0.01	0.09
GA (No Attribute)	13.09	4.08	20.00	2.99	0.04	0.17
ANN (Hyperbolic tangent layer 2)	5.32	1.66	8.50	1.93	0.02	0.12
GAIL						
ARIMA (0,1,1)	5.69	1.58	3.36	1.32	0.02	0.11
GA (No Attribute)	29.03	8.06	61.22	6.66	0.08	0.26
ANN (Hyperbolic tangent layer 2)	13.19	3.67	35.43	4.52	0.04	0.17
HERO MOTOR						
ARIMA (1,1,1)	3.13	0.16	0.54	0.73	0.00	0.04
GA (No Attribute)	350.03	17.40	7757.46	80.23	0.17	0.40

ANN (Zero Based Log-Sigmoid-Layer 1)	55.60	2.74	1561.72	25.04	0.03	0.15
NTPC						
ARIMA (0,1,2)	0.95	0.72	0.13	0.22	0.01	0.07
GA (No Attribute)	15.59	11.96	16.81	3.66	0.12	0.33
ANN (Hyperbolic tangent layer 2)	2.03	1.56	0.61	0.62	0.02	0.11
RELIANCE						
ARIMA (1,1,1)	8.39	0.82	4.91	1.95	0.01	0.09
GA (No Attribute)	34.41	3.40	101.57	8.05	0.03	0.17
ANN (Zero Based Log-Sigmoid-Layer 1)	61.45	5.97	811.65	23.16	0.06	0.24
SUN PHARMACEUTICALS						
ARIMA (1,1,1)	5.44	0.91	2.88	1.27	0.01	0.08
GA (No Attribute)	51.24	8.44	243.71	11.47	0.08	0.26
ANN (Bipolar-Sigmoid-Layer 2)	21.15	3.56	127.64	8.60	0.04	0.18

INTERPRETATION

It is observed from the test statistics of predicted prices from different models of time series for Coal India whose time series stock prices are normally distributed that:

a) Predicted stock prices has the least MAE value (2.93) for ARIMA Model (1,1,1) when compared with MAE (5.32) for ANN-Hyperbolic tangent Layer 2 model and MAE (13.09) for Genetic Algorithm (No Attribute) model respectively.

b) Predicted stock prices has the least MAPE (0.92) for ARIMA Model (1,1,1) when compared with MAPE (1.66) for ANN-Hyperbolic tangent Layer 2 model and MAPE (4.08) for Genetic Algorithm (No Attribute) model respectively.

c) Predicted stock prices has the least RMSE (0.85) for ARIMA Model (1,1,1) when compared with RMSE (18.50) for ANN-Hyperbolic tangent Layer 2 model and RMSE (20.00) for Genetic Algorithm (No Attribute) model respectively.

d) Predicted stock prices has the least RRMSE (0.70) for ARIMA Model (1,1,1) in comparison to RRMSE (1.93) for ANN-Hyperbolic tangent Layer 2 model and RRMSE (2.99) for Genetic Algorithm (No Attribute) model respectively.
e) Predicted stock prices has the least RAE (0.01) for ARIMA Model (1,1,1) when compared with RAE (0.02) for ANN-Hyperbolic tangent Layer 2 model and RAE (0.04) for Genetic Algorithm (No Attribute) model respectively.
f) Predicted stock prices has the least RRSE (0.09) for ARIMA Model (1,1,1) when compared with RRSE (0.12) for ANN-Hyperbolic tangent Layer 2 model and RRSE (0.17) for Genetic Algorithm (No Attribute) model respectively.

In all the above test statistics, the least value for goodness of fit statistics are found for ARIMA (1,1,1) Model. Hence, ARIMA (1,1,1) is considered as the best fit model for forecasting the stock prices.

Appraisal of the experiment:

Similarly, ARIMA (0,1,1) model for GAIL, ARIMA (0,1,2) model for Hero Motor, ARIMA (0,1,2) model for NTPC, ARIMA (1,1,1) model for Reliance and Sun Pharmaceuticals has the least value of test statistics, i.e., MAE, MAPE, RMSE, RRMSE, RAE and RRSE for prediction of stock prices using different model of time series (ARIMA, ANN and Genetic Algorithm). Hence it is concluded that out of three models ARIMA model is proved as the best forecasting model for the normally distributed time series stock prices data.

Table 7.8: Result analysis of stocks (non-normal) using different forecasting models.

TESTS STATISTICS	MAE	MAPE	RMSE	RRMSE	RAE	RRSE
ADANI PORT						
ARIMA (1,1,1)	0.50	0.34	0.01	0.12	0.00	0.06
GA (No Attribute)	6.15	4.16	2.76	1.42	0.04	0.19
ANN (Zero Based Log-Sigmoid-Layer 1)	48.75	33.13	382.14	17.45	0.33	0.57
AXIS BANK						
ARIMA (0,1,2)	3.24	1.43	0.93	0.75	0.01	0.11
GA (No Attribute)	10.51	4.58	8.19	2.44	0.05	0.20
ANN (Zero Based Log-Sigmoid-Layer 1)	30.96	13.72	91.97	9.29	0.14	0.36

AIRTEL						
ARIMA (0,1,2)	2.53	0.79	0.65	0.60	0.01	0.08
GA (No Attribute)	11.88	3.60	12.79	2.97	0.04	0.17
ANN (Zero Based Log-Sigmoid-Layer 1)	6.51	2.01	6.46	2.13	0.02	0.13
BAJAJ AUTO						
ARIMA (1,1,1)	8.31	0.55	3.76	1.92	0.01	0.07
GA (No Attribute)	1052.13	68.99	60183.85	244.19	0.69	0.83
ANN (Threshold Layer 1)	4746.00	311.79	3609338.05	1693.44	3.12	1.77
CIPLA						
ARIMA (1,1,1)	2.96	0.73	0.67	0.69	0.01	0.08
GA (No Attribute)	64.32	16.37	394.81	14.46	0.16	0.34
ANN (Zero Based Log-Sigmoid-Layer 1)	14.59	3.64	36.94	5.08	0.04	0.18
DR. REDDY						
ARIMA (0,1,2)	1.87	0.07	0.35	0.44	0.00	0.02
GA (No Attribute)	2165.50	82.12	253122.63	502.27	0.82	0.91
ANN (Log Sigmoid Layer 1)	43.58	1.66	302.39	14.49	0.02	0.12
HDFC BANK						
ARIMA (0,1,2)	8.02	0.67	5.86	1.87	0.01	0.07
GA (No Attribute)	66.89	5.68	336.67	15.60	0.06	0.22
ANN (Hyperbolic tangent layer 1)	3.00	0.25	2.41	1.16	0.00	0.05
HDFC FINANCE						
ARIMA (0,1,2)	1.19	0.18	0.13	0.28	0.00	0.04
GA (No Attribute)	210.62	32.52	2388.73	48.73	0.33	0.57
ANN (Zero Based Log-Sigmoid-Layer 2)	91.95	14.23	1095.83	31.08	0.14	0.38
ICICI BANK						
ARIMA (2,1,0)	6.19	3.09	2.91	1.44	0.03	0.16
GA (No Attribute)						
ANN (Zero Based Log-Sigmoid-	21.70	10.65	123.61	8.63	0.11	0.32

Layer 1)						
INFOSYS						
ARIMA (2,2,1)	9.43	0.86	6.71	2.16	0.01	0.09
GA (No Attribute)	15009.53	1359.35	26674773.6	3532.24	13.59	3.20
ANN (Hyperbolic tangent layer 2)	20.19	1.84	232.97	9.51	0.02	0.12
L&T						
ARIMA (0,2,1)	3.52	0.35	0.69	0.82	0.00	0.06
GA (No Attribute)	131.98	13.20	2071.68	29.22	0.13	0.31
ANN (Zero Based Log-Sigmoid-Layer 3)	237.93	23.97	5868.42	75.06	0.24	0.48
LUPIN						
ARIMA (0,1,2)	20.95	1.20	43.73	4.90	0.01	0.10
GA (No Attribute)	150.78	8.55	1358.73	34.86	0.09	0.28
ANN (Hyperbolic tangent layer 2)	46.20	2.67	1307.95	21.78	0.03	0.15
MARUTI						
ARIMA (0,1,2)	29.04	0.65	69.02	6.72	0.01	0.07
GA (No Attribute)	420.25	9.71	36548.31	98.76	0.10	0.26
ANN (Hyperbolic tangent layer 2)	13.28	0.31	63.91	5.42	0.00	0.05
ONGC						
ARIMA (0,1,2)	2.06	0.91	0.35	0.48	0.01	0.09
GA (No Attribute)	30.60	13.38	83.85	6.86	0.13	0.33
ANN (Zero Based Log-Sigmoid-Layer 3)	3.45	1.52	4.32	1.34	0.02	0.11
POWER GRID						
ARIMA (0,1,2)	0.07	0.05	0.00	0.02	0.00	0.02
GA (No Attribute)	17.64	12.57	18.64	4.12	0.13	0.35
ANN (Hyperbolic tangent layer 1)	0.09	0.06	0.00	0.03	0.00	0.02
SBI						
ARIMA (0,1,2)	2.51	1.18	0.61	0.58	0.01	0.10
GA (No Attribute)	3.00	1.38	0.60	0.69	0.01	0.11
ANN (Zero Based Log-Sigmoid-	1.45	0.69	0.75	0.53	0.01	0.07

Layer 2)						
TATA STEEL						
ARIMA (1,1,1)	0.34	0.13	0.01	0.08	0.00	0.03
GA (No Attribute)	11.82	4.72	10.29	2.74	0.05	0.20
ANN (Hyperbolic tangent layer 1)	3.84	1.52	4.53	1.49	0.02	0.12
TCS						
ARIMA (1,1,1)	11.62	0.53	10.50	2.69	0.01	0.07
GA (No Attribute)	61.07	2.81	294.90	14.05	0.03	0.15
ANN (Hyperbolic tangent layer 1)	37.33	1.69	670.39	15.74	0.02	0.12
WIPRO						
ARIMA (0,1,2)	3.97	0.72	1.19	0.93	0.01	0.08
GA (No Attribute)	5.69	1.03	3.30	1.30	0.01	0.09
ANN (Zero Based Log-Sigmoid- Layer 1)	13.22	2.40	41.56	5.11	0.02	0.15

INTERPRETATION

It is observed from the test statistics of predicted prices from different models of time series for Adani Port whose time series stock prices are non-normally distributed that:

a) Predicted stock prices has the least MAE value (0.50) for ARIMA Model (1,1,1) when compared with MAE (48.75) for ANN-Hyperbolic tangent Layer 2 model and MAE (6.15) for Genetic Algorithm (No Attribute) model respectively.

b) Predicted stock prices has the least MAPE value (0.34) for ARIMA Model (1,1,1) when compared with MAPE (33.13) for ANN-Hyperbolic tangent Layer 2 model and MAPE (4.16) for Genetic Algorithm (No Attribute) model respectively.

c) Predicted stock prices has the least RMSE value (0.01) for ARIMA Model (1,1,1) when compared with RMSE (382.14) for ANN-Hyperbolic tangent Layer 2 model and RMSE (2.76) for Genetic Algorithm (No Attribute) model respectively.

d) Predicted stock prices has the least RRMSE value (0.12) for ARIMA Model (1,1,1) when compared with RRMSE (17.45) for ANN-Hyperbolic tangent Layer 2 model and RRMSE (1.42) for Genetic Algorithm (No Attribute) model respectively.

e) Predicted stock prices has the least RAE value (0.00) for ARIMA Model (1,1,1) when compared with RAE (0.33) for ANN-Hyperbolic tangent Layer 2 model and RAE (0.04) for Genetic Algorithm (No Attribute) model respectively.

f) Predicted stock prices has the least RRSE value (0.06) for ARIMA Model (1,1,1) when compared with RRSE (0.57) for ANN-Hyperbolic tangent Layer 2 model and RRSE (0.19) for Genetic Algorithm (No Attribute) model respectively.

On the basis of the experiments conducted above the least value for goodness of fit statistics are found least for ARIMA (1,1,1) model. Hence, ARIMA (1,1,1) model is considered as the best fit model for forecasting the stock prices of non-normal time series distribution.

Appraisal of the experiment:

ARIMA (0,1,1) model for Axis Bank, ARIMA (0,1,2) model for Bharti Airtel, ARIMA (0,1,2) model for Bajaj Auto, ARIMA (1,1,1) model for CIPLA, ARIMA (0,1,2) model for Dr. Reddy, ARIMA (0,1,2) model for HDFC Bank, ARIMA (0,1,2) model for HDFC Finance, ARIMA (2,1,0) model for ICICI Bank, ARIMA (2,2,1) model For Infosys, ARIMA (0,2,1) model for L&T, ARIMA (0,1,2) model for Lupin, ARIMA (0,1,2) model for ONGC, ARIMA (0,1,2) model for Power Grid Corporation, ARIMA (1,1,1) model for Tata Steel, ARIMA (1,1,1) model for TCS, and ARIMA (0,1,2) model for WIPRO and ANN (Hyperbolic tangent Layer 2) Model for Maruti Suzuki and ANN (Zero Based Log-Sigmoid-Layer 2) Model for State Bank of India are showed the least value of test statistics , i.e., MAE, MAPE, RMSE, RRMSE, RAE and RRSE for prediction of stock prices using different model of time series (ARIMA, ANN and Genetic Algorithm). Hence, in most of the cases best predictions are obtained through ARIMA models except for two stocks, i.e., Maruti Suzuki India Limited and State Bank of India where ANN models gave the best prediction for stocks price data.

7.6 CONCLUSION AND SUGGESTIONS

It can be inferred from the results obtained from select BSE 25 companies using three algorithms (ARIMA, ANN and GA) that GA model "No Attribute Selection" is providing forecasting of stock prices with minimum errors for all 25 companies.

Table : 7.9: Snapshot of algorithms, goodness of fit models and normality of stock prices

Parameter	Description/Details		
Normality	6 companies stocks prices confirm to normality and 19 not confirm to normality		
Algorithms	ARIMA	ANN	GA
Models based of Algorithms	18	15	3
Criteria of Goodness of fit	11	6	7
No of values	523	523	523

Table : 7.10: Snapshot of analysis in relation to algorithms and voting of best fit based on different criteria

Companies	Normal (N) Non-normal (NN)	Model used ARIMA	Total No. of votes (11)	Model used ANN	Total No. of votes (6)	Model used GA	Total No. of votes (7)
ADANI PORT	NN	(1,1,1)	5	Zero Based Log-Sigmoid-Layer 1	6	M5, Greedy	4
AXIS BANK	NN	(0,1,2)	9	Zero Based Log-Sigmoid-Layer 1	6	M5, No attribute	3
AIRTEL	NN	(0,1,2)	9	Zero Based Log-Sigmoid-Layer 1	4	M5, No attribute	3
BAJAJ AUTO	NN	(1,1,1)	5	Threshold-Layer 1	6	No Attribute	7
CIPLA	NN	(1,1,1)	10	Zero Based Log-Sigmoid-Layer 1	6	No Attribute	7
DR. REDDY	NN	(0,1,2)	10	Log Sigmoid Layer 1	6	No Attribute	6
HDFC BANK	NN	(0,1,2)	6	Hyperbolic tangent layer 1	6	Greedy Method	4

HDFC FINANCE	NN	(0,1,2)	9	Zero Based Log-Sigmoid-Layer 2	4	No Attribute	7
ICICI BANK	NN	(2,1,0)	5	Zero Based Log-Sigmoid-Layer 1	6	No Attribute	6
INFOSYS	NN	(2,2,1)	9	Hyperbolic tangent layer 2	4	No Attribute	7
L&T	NN	(0,2,1)	10	Zero Based Log-Sigmoid-Layer 3	4	No Attribute	7
LUPIN	NN	(0,1,2)	6	Hyperbolic tangent layer 2	6	No Attribute	6
MARUTI	NN	(0,1,2)	6	Hyperbolic tangent layer 2	6	No Attribute	7
ONGC	NN	(0,1,2)	9	Zero Based Log-Sigmoid-Layer 3	4	No Attribute	6
POWER GRID	NN	(0,1,2)	9	Hyperbolic tangent layer 1	6	M5, No attribute	3
SBI	NN	(0,1,2)	9	Zero Based Log-Sigmoid-Layer 2	6	No Attribute	6
TATA STEEL	NN	(1,1,1)	5	Hyperbolic tangent layer 1	6	No Attribute	6
TCS	NN	(1,1,1)	6	Hyperbolic tangent layer 1	6	No Attribute	7
WIPRO	NN	(0,1,2)	10	Zero Based Log-Sigmoid-Layer 1	6	No Attribute	7
COAL INDIA	N	(1,1,1)	6	Hyperbolic tangent layer 2	6	No Attribute	4
GAIL	N	(0,1,1)	9	Hyperbolic tangent layer 2	6	No Attribute	4
HERO MOTOR	N	(1,1,1)	5	Zero Based Log-Sigmoid-Layer 1	6	No Attribute	4
NTPC	N	(0,1,2)	6	Hyperbolic tangent layer 2	6	Greedy, No attribute	3
RELIANCE	N	(1,1,1)	6	Zero Based Log-Sigmoid-Layer 1	6	No Attribute	4
SUN PHARMA	N	(1,1,1)	5	Bipolar-Sigmoid-Layer 2	4	No Attribute	5

It can be seen from the summary data presented in the table 7.9 and table 7.10 that ARIMA models are better for some data sets and in other-artificial neural networks or genetic algorithms are proved the best fit algorithms. It is inferred that the single algorithm cannot be fitted to all data sets. Further, it is not an exhaustive list of criteria for goodness of fit but a selective list (due to limitations of software used for the purpose of analysis).

Based on the summary presented in table 7.10 following can be further inferred:
1. All models given in table 7.10 are the best fit based on six criteria, i.e., MAE, MAPE, RMSE, RRMSE, RAE and RRSE.
2. No Single model is the best model for the data set of 25 companies and against the all criteria of goodness of fit applied in this research dissertation.
3. Efficiency of forecasting models can be enhanced by changing parameters, i.e., p, q, and d.
4. For the given data sets GA models with "no attribute selection" algorithm are the best fit for forecasting stock price data.
5. In view of the above observations, to declare a model as "best fit model" criteria of maximum vote was considered. The voting distribution for three category of algorithms is as under:
    (i) Voting for ARIMA models varies from 5 to 10 out of 11.
    (ii) Voting for ANN models varies from 4 to 6 out of 6.
    (iii) Voting for GA models varies from 3 to 7 out of 7.

Limitations of the present research are (i) algorithms that are used depends on the features of different software's, i.e., Weka, XLstat, Neuro XL-Predictor and SPSS used for the purpose of analysis in the study, (ii) the results could not be augmented by analyzing data with additional algorithms (hybrid models), (iii) only maximum voting method was used
Researchers in future may use hybrid models to this data set to improve results for financial forecasting purpose especially for learning algorithms that can handle business cycles, market and financial crisis. Finally, there are many other learning algorithms in the category of artificial neural networks to be explored for some more possible forecasting of stock prices.